CRIC

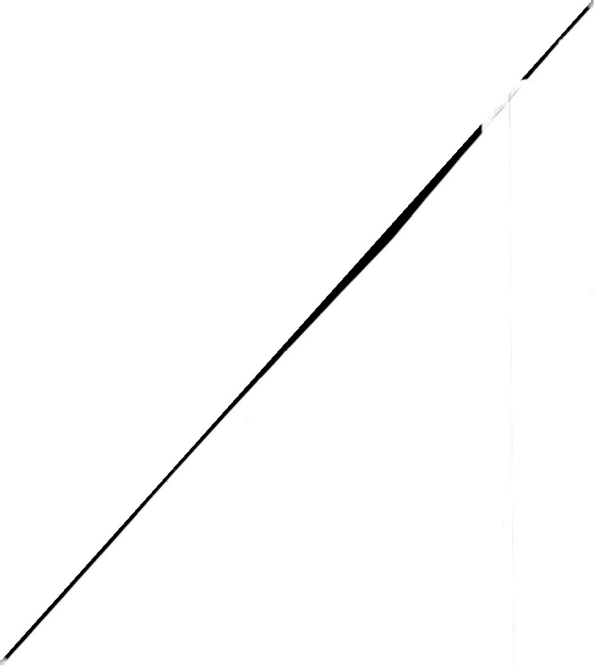

CRICKET EXTRAS 2

CRICKET'S GREATEST FEATS AND UNUSUAL FACTS AND FIGURES

Marc Dawson

Forewords by
IAN HEALY AND DAVID BOON

Kangaroo Press

First published in 1994 by Kangaroo Press Pty Ltd
3 Whitehall Road Kenthurst NSW 2156 Australia
P.O. Box 6125 Dural Delivery Centre NSW 2158
Typeset by G.T. Setters Pty Limited
Printed by Australian Print Group, Maryborough, Victoria 3465

ISBN 0 86417 642 2

Contents

Foreword by David Boon

Cricket is a game renowned throughout history as a gentleman's game, and thus quite a serious one. Throughout Marc Dawson's book, *Cricket Extras 2*, we can see there is much more to this great game than meets the eye.

From the more obscure cricket records and statistics to many humorous happenings, trivia, photographs and much more, this book has it all.

For the statistician, the cricket lover and even the non-committed, *Cricket Extras 2* has many hours of enjoyment and pleasure contained within its pages.

David Boon

Foreword by Ian Healy

It's quite ironic that I should be asked to pen the foreword for a book on cricket extras, something that I've learnt to hate in my job as a wicket-keeper. Extras never offer me pleasant times, whether I'm battling within myself for calm and peace or chastising our bowlers for not bowling them straight to me!

Marc Dawson once again exposes cricket's universal appeal, bridging not only many nationalities but so many lifestyles from the poorest to the most wealthy.

We as players, and I guess the same goes for the public, become so focused on the game at hand that it takes someone such as Marc to step back and allow us to become aware of the many varied ways that cricket has touched people worldwide.

The big picture, the way in which cricket has affected so many, reinforces for me the broader niceties and traditions of our magnificent game—traditional etiquette, the incredible statistical records, what players do outside the game, where many players end up after their playing days, as well as many skilful cricketing feats that get lost in the total match outcome. These are the very same qualities and personal pressures that are so readily forgotten in the heat of battle. The *battle*, I believe, is the most appealing aspect and is the constant which generates all the 'extras'.

With my copy of *Cricket Extras 2* I have the perfect way of filling in the many idle dressing room hours as we, the current players, endeavour to provide many more battles in the rich tradition of cricket.

Ian Healy

1 Famous Firsts

The first international cricket matches were between the U.S.A. and Canada, played in New York in 1844.

•

When India met South Africa in a Test match for the first time, at Durban in 1992–93, it became the first country to play Test cricket against all the other eight countries.

•

Billy Midwinter was the first man to play Test cricket both for and against Australia. He appeared in eight Tests for Australia, all against England, between 1877 and 1887. After his initial two Tests, he played in four Tests for England (1881–82) and then reappeared for Australia. At Melbourne in 1993–94, South Africa's Kepler Wessels became the second to play Test cricket both for and against Australia.

•

Jack Marsh, a right-arm fast bowler from New South Wales, was the first Aborigine to take five wickets in a first-class innings, achieving the feat on his debut against South Australia at Adelaide in 1900–01. His last two appearances for NSW coincided with the first two in the career of Queensland's first Aboriginal player, Alex Henry. When the two played at Brisbane in 1901–02 and 1902–03, each opened the bowling for his state, the only occasions that Aborigines have opposed each other in first-class cricket.

The first Aborigine to play at first-class level was Twopenny, who represented New South Wales once in 1869–70. The first Maori to play first-class cricket was W.T. Wynyard for Wellington v Canterbury in 1890–91; the first Samoan first-class cricketer was S.W. Kohlhase for Northern Districts in 1963–64.

•

The first black man to appear in a Test match was an Australian, Sam Morris, who was born in Hobart of West Indian parents. He appeared in his only Test match against England at Melbourne in 1884–85.

•

Test cricket was played on Christmas Day for the first time during the third Test between Australia and the West Indies at Adelaide in 1951–52. Santa Claus was kinder to the tourists, with the West Indies receiving a six-wicket win midway through the first Christmas Day Test match.

When Transvaal met Griqualand West in 1890–91, 1,402 runs were scored over seven days. It was the first first-class match in the world to progress past the fifth day.

•

Shane Warne was the first graduate of the Australian Cricket Academy to play Test cricket.

•

The Test match against New Zealand at Hobart in 1993–94 was the first one in which an Australian side had 500 Test caps between them.

•

When England's 'Dickie' Bird officiated in the second Test between Zimbabwe and New Zealand at Harare in 1992–93 he became the first umpire to stand in 50 Test matches.

•

Organised competitive club cricket matches were first played in Australia in Melbourne in 1860–61, with Richmond being the first winners. Hobart was next in line, with Wellington taking the first title in 1869–70. For the other capital cities, Sydney followed in 1871–72 (Albert Cricket Club the first winners), Adelaide in 1873–74 (Norwood), Brisbane in 1876–77 (Albert CC), Perth in 1900–01 (Claremont-Cottesloe) and Canberra in 1922–23 (Ainslie).

•

During the third Pakistan–New Zealand Test at Karachi in 1976–77, Imran Khan was warned by umpires Shakoor Rana and Shujauddin for bowling too many short-pitched balls. He became the first bowler in Test history to be banned from bowling during a match for intimidatory bowling.

•

The first women's Test match was played between Australia and England at Brisbane in 1934–35. The visitors recorded a decisive first-up victory, beating Australia by nine wickets, Myrtle Maclagan starring with a score of 72 and recording the first instance of five wickets in an innings (7–10) in a women's Test. In the second Test at Sydney she became the first woman to score a Test century (119).

The first Australian to hit a century in a women's Test was Una Paisley, who scored 108 against New Zealand at Wellington in 1948. Playing alongside Paisley was Betty Wilson, who later became the first to score a century and take five innings wickets in the same match—111 and 6–23 v England at Adelaide in 1948–49.

NOTABLE WORLD FIRSTS BY AUSTRALIAN WOMEN CRICKETERS

First woman to score a century in each innings of a match
Rosalie Dean (195 & 104)—Inter-Colonial Ladies v Sydney at Sydney in 1891
First team score of 500
567 by Tarana v Rockley at Rockley in New South Wales in 1896–97
First woman to record the 1000 run–100 wicket double in a season
Miss F. Tamsett (1,009 runs and 159 wickets) at Goulburn in New South Wales in 1929–30
First triple-century
Dot Laughton (390*)—YWCA Golds v Wyverns in 1948–49
First woman to take a Test hat-trick
Betty Wilson—Australia v England at St Kilda, Victoria in 1957–58
First cricketer to score a century and take 10 wickets in the same Test
Betty Wilson (100 and 11–16)—Australia v England at St Kilda in 1957–58
First triple-century partnership in a women's Test match
309 for the 3rd wicket by Denise Annetts (193) and Lindsay Reeler (110*) v England at Collingham in 1987

•

The Queensland–Western Australia match at Brisbane in 1964–65 was the first Sheffield Shield game to include play on a Sunday. Queensland's Bill Buckle celebrated the event by registering his highest score in first-class cricket, an innings of 207. Sunday play was introduced in England's County Championship for the first time in the Essex–Somerset match at Ilford in 1966.

•

One of the first recorded accounts of cricket in New Zealand was in 1835 in the diary of Charles Darwin during his voyage on HMS *Beagle*. He noted the game being played by Maoris on a farm at Waiwata.

•

Zimbabwe found itself in the unusual position of staging its first Test match without having in place a domestic first-class competition. Zimbabwe's inaugural Test match was played against India at Harare in 1992–93. A little over a year later the new Logan Cup was introduced with two matches commenced on 14 January 1994. The first teams to take part in the competition were Mashonaland Country Districts and Mashonaland at the Harare South Country Club and Matabeleland and the Mashonaland Under-24s at the Queens Ground in Bulawayo.

THE FIRST TEST FOR EACH COUNTRY

Country	Date	Opposition	Venue	Result
Australia	15.3.1877	England	Melbourne	Won by 45 runs
England	15.3.1877	Australia	Melbourne	Lost by 45 runs
South Africa	12.3.1889	England	Port Elizabeth	Lost by 8 wickets
West Indies	23.6.1928	England	Lord's	Lost by innings & 58 runs
New Zealand	10.1.1929	England	Christchurch	Lost by 8 wickets
India	25.6.1932	England	Lord's	Lost by 158 runs
Pakistan	16.10.1952	India	Delhi	Lost by innings & 70 runs
Sri Lanka	17.10.1982	England	Colombo	Lost by 7 wickets
Zimbabwe	18.10.1992	India	Harare	Drawn

•

The first first-class cricket match in Australia began on 11 February 1851 between a Van Diemen's Land XI and a Port Phillip XI from Melbourne. The historic match was played at the Launceston Racecourse and was over in two days with victory to the Tasmanians. Victoria's D.E. Cooper faced the first ball in Australian first-class cricket from Bill Henty. Victoria's Tom Antill, in his only first-class match, recorded Australia's first duck and the first haul of 10 wickets (7–33 & 6–19).

AUSTRALIA'S FIRST FIRST-CLASS CRICKET MATCH
TASMANIA V VICTORIA
Played at Launceston, 1850–51
Tasmania won by three wickets

VICTORIA

D.E. Cooper	b McDowall	4	(7) b Henty		0
W. Philpott (c)	c Maddox b McDowall	17	(6) run out		3
T.F. Hamilton	b McDowall	10	(1) lbw b McDowall		35
C. Lister	run out	10	c Maddox b Field		3
A.T. Thomson	b McDowall	1	b Henty		0
R.S. Philpott	b Henty	12	(8) c Westbrook b Henty		1
T.W. Antill	st Marshall b Henty	0	(11) not out		0
J.C. Brodie	c Henty b McDowall	17	(2) c Tabart b Henty		5
F.W. Marsden	b Henty	2	b McDowall		2
M. Hall	not out	6	(3) lbw b McDowall		6
M. Hervey	b Henty	0	(10) c McDowall b Henty		1
Extras	(b1, lb2)	3	(b1)		1
	(26 overs)	82	(17 overs)		57

TASMANIA

G.B. Du Croz	b Antill	27	(2) b Antill		6
J. Marshall (c)	c Lister b Antill	13	(7) c & b Antill		0
W. Field	b Antill	0	(5) c Thomson b Brodie		1
G. Maddox	b Antill	1			
G. Gibson	b Hamilton	8	(6) b Antill		1
W.H. Westbrook	b Antill	10	(3) c Cooper b Antill		4
C. Arthur	b Antill	1	(8) c Hervey b Antill		0
J.L.B. Tabart	b Hamilton	2	(4) not out		15
V.W. Giblin	not out	7	(1) b Antill		1
W. Henty	b Antill	0			
R.M. McDowall	c Antill b Hamilton	11	(9) not out		4
Extras	(b11, lb5, nb8)	24	(b3, lb2)		5
	(32 overs)	104	(13 overs) (7 wkts)		37

TASMANIA	O	M	R	W	O	M	R	W
Henty	13		52	4	9		26	5
McDowall	13		27	5	5		21	3
Field					3		9	1
VICTORIA								
Lister	12		23	0				
Hamilton	8		24	3				
Antill	12		33	7	6		19	6
Brodie					7		13	1

•

Charles Bannerman, who scored the first run in Test cricket, at Melbourne in 1876–77, later became the first Australian to reach the milestone of 1,000 Test runs, at The Oval in 1893. A month before, England's Arthur Shrewsbury, in the first Test at Lord's, became the first batsman from any country to score 1,000 Test runs.

•

The first known artwork depicting cricket dates back to 1739 when the French artist Gravelot painted *The Game of Cricket*. 'Lumpy' Stevens, one of the game's most accurate fast bowlers, was the first cricketer to be the subject of a portrait, in 1783.

•

S.T. Gill's painting of the first first-class match played in Sydney, between New South Wales and Victoria at the Domain in 1856–57. In a low-scoring affair, NSW (80 & 86) defeated Victoria (63 & 38) by 65 runs.

Australian Cricketers at Chilham Castle, Kent, August 1878—a painting by an unidentified artist depicting a match between Wilsher's Gentlemen and the 1878 Australians, the first representative Australian team to tour England

TEST CRICKET FIRSTS

First player to score a 50 and take a hat-trick in the same Test
Billy Bates—England v Australia at Melbourne in 1882–83
First player to score a century and take five wickets in an innings in the same Test
Jimmy Sinclair (106 & 6–26)—South Africa v England at Cape Town in 1898–99
First player to appear in 50 Tests against one country
Jack Gregory—Australia v England in 1912
First batsman to score centuries in his first two Tests
Bill Ponsford (110 & 128)—Australia v England in 1924–25
First player to be on the field throughout a Test
Nazar Mohammad—Pakistan v India at Lucknow in 1952–53
First batsman to score 200 runs in boundaries in a Test match
John Edrich (238 out of 310*)—England v New Zealand at Leeds in 1965
First player to score a 50 and take 10 wickets on his Test debut
John Lever (53 & 10–70)—England v India at Delhi in 1976–77
First batsman to score three consecutive 150s
Zaheer Abbas (215, 186 & 168)—Pakistan v India in 1982–83
First substitute to claim four catches in a Test
Gursharan Singh—India v West Indies at Ahmedabad in 1983–84
First batsman to score centuries in his first three Tests
Mohammad Azharuddin (110, 105 & 122)—India v England in 1984–85
First batsman to stay at the crease for over 90 minutes without scoring
Jeff Crowe—New Zealand v West Indies at Bridgetown in 1984–85
First batsman to score 10,000 Test runs
Sunil Gavaskar—India v Pakistan at Ahmedabad in 1986–87
First wicket-keeper to stump six batsmen in a Test
Kiran More—India v West Indies at Madras in 1987–88
First batsman to score 400 runs in a Test
Graham Gooch (456–333 & 123)—England v India at Lord's in 1990
First player to reach the Test double of 4,000 runs and 400 wickets
Kapil Dev—India v Australia at Perth in 1991–92
First player to be given out by a third umpire (video replay) in a Test
Sachin Tendulkar—India v South Africa at Durban in 1992–92
First player to bat in 250 Test innings
Allan Border—Australia v England at Edgbaston in 1993
First player to appear in 150 Tests
Allan Border—Australia v New Zealand at Brisbane in 1993–94
First batsman to score 11,000 Test runs
Allan Border—Australia v South Africa at Adelaide in 1993–94

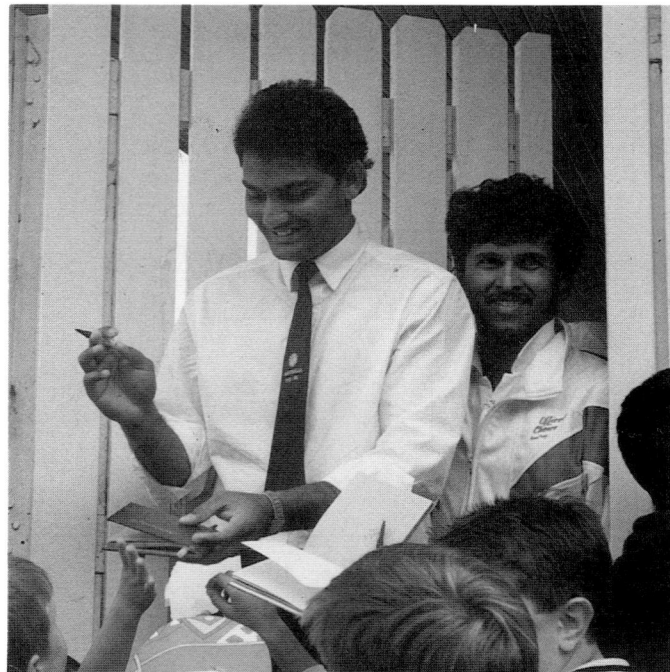

Mohammad Azharuddin and Kiran More, Indian Test players who both completed Test cricket 'firsts' during the 1980s

•

Samuel Jackson only played in one first-class match, for Yorkshire v Lancashire at Manchester in 1891. He got his chance when Arthur Sellers fell ill and batted in both innings as a substitute—the first player to do so in English first-class cricket.

•

2 Literary Links

•

Edmund Blunden, the poet and cricket-lover who wrote *Cricket Country*, kept wicket in a team run by fellow poet and author J.C. Squire. The Invalids' XI also included Alec Waugh, J.B. Priestley and Hilaire Belloc.

•

Richard Keigwin, who appeared in around 70 first-class matches for Essex, Gloucestershire and Cambridge between 1903 and 1923, later became a leading translator of Danish writings, and a recognised authority on the works of Hans Christian Andersen. Keigwin was later awarded a knighthood for his services to Danish literature.

•

One of the most remarkable victories in the history of first-class cricket was due in part to the batting exploits of a butler to Lionel Tennyson, grandson of the Poet Laureate Lord Tennyson. Walter Livsey, who kept wicket for Hampshire under the captaincy of his employer, was at the crease when they beat Warwickshire at Birmingham in 1922 by 155 runs, after being dismissed in their first innings for 15. Following on, Hampshire scored 521, thanks largely to Livsey who scored 110 not out batting at No. 10.

•

The first full description of a cricket match was in a Latin poem by William Goldwin, of Cambridge, in 1706.

•

A.A. Milne, the author of *When We Were Very Young* and *Winnie-the-Pooh*, played cricket for his school Westminster in 1899 and 1900. He made 294 runs in his two seasons at 10.50—top score 44—and took 28 wickets at 23.11.

But what care I? It's the game that calls me,
    Simply to be on the field of play;
How can it matter what fate befalls me,
    With ten good fellows and one good day!

—**A.A. Milne, 'The First Game'**

•

E.W. Hornung, the English novelist who created Raffles, the cricketing burglar, was himself a keen player, being a slow bowler and competent middle-order batsman. The fictional A.J. Raffles turned out to be a much better player than his creator, who described him as 'a dangerous bat, a brilliant field, and perhaps the very finest slower bowler of his decade'. It was on a tour of Australia that Raffles first combined cricket and crime, stealing money from a bank after losing heavily on a bet at the Melbourne Cup.

Another literary character involved in both cricket and crime was Dorothy L. Sayers' Lord Peter Wimsey, the hero of many bestselling crime novels of the 1920s and '30s. A first-class cricketer, his batting exploits, when he scored two successive hundreds for Oxford, are referred to in *Murder Must Advertise*. Sayers also mentions cricket in *The Nine Tailors, Have His Carcase, Unnatural Death* and *Gaudy Night*.

•

Two England captains wrote novels with a cricketing theme—C.B. Fry's *A Mother's Son* and Ted Dexter's *Testkill* (co-written with Clifford Makins).

•

Charles Dickens was indirectly responsible for the birth of Anglo-Australian cricket. In 1861–62 Spiers & Ponds, the owners of a Melbourne cafe, brought to Australia the first English cricket team to promote its business, but only after Dickens had turned down, at the last minute, an invitation to undertake a lecture tour.

•

THE ALL ENGLAND ELEVEN.—ARRIVAL AT THE CAFE DE PARIS, MELBOURNE.

The arrival at Melbourne's Cafe de Paris in 1861–62 of Heathfield Stephenson's England team, a tour that replaced one cancelled by Charles Dickens

Jeffrey Archer

Jeffrey Archer, one of England's most successful contemporary novelists, is a cricket nut, who one day in 1985 had a dream come true when invited to join the Somerset team for a testimonial match in honour of Viv Richards. Archer acquitted himself reasonably well in a team that included Peter Roebuck, Brian Rose, Joel Garner and Ian Botham. With the bat he scored 3 runs surviving 17 deliveries, and claimed one wicket; Rose commenting 'One for nine—you can live with those figures for the rest of your life'. He has.

JEFFREY ARCHER'S ALL-TIME BEST TEST XI
1 Len Hutton
2 Sunil Gavaskar
3 Jack Hobbs
4 Don Bradman (c)
5 David Gower
6 Garry Sobers
7 Keith Miller
8 Godfrey Evans
9 Jim Laker
10 Dennis Lillee
11 Michael Holding

•

Of all the leading literary figures who've taken an interest in cricket, two have gone on to play the game at first-class level—Samuel Beckett for Dublin University and Sir Arthur Conan Doyle for the MCC. The man who brought us Sherlock Holmes appeared in 10 first-class matches at the turn of the century, recording 231 runs with the bat, but just one wicket. However, his victim was a prized scalp. On his first-class debut for the MCC in 1900, Conan Doyle dismissed the great W.G. Grace, who was playing for London County. Conan Doyle was so pleased with his effort, he wrote a poem—'A Reminiscence of Cricket'— to commemorate the event.

Once in my heyday of cricket,
    Oh day I shall ever recall!
I captured that glorious wicket,
    The greatest, the grandest of all.

Before me he stands like a vision,
    Bearded and burly and brown,
A smile of good-humoured derision
    As he waits for the first to come down.

A statue from Thebes or from Cnossus,
    A Hercules shrouded in white,
Assyrian bull-like Collossus,
    He stands in his might.

With the beard of a Goth or a Vandal,
    His bat hanging ready and free,
His great hairy hands on the handle,
    And his menacing eyes upon me.

And I—I had tricks for the rabbits
    The feeble of mind or of eye,
I could see all the duffer's bad habits
    And guess where his ruin might lie.

The capture of such might elate one,
    But it seemed like some horrible jest
That I should serve tosh to the great one,
    Who had broken the hearts of the best.

Well, here goes! Good Lord, what a rotter!
    Such a sitter as never was dreamt;
It was clay in the hands of the potter,
    But he tapped it with quiet contempt.

The second was better—a leetle;
    It was low, but was nearly long-hop;
As the housemaid comes down on the beetle
    So down came the bat with a chop.

He was sizing me up with some wonder,
    My broken-kneed action and ways;
I could see the grim menace from under
    The striped peak that shaded his gaze.

The third was a gift or it looked it—
    A foot off the wicket or so;
His huge figure swooped as he hooked it,
    His great body swung to the blow.

Still when my dreams are night-marish,
    I picture that terrible smite,

It was meant for a neighbouring parish,
Or any old place out of sight.

But—yes, there's a but to the story—
The blade swished a trifle too low;
Oh wonder, and vision of glory!
It was up like a shaft from a bow.

Up, up, like the towering game-bird,
Up, up, to a speck in the blue,
And then coming down like the same bird,
Dead straight on the line that it flew.

Good Lord, was it mine! Such a soarer
Would call for a safe pair of hands;
None safer than Derbyshire Storer,
And there, face uplifted, he stands.

Wicket-keeper Storer, the knowing,
Wary and steady of nerve,
Watching it falling and growing
Marking the pace and the curve.

I stood with my two eyes fixed on it,
Paralysed, helpless, inert;
There was 'plunk' as the gloves shut upon it,
And he cuddled it up in his shirt.

Out—beyond question or wrangle!
Homeward he lurched to his lunch!
His bat was tucked up at an angle,
His great shoulders curved to a hunch.

Walking he rumbled and grumbled,
Scolding himself and not me;
One glove was off, and he fumbled,
Twisting the other hand free.

Did I give Storer the credit
The thanks he so splendidly earned?
It was mere empty talk if I said it,
For Grace was already returned.

•

The infamous Hill at the SCG claimed a literary casualty in 1974 when Laurie Lee, the British poet and author famed for his autobiographical novel *Cider With Rosie*, was knocked unconscious by a beer bottle. He was hit by the flying missile during the third day's play of the second Australia–New Zealand Test match.

•

J.H.L. Aubrey-Fletcher, who appeared in a couple of first-class matches in England in 1933, was a successful novelist, writing detective stories under the nom-de-plume Henry Wade.

•

Alfred Dryden, who played cricket at his school Winchester, and at Oxford, was a descendant of the famous English poet and first official Poet Laureate, John Dryden.

•

Henry Dickens, the last surviving grandson of Charles Dickens, was an enthusiastic cricketer and a member of the MCC.

•

The Bank of England issued a £10 note (below) in 1992 that featured one of fiction's most famous cricket matches, the one between Dingley Dell and All Muggleton, from Charles Dickens' 1836 novel, *The Pickwick Papers*.

Poet Lord Byron played in a match for Harrow v Eton at Lord's in 1805, scoring 7 and 2 with the assistance of a runner. Also appearing in the match for Harrow was a player by the name of Shakespeare.

SHAKESPEARIAN CRICKET QUOTES

'A very good bowler'—*Love's Labour's Lost*, Act 5, Scene 2

'Where go you? With bats and clubs?'—*Coriolanus*, Act 1, Scene 1

'A hit, a very palpable hit'—*Hamlet*, Act 5, Scene 2

'Sing willow, willow, willow'—*Othello*, Act 4, Scene 3

'Gower is a goot captain'—*Henry V*, Act 4, Scene 7

'Have I caught thee?'—*The Merry Wives of Windsor*, Act 1, Scene 3

'I see you stand like greyhounds in the slips'—*Henry V*, Act 3, Scene 1

'Doubly redoubled strokes'—*Macbeth*, Act 1, Scene 2

'This is the bloodiest shame, the wildest savagery, the vilest stroke'—*King John*, Act 4, Scene 3

'Bring me to the test'—*Hamlet*, Act 3, Scene 4

'Fetch my bail'—*All's Well That Ends Well*, Act 5, Scene 3

'How's that?'—*King Lear*, Scene 5, Act 1

'Ah, ah! You're caught'—*Antony and Cleopatra*, Act 2, Scene 5

'...Sweet duck...What a pair of spectacles is here!'—*Troilus and Cressida*, Act 4, Scene 4

'Let me be umpire'—*Henry VI (Part 1)*, Act 4, Scene 1

'Give me a bowl'—*Julius Caesar*, Act 4, Scene 3

•

The prolific comic novelist P.G. Wodehouse, creator of Bertie Wooster and the inimitable Jeeves, was an opening bowler for his school who later turned out for an Author's XI side, which occasionally featured Sir Arthur Conan Doyle. Wodehouse's proudest cricketing moment came in 1899 when, bowling for Dulwich College against Tonbridge School, he took seven wickets setting up his side's 170 run victory.

It's thought that both Wodehouse *and* Conan Doyle named their most famous literary characters after first-class cricketers. Wodehouse borrowed the name of Warwickshire fast bowler Percy Jeeves for Jeeves the butler, while it's been suggested that Conan Doyle named Sherlock Holmes after England Test player Mordecai *Sher*win, Derbyshire fast bowler Francis Shack*lock* and Hampshire all-rounder Henry *Holmes*.

> Oh, I am so glad you have begun to take an interest in cricket. It is simply a social necessity in England.
>
> **P.G. Wodehouse, *Piccadilly Jim***

•

Matthew Fleming, who made his first-class debut for Kent in 1988, is a cousin of the *James Bond* creator Ian Fleming.

•

In 1994 cricket commentator Henry Blofeld sold his collection of 150 first-edition books by Ian Fleming and P.G. Wodehouse at auction for £42,000. Blofeld's family were friends of Fleming, who named one of his arch-villains after them.

•

Australian author Jon Cleary

JON CLEARY'S ALL-TIME BEST TEST XI

1. Sunil Gavaskar
2. Arthur Morris
3. Don Bradman (c)
4. Denis Compton
5. Viv Richards
6. Garry Sobers
7. Keith Miller
8. Don Tallon
9. Dennis Lillee
10. Lance Gibbs
11. Bill O'Reilly

There are others who have scored more runs or taken more wickets—Hutton, Ponsford, Hammond, Botham to name some—and I gave some thought to one or two Pakistani players (but none to South African players, since I haven't seen enough of them) and to a couple of New Zealanders, but in the end my criterion was the pleasure that particular players had given me, and how they played the game.

Hutton and Ponsford would have to be compared to Morris, but I preferred to watch Morris. Hammond and Gower could be compared to Compton, but again Compton was the one who left me the most memories.

It was a toss-up between Miller and Botham, but Miller got the vote because I thought he was the most naturally gifted cricketer I've ever seen.

Australians predominate in my team, but I guess that's natural—I wouldn't quarrel with an Englishman or Pakistani or Indian or West Indian or Kiwi who chose another team altogether with only one or two Australians in it.

In the end we all choose out of our own eye.

Lord Dunsany, the prolific Irish poet and novelist, was a great devotee of the game, who staged regular cricket matches at his castle in County Meath at the turn of the century. Apart from his more famous works, such as *The Gods of Pagena* and *Patches of Sunlight*, Dunsany wrote many cricketing stories including 'The Unrecorded Test Match' and 'How Jembu Played for Cambridge'.

•

The English poet John Keats received a black eye after being hit by a cricket ball in 1819.

> I felt so much pleasure from the simple idea of your playing a game of cricket.
>
> —John Keats, to his brother

•

Although it is not regarded as a first-class match, Charles Wordsworth—a nephew of the poet William Wordsworth—took a five-wicket haul for Oxford when they dismissed Cambridge for 92 at Lord's in 1827. This was the first recognised match between the two universities.

•

Donald Woods—the author of the books *Biko* and *Asking for Trouble*, which were used for the film *Cry Freedom*—was arrested for anti-apartheid activities in 1977. At the time he was the only white member of the governing council of the South African Cricket Board.

•

Alec Waugh, a novelist like his brother Evelyn, was a great lover of the game who for nearly 50 years attended Test matches at Lord's. He played the game himself, appearing in the 1916 *Wisden* heading the batting averages for his school Sherbourne. He continued his cricket in later life, representing a number of teams including the MCC and the Old Broughtonians. Waugh's other cricketing claim to fame was being immortalised as Bobby Southcott, one of the main characters in the village match story contained in A.G. Macdonell's 1933 book, *England, Their England*.

ALEC WAUGH'S DREAM TEAM OF CRICKET WRITERS

1 W.A. Darlington
2 Herbert Farjeon
3 S.J. Snaith
4 Sir Arthur Conan Doyle (c)
5 Nigel Balchin
6 P.G. Wodehouse
7 Clifford Bax
8 Hugh de Selincourt
9 Reginald Berkeley
10 Hesketh Pritchard
11 Rupert Brooke

•

When George Bernard Shaw was told that England had won a Test series against Australia, he asked what they'd been testing.

•

Bryce Courtenay, author of the bestselling books *The Power of One, Tandia* and *April Fools Day*

BRYCE COURTENAY'S ALL-TIME BEST TEST XI

I imagine they play a lot of cricket in Heaven, this side will play there one day. It could win against the Devil himself. There are some very individual preferences here, which I will briefly comment upon after the list.

1 W.G. Grace
2 Jack Hobbs
3 Don Bradman (c)
4 K.S. Ranjitsinhji
5 Graeme Pollock
6 Garry Sobers
7 Bert Oldfield
8 Jim Laker
9 Bill O'Reilly
10 Dennis Lillee
11 Sydney Barnes

Purists might say this team has a long tail, with Oldfield, the wicket-keeper, coming in at seven, with the rest of the batting order to follow him all bunnies. However I would argue that by the time Oldfield went out to bat the score would be 6 for about 900, so it really wouldn't matter.

To the team itself, if you're going to have a game you might as well have the Father of Cricket opening the batting, that's why W.G. heads my list. You can't leave Hobbs out on figures alone, and he was an aristocrat at the crease.

Bradman is Bradman. With the possible exception of Walter Lindrum, no sportsman has dominated his chosen game like him, and he has to be the captain.

Ranji comes in next. A controversial choice I'm sure. But all reports say that he was a glorious and graceful player. Other choices to fill the number four position could have been Barrington from England, or indeed that giant, Trumper. But for sheer artistry we'll leave it with the Black Prince.

Pollock is five. A gifted left-hander who was the epitome of power and grace.

Six is Sobers, the greatest all-round cricketer of all time. He could open the bowling, bowl Chinamen or orthodox spin, take miracle catches anywhere on the field, and then come in and tear the opposing attack apart with his bat. Anyone who saw his 254 in Melbourne in 1971 will never forget it. He's also my vice-captain.

The keeper is Oldfield. He was a genius with the gloves, and could also take O'Reilly's spinners.

Laker comes in at eight. The off-spinner who took 19 wickets at Manchester in 1956. A feat that will never be equalled. A great genius with the ball.

'Tiger' O'Reilly is a natural at nine. He was claimed by Bradman to be the greatest bowler he ever faced. That's good enough for me.

Lillee is ten. Opening the bowling or using the old ball Lillee stamped his class on the game with sheer speed, controlled aggression and brains—he was a very smart bowler.

Sydney Barnes of England is my number eleven. Barnes was the greatest bowler of his age, and those who saw him claim him as The Greatest of All Time. He bowled fast-medium and his record speaks for itself. He claimed 189 wickets in just 27 Tests. Finally to carry the drinks, probably the second greatest all-rounder who ever lived, Alan Davidson.

What a team. And yet I've left out Lindwall, Miller, Trueman, Larwood, Mohammad, Trumper, Jackson, Ponsford, Freeman, Richards, Botham, etc, etc, etc.

This World XI on any wicket made by God or man would have thrashed the rest of the world.

●

J.M. Barrie, the British novelist and playwright best remembered for *Peter Pan*, had his own cricket team, The Allahakbarries, and once played in a cricket match at Lord's, for the Authors Club against the Press Club in 1896.

> **A loving wife is better than making 50 at cricket, or even 99. Beyond that I will not go.**
>
> **—J.M. Barrie**

●

THE FAVOURITE AUTHORS OF SOME MODERN-DAY TEST CRICKETERS

David Boon—Stephen King
Hansie Cronje—Bryce Courtenay, John Grisham
Martin Crowe—Robert Ludlum, Jeffrey Archer
Tony Dodemaide—Jeffrey Archer
Neil Fairbrother—Wilbur Smith
Neil Foster—Frederick Forsyth, John Mortimer, Tom Sharpe
Mike Gatting—J.R. Tolkein
Ian Healy—Wilbur Smith
Dean Jones—Thomas Harris
Chris Lewis—Tom Sharpe
Malcolm Marshall—Robert Ludlum, Sidney Sheldon
Tom Moody—Wilbur Smith
Derek Pringle—Paul Theroux, Don Delillo
Jonty Rhodes—Robert Ludlum, Jeffrey Archer
Richie Richardson—Sidney Sheldon
Jack Russell—Charles Dickens
Robin Smith—Sidney Sheldon, Wilbur Smith, Jeffrey Archer
Alec Stewart—Dick Francis
Peter Such—Wilbur Smith, Doris Lessing, F. Scott Fitzgerald

3 Caught in Court

One of the first recorded instances of cricket being the subject of a court case was in 1640 in England when a Maidstone court found a group of cricketers guilty of playing the game on Sunday.

•

One cricketer's fixation with the game was deemed sufficient grounds for divorce. In 1981 Mildred Rowley filed for divorce in a Wolverhampton court on the grounds of her husband's unreasonable behaviour, complaining that he was 'cricket mad'. 'Cricket was not just a hobby, it was a total obsession.' Her husband, Michael Rowley was unable to attend the court proceedings as he was playing cricket with his club, Stourbridge. Quizzed on the verdict by journalists, he said he had nothing to say, except 'I cannot stop—we have to get on with the game.'

•

Two days after he became Test cricket's first streaker, the artistically named Michael Angelow was fined on a charge of insulting behaviour when he appeared in the Marylebone Magistrates Court in London. Angelow made his history-making run on the fourth afternoon of the England–Australia Test match at Lord's in 1975, hurdling over each set of stumps. In court, the merchant seaman said he did it for a £20 bet, to which the judge replied: 'The court will have that £20. Please moderate your behaviour in future.'

•

In 1993 the former Pakistan fast bowler Sarfraz Nawaz found himself in court three times. On his first visit he was fined £100 and banned from driving for 15 months on a drink-driving charge. He then appeared in the Old Bailey charged with holding a woman prisoner. The incident allegedly took place in a London flat in 1992—he was also charged with stealing £200. Sarfraz walked a free man after the woman declined to give evidence against him. A few months later Sarfraz brought a libel action, that was later dropped, against Allan Lamb over allegations of ball tampering, made by his former Northamptonshire team-mate in a newspaper article the previous year.

•

In 1992 Torrel James, a former Trinidad and Tobago Youth Team representative, received a 15-year gaol sentence and 20 lashes with a tree branch after he was found guilty of the attempted murder of his girlfriend and her father.

•

Former Australian Test spinner Terry Jenner served 18 months of a six and a half year gaol term handed down in 1988 on embezzlement charges. The Adelaide judge who passed sentence described Jenner as a 'pathological gambler'. Jenner spent a year of his term at the Mobilong prison near Murray Bridge and six months on home detention.

> When I went to prison, of all the people I know, I would have voted myself the most unlikely to get through it because I thought I was as weak as water.
>
> —Terry Jenner

•

Bruce Taylor, a former New Zealand all-rounder, was sentenced to two years gaol in 1993 for theft. Taylor, the only player to record a century and five wickets in an innings on his Test debut (at Calcutta in 1964–65), was found guilty of stealing $A287,000 from a Dunedin Presbyterian high school where he'd been employed as an administrator.

•

Rusi Surti, the former Indian Test all-rounder, took his employer the Queensland Fire Service to court in 1992 seeking over $200,000 compensation on the grounds of racial abuse. The one-time Queensland Sheffield Shield representative lost the case, the court contending that much of the abuse was 'mere banter'.

•

A courtroom drama played out in Sydney in 1899 had all the ingredients for a gripping film script—a divorce, sex with a priest, a gun, and an Australian Test cricketer.

Arthur Coningham, an all-rounder who scored Queensland's first first-class century as an opening batsman, hit the headlines in 1894–95 when he became the first bowler to take a wicket with his first delivery on his Test debut. But it was for the something that happened off the field, rather than on, that Coningham will be probably best remembered.

In 1899 Coningham sued his wife for divorce on the grounds that a Sydney priest, D.F. O'Haran, had fathered one of his children. During the trial, in which he conducted his own case, evidence was tendered that it was highly unlikely that Coningham could have been the father due to an injury sustained by a cricket ball 10 years earlier. At the end of proceedings the jury could not agree on a verdict and another trial was scheduled—one that saw

Coningham produce a gun. He also had to be forcibly restrained after trying to attack the priest and breaking courtroom furniture.

Coningham failed to get his divorce, although a few years later, in Wellington, his wife managed to divorce *him* on the grounds of adultery. He also spent six months in gaol on fraud charges.

•

In 1944 the West Indies cricketer Learie Constantine took the owners of a London hotel chain to the High Court, charging that they'd denied him accommodation because of his colour. He won the case and was awarded nominal damages, an amount of five guineas.

•

Gloucestershire batsman Mark Alleyne was sentenced to 30 days gaol by a Nairobi court in 1990 after ripping up Kenyan banknotes. On appeal his sentence was suspended for a year.

•

In 1968 England's Test selectors Doug Insole, Alec Bedser, Don Kenyon, Peter May and Brian Close successfully brought a libel action in the High Court of Justice against Times Newspapers Limited. Michael Parkinson had written an article for the *Sunday Times* in 1967, highly critical of the selectors' decision to axe Geoff Boycott from the Test side, even though he'd scored a double-century in the previous Test. Parkinson suggested the selectors had done Boycott a considerable injustice and that they'd been influenced by 'unworthy and discreditable motives'. The newspaper publishers and Parkinson apologised to the selectors for the distress caused by the article and paid their legal costs.

•

Miles Giffard, who played cricket for Minor Counties in England in 1948, appeared in court four years later charged with the murder of his mother and father. Giffard, who'd been diagnosed as a schizophrenic, killed his parents by hitting them with an iron pipe and disposed of their bodies over a cliff. He was found guilty by the court and later executed.

•

In 1958 the former England opener Herbert Sutcliffe was fined 20 shillings in a London court for driving through a red light. In a letter to the court Sutcliffe wrote: 'I have no wish to doubt the accusation made by the police, but I should like to state that my eyesight and concentration are almost as good now as when I had the honour of playing for England along with my old partner Sir J.B. Hobbs'.

•

Imran Khan was fined nearly £300 after being charged with speeding on England's M1 motorway in 1993. Later in the year, England batsman Matthew Maynard received a £500 fine and an 18-month driving ban after being charged with driving three times over the limit.

•

During the World Series Cricket tour of the West Indies in 1978–79, Ian Chappell was charged and convicted in a Guyana court of assaulting a cricket official and using offensive language.

•

At a court hearing in Adelaide in 1993, one of cricket's most prominent authors was charged with the theft of property valued at $20,000 from the South Australian Cricket Association. In 1990 Chris Harte, an Englishman who'd lived and worked in Adelaide for 16 years, met Neil Hawke and offered to sell, on his behalf, some of the former Test player's cricket memorabilia in England. Some time later, Harte informed Hawke that the collection had been virtually destroyed in transit and that he was having some problems getting the insurance money. However, Hawke had discovered that one of the items, an Australian team blazer, had been sold for £500 at auction. In 1993 Harte returned to Adelaide to promote his latest book—*A History of Australian Cricket*—and upon arrival was arrested, spent the night in gaol and charged with false pretences. On bail, Harte was arrested a second time attempting to leave Australia on a flight to London. Although Hawke's case never proceeded to court, Harte was made to pay compensation, an amount of several thousand dollars.

Harte then appeared in the Adelaide Magistrate's court on a charge of stealing photographs and film from the SACA, who'd engaged him to write a history of the association. He was also charged with stealing approximately 1,000 copies of his book, *The History of the South Australian Cricket Association*, valued at $11,000. The magistrate gave him a suspended gaol sentence, a $1,000 fine and ordered him to pay compensation of $20,000.

•

A case being tried at the Kingston High Court in 1974 was unexpectedly interrupted by the judge, when he exclaimed: 'I have to tell you, gentlemen, that Boyce has been dismissed'. The defense counsel quickly replied that 'My client's name is Bryce!' 'Ah, quite so, but I thought you'd like to know the latest Test score from Sabina Park.' The trial, involving a man charged with robbery, was temporarily halted while the judge gave details of the second Test match against England.

•

A village cricket club in Durham pulled off its biggest victory in 1977 when the Appeal Court of London upheld its right to continue playing and to hit sixes into a neighbouring garden. John and Brenda Miller, whose house was situated near the Lintz Cricket Club in Burnopfield, took the cricketers to court in an attempt to ban their games. In 1976 a judge upheld their application until the club took steps to prevent balls landing on the Millers' property.

Lord Denning, sitting in the Appeal Court, overturned the ban and suggested the Millers move house. 'For over seventy years the game of cricket has been played on this ground to the great benefit of the community as a whole, and to the injury of none.' In summing up, he suggested that when cricket was being played Mr Miller should sit on the other side of the house, or go out.

•

A man who tried to strangle his girlfriend with an MCC tie after an argument following the 1989 NatWest Bank Trophy at Lord's was given a suspended gaol sentence at the Old Bailey in 1990.

•

Vallance Jupp, who appeared in eight Tests for England during the 1920s, was sent to gaol after being found guilty of manslaughter following the death of a person in a car accident.

4 Batting to Remember

On the day that thousands commemorated the 50th anniversary of D-Day in Normandy, across the channel at Edgbaston the cricket world was applauding another battle, one led single-handedly by West Indies batsman Brian Lara. Playing for Warwickshire against Durham in the 1994 County Championship, Lara became the first batsman in first-class cricket to score 500. His innings of 501 not out was his seventh hundred in eight consecutive first-class innings; a world record sequence which began with 375 against England at St John's—the highest individual score in Test cricket.

The first six months of 1994 were a breathtaking period for the young left-hander who smashed record after record with seemingly consummate ease. He began the year by amassing a record 715 runs for Trinidad and Tobago in the Red Stripe Cup, hitting three big centuries along the way—180, 169 and 206—the three highest individual scores of the season. A five-match Test series against England followed, in which he scored two centuries (167 & 375) and a total of 798 runs at the Bradman-like average of 99.75. Now rated the world's No. 1 batsman, Lara headed off to England for his first stint on the county circuit and celebrated his first-class debut for Warwickshire by scoring 147 against Glamorgan at Edgbaston. He then hit hundreds in his next five Championship matches, culminating in his world-record undefeated 501 against Durham. Starting the day at 111, Lara passed 'Tip' Foster's Warwickshire record of 305 not out which had stood since 1914; Archie MacLaren's 99-year English record of 424; and finally Hanif Mohammad's world record 499 against Bahawalpur at Karachi in 1958–59.

Despite a swag of world records collected in such a short space of time, Lara appeared totally unfazed by his front-page achievements. Asked to reflect on his 501, he modestly replied: 'I still don't think this makes me a great cricketer. It's nice to have records and be on top, but I've still got a lot of cricket ahead of me and I need to be more consistent.'

WARWICKSHIRE v DURHAM
Edgbaston 1994

D.P. Ostler	c Scott b Cummins	8
R.G. Twose	c Cox b Brown	51
B.C. Lara	not out	501
T. Penney	c Hutton b Bainbridge	44
P.A. Smith	lbw Cummins	12
K.J. Piper	not out	116
Extras	(b28, lb22, w2, nb26)	78
	4 declared for	810

BRIAN LARA'S 501* v DURHAM
The milestones

- His 501* is the highest individual score in first-class cricket and was his seventh hundred in eight first-class innings, another world record—375 v England at St John's, 147 v Glamorgan at Edgbaston, 106 & 120* v Leicestershire at Edgbaston, 136 v Somerset at Taunton, 26 & 140 v Middlesex at Lord's and 501*.
- Despite playing only one innings he became the first batsman to score 500 runs in a first-class match.
- His innings included a world record number of boundaries—62 fours and 10 sixes.
- He scored 390 runs in a day—another world record.
- During his knock he passed the milestone of 1,000 first-class runs in just seven innings—a record for Warwickshire and one that equalled Don Bradman's achievement in England in 1938. From seven innings for Warwickshire Lara had scored 1,176 runs at 235.20.

HOW BRIAN LARA SCORED HIS WORLD RECORD 501*

Score	Mins	Balls	4s	6s
100	144	138	14	–
150	201	193	22	–
200	224	220	30	2
250	246	245	37	5
300	280	278	44	7
350	319	311	49	8
400	367	350	53	8
450	430	398	55	9
501	474	427	62	10

THE TOP FIVE HITS OF ALL-TIME

First-class

501*	Brian Lara	Warwickshire v Durham at Edgbaston in 1994
499	Hanif Mohammad	Karachi v Bahawalpur at Karachi in 1958–59
452*	Don Bradman	NSW v Queensland at Sydney in 1929–30
443*	B.B. Nimbalkar	Maharashtra v Kathiawar at Poona in 1948–49
437	Bill Ponsford	Victoria v Queensland at Melbourne in 1927–28

Test

375	Brian Lara	West Indies v England at St John's in 1993–94
365*	Garry Sobers	West Indies v Pakistan at Kingston in 1957–58
364	Len Hutton	England v Australia at The Oval in 1938
337	Hanif Mohammad	Pakistan v West Indies at Bridgetown in 1957–58
336*	Walter Hammond	England v New Zealand at Auckland in 1932–33

●

The irrepressible Brian Lara who, in a three-month period in 1994, made a Test record 375, a world record 501*, seven centuries in eight first-class innings and eight in 11 innings

Greg Matthews was the surprise batsman to come out on top of the aggregates in the three-match Test series against Sri Lanka in 1992–93. He was the only batsman from either side to get 300 runs, his total of 329 including five consecutive half-centuries—64, 55 & 51 and 57 & 96.

•

Chris Tavaré, one of the great stonewallers, surprised all in a County Championship match in 1985, hitting three sixes in four balls against Hampshire at Southampton. In a Test match against Australia at Manchester in 1981 Tavaré made history by scoring 69 in 287 minutes and 78 in 423 minutes.

•

When Leicestershire suffered a 10-wicket defeat at Old Trafford in 1956, only two Lancashire batsmen were required to bat. Lancashire secured an easy win, scoring nought declared for 166 and none for 66 thanks to the two openers Jack Dyson (75* & 31*) and Alan Wharton (87* & 33*).

•

A South African batting record of 54 years standing was broken in 1993–94, not once, but twice within a few weeks. During the 1939–40 season Eric Rowan scored an unbeaten 306 for Transvaal v Natal at Johannesburg, the highest individual innings in South African history. The first batsman to extinguish Rowan's record in '93–94 was Terence Lazard with 307 for Boland against Western Province at Worcester. Lazard was to hold the record for just a short time, with Transvaal's Daryll Cullinan scoring 337 not out against Northern Transvaal at Johannesburg a month later.

•

Mark Waugh completed an extraordinary double in 1993, scoring consecutive centuries in the same fixture but for rival teams. In 1989 while playing county cricket for Essex, Waugh scored 100 not out against the touring Australians and in 1993 made 108 for the Australians *against* Essex.

•

Mohammad Azharuddin made history in 1984–85 when he became the first batsman to score centuries in his first three Tests. Just prior to his first Test at Calcutta, Azharuddin made centries in the three first-class innings leading up to his international debut. In 11 successive innings he hit nine fifties, going on to the century-mark six times.

Score	Match
52*	Indian Cricket Board President's XI v England XI at Jaipur
151	Indian Under-25 XI v England XI at Ahmedabad
121 & 105*	Hyderabad v Andhra at Machillipatnam
110	India v England at Calcutta
18 & 52	South Zone v England XI at Secunderabad
48 & 105	India v England at Madras
122 & 54*	India v England at Kanpur

•

In the space of four days during the 1993–94 Champions Trophy tournament at Sharjah, Pakistan opener Saeed Anwar hit three consecutive one-day international centuries—107 v Sri Lanka, 131 v West Indies and 111 v Sri Lanka.

•

In 1936 two batsmen named Wensley and Ashdown were asked to take on an entire eleven to mark the anniversary of a match in England in 1834 in which E.G. Wenham and Richard Mills single-handedly defeated the Isle of Oxney cricket team. History repeated itself with the Oxney XI making 153 in 24.4 overs, and Wensley and Ashdown then knocking off the required total in 36.4 overs.

•

> I was on 99 . . . I got really scared. I pooped my pants, missed the next ball and was bowled.
>
> —Victorian batsman Brad Hodge
> on his dismissal in a Melbourne under-12 cricket final

Gordon Greenidge, the scorer of 19 Test hundreds, set an unusual record in 1979–80 when he became the first batsman to make a pair of nineties in the same Test more than once. His double of 91 and 97 at Christchurch followed his 91 and 96 against Pakistan at Georgetown

24   CRICKET EXTRAS 2

in 1976–77. Before him, only Australia's Clem Hill and England's Frank Woolley had been unlucky enough to fall in the nineties twice in the same Test.

•

India's Vinod Kambli, at the age of just 21, hit the headlines in 1993 when he became the first batsman to score two double-centuries and another century in successive Test innings. After a memorable 224 against England at Bombay in 1992–93, Kambli scored 227 against Zimbabwe at New Delhi and, in his next innings, 125 against Sri Lanka at Colombo. In the following Test, also at Colombo, the left-hander scored 120—his fourth hundred in five innings in which he batted.

•

John Emburey, who topped England's batting averages with 92.00 in the 1993 Ashes series, once hit six sixes in seven balls when playing for Western Province in the Currie Cup. The off-spinner established a new South African record with his big hitting, scoring 52 not out at No. 9 in the match against Eastern Province at Cape Town in 1983–84.

John Emburey

During the summer of 1993–94 Test opener Michael Slater was three times dismissed in the nervous nineties—for 99 against New Zealand at Perth and for 92 against South Africa at Sydney and 95 at Durban. His unlucky hat-trick of outs was the first instance of an Australian opener dismissed three times in the nineties in a single season.

On a slightly brighter note, it was during the second Test against the South Africans at Cape Town that Slater reached the landmark of 1,000 Test runs. He got there only 293 days after making his debut—an Australian Test record, one that was previously held by his batting partner Mark Taylor.

The Australian record for the fastest 1,000 Test runs in terms of innings is held by Don Bradman, who managed the magic milestone in just 13 knocks.

FEWEST INNINGS TO REACH EACH 1,000-RUN LANDMARK

Runs	Innings	Batsman
1,000	12	Herbert Sutcliffe (England)
	12	Everton Weekes (West Indies)
2,000	22	Don Bradman (Australia)
3,000	33	Don Bradman (Australia)
4,000	48	Don Bradman (Australia)
5,000	56	Don Bradman (Australia)
6,000	68	Don Bradman (Australia)
7,000	131	Walter Hammond (England)
8,000	157	Garry Sobers (West Indies)
9,000	192	Sunil Gavaskar (India)
10,000	212	Sunil Gavaskar (India)
11,000	260	Allan Border (Australia)

•

On his Test debut at The Oval in 1981, Dirk Wellham made history by scoring 103 which followed a century (100) on his first-class debut for New South Wales against Victoria the previous summer. He was the first Australian to achieve the feat and only the second after India's Gundappa Viswanath. However, Wellham suffered the extreme misfortune of being dropped for the next match for both New South Wales and Australia.

•

When England played the West Indies at Port-of-Spain in 1947–48 all four openers scored centuries—Jack Robertson 133, 'Billy' Griffith 140, George Carew 107 and Andy Ganteaume 112. This Test match remains unique with two batsmen—Griffith and Ganteaume—scoring centuries on debut and then both being dropped for the following Test.

A CENTURY IN FIRST TEST THEN OUT OF THE NEXT

Batsman and score	Test debut	Total Tests	Total inns
Roger Hartigan (116)	Australia v England at Adelaide in 1907–08	2	4
'Billy' Griffith (140)	England v West Indies at Port-of-Spain in 1947–48	3	5
Andy Ganteaume (112)	West Indies v England at Port-of-Spain in 1947–48	1	1
Arthur Milton (104*)	England v New Zealand at Leeds in 1958	6	9
Khalid Ibadulla (166)	Pakistan v Australia at Karachi in 1964–65	4	8
Rodney Redmond (107)	New Zealand v Pakistan at Auckland in 1972–73	1	2
Dirk Wellham (103)	Australia v England at The Oval in 1981	6	11

In the same Test series that Sunil Gavaskar scored his record 774 runs (v West Indies 1970–71) another debutant batsman also impressed. For Desmond Lewis, a wicket-keeper, this was his only taste of big-time cricket and he made the most of it scoring 81 not out on debut at Georgetown, and 88 and 72 in the following matches. His three-match Test career yielded him 259 runs, average 86.33.

•

When New Zealand fast bowler Richard Collinge made his highest Test score of 68 not out, against Pakistan at Auckland in 1972–73, it was the highest innings by a No. 11 batsman in Test cricket. He set another Test record during his stay at the crease, putting on a 10th wicket stand of 151 with Brian Hastings which beat the partnership of 130 between England's 'Tip' Foster and Wilfred Rhodes in the first Test at Sydney in 1903–04.

		HIGHEST TEST SCORES FOR EACH BATTING POSITION	
1	364	Len Hutton	England v Australia at The Oval in 1938
2	325	Andy Sandham	England v West Indies at Kingston in 1929–30
3	375	Brian Lara	West Indies v England at St John's in 1993–94
4	307	Bob Cowper	Australia v England at Melbourne in 1965–66
5	304	Don Bradman	Australia v England at Leeds in 1934
6	250	Doug Walters	Australia v New Zealand at Christchurch in 1976–77
7	270	Don Bradman	Australia v England at Melbourne in 1936–37
8	209	Imtiaz Ahmed	Pakistan v New Zealand at Lahore in 1955–56
9	173	Ian Smith	New Zealand v India at Auckland in 1989–90
10	117	Walter Read	England v Australia at The Oval in 1884
11	68*	Richard Collinge	New Zealand v Pakistan at Auckland in 1972–73

•

The New South Wales batsman Wendell Bill hit a century in his first first-class match and his last—115 v Tasmania at Sydney in 1929–30 and 118 for the Australians against a Patiala XI at Patiala in 1935–36. South Australia's Ron Hamence is the only other Australian batsman to record a similar double—121 on his first-class debut, against Tasmania at Adelaide in 1935–36 and 114 in his farewell match, against the MCC at Adelaide in 1950–51.

•

When the West Indians played Cambridge University in 1950 the average number of runs scored per wicket established a new record in first-class cricket. The students scored 4 declared for 594, and in reply the tourists made 3 for 730, for an average of 189 runs per wicket. The match included two triple-century partnerships, one for each side—343 for the first wicket by John Dewes and David Sheppard and 350 for the third wicket by Frank Worrell and Everton Weekes.

•

England's Colin Cowdrey, the first player to appear in 100 Test matches, celebrated the event by scoring a century

Rohan Kanhai, the West Indies batsman who scored six Test-match nineties

Although Alvin Kallicharran scored 12 Test match centuries, he got close on numerous other occasions, making it into the nineties without reaching 100 a record eight times. Fellow West Indians Gordon Greenidge and Rohan Kanhai were each out in the nineties six times during their Test careers, while Garry Sobers made five Test nineties.

THE MOST TEST SCORES BETWEEN 90 AND 99 BY ONE BATSMAN		
A.I. Kallicharran (8)	91	v England at Port-of-Spain in 1972–73
	93	v England at Kingston in 1973–74
	98	v India at Bombay in 1974–75
	92*	v Pakistan at Lahore in 1974–75
	93	v India at Bridgetown in 1975–76
	97	v England at Nottingham in 1976
	92	v Australia at Port-of-Spain in 1977–78
	98	v India at Madras in 1978–79

•

On his Test debut, Australia's Bruce Laird set a new record by scoring 167 runs, the highest aggregate in a batsman's first match without the aid of a century—92 & 75 v West Indies at Brisbane in 1979–80.

•

(104 v Australia at Birmingham in 1968). On his way to the hundred, Cowdrey became the second batsman after Walter Hammond to pass 7,000 Test runs. Against New Zealand at Brisbane in 1993–94, Allan Border became the first to appear in 150 Tests and, like Cowdrey, he too marked the occasion by scoring a century (105).

COLIN COWDREY'S ALL-TIME BEST TEST XI

1 Jack Hobbs
2 Bill Ponsford
3 Don Bradman (c)
4 Walter Hammond
5 Denis Compton
6 Garry Sobers
7 Godfrey Evans
8 Ray Lindwall
9 Wes Hall
10 Jim Laker
11 Bill O'Reilly

•

David Lloyd passed the half-century mark just once in his nine-match Test career for England, but converted that 50 into a double-century—214 not out against India at Edgbaston in 1974.

Former England opener David Lloyd

•

In only his sixth match of 1993–94, Queensland's Matthew Hayden passed the coveted milestone of 1,000 first-class runs, becoming just the fourth batsman after Don Bradman, Greg Chappell and Allan Border to attain the feat in three consecutive domestic seasons, and the first to do it at the beginning of his career. In 1991–92 he made 1,028 runs, the first Australian, and only the 33rd batsman worldwide, to crack the 1,000-run target in the season of his first-class debut. Selected in the 1993 Ashes squad, Hayden then became the first Australian batsman to score 1,000 first-class runs on an overseas tour without playing in a Test. In 13 matches, the Queensland opener made 1,150 runs at 57.50, but so good was the Australian side he was unable to break into the first XI.

Still unable to gain a Test berth, Hayden developed an insatiable appetite for big scores in 1993–94, hitting seven centuries, with three in successive innings *twice*, and an unbeaten 96 in his only six matches of the season at the phenomenal average of 126.22.

1,000 FIRST-CLASS RUNS IN FIRST FOUR SEASONS

	M	I	NO	Runs	HS	100s	Avge
1991–92 Australia	11	21	2	1,028	149	3	54.10
1992–93 Australia	14	26	2	1,249	161*	2	52.04
1993 England	13	21	1	1,150	151*	3	57.50
1993–94 Australia	6	12	3	1,136	173*	7	126.22

Against South Australia at Adelaide he scored twin centuries (165 & 116), sharing with Trevor Barsby two 150-plus-run opening partnerships (183 & 243). Hayden and Paul Nobes (140 & 106) made history in this match by both making twin hundreds, the first example of opposing opening batsmen recording the feat in a first-class match in Australia. And along the way, Hayden entered the Sheffield Shield hall of fame by passing the milestone of 2,500 runs in his first 25 matches. Only greats such as Bradman, Bill Ponsford and Arthur Morris have bettered his performance.

2,000 RUNS IN FIRST 25 SHEFFIELD SHIELD APPEARANCES

Batsman	State	Runs	100s	50s	Avge
Bill Ponsford	Victoria	3,948	16	9	98.70
Don Bradman	New South Wales	3,558	13	8	98.83
Arthur Morris	New South Wales	2,709	10	10	69,46
Matthew Hayden	Queensland	2,661	9	11	63.35

Batting against Victoria at the Gabba he completed another batch of twin hundreds (126 & 155), the second of which was his sixth in seven innings. His 155, the seventh hundred he'd scored in the summer, gave Hayden yet another record—the most Sheffield Shield centuries in a season—one held previously by Queensland's David Ogilvie.

MOST SHEFFIELD SHIELD CENTURIES IN A SEASON

Batsman	Scores	Season
Matthew Hayden (Qld – 7)	125, 173*, 165, 116, 121*, 126, 155	1993–94
David Ogilvie (Qld – 6)	194, 109, 100, 104, 106, 168*	1977–78

MOST CENTURIES IN AN AUSTRALIAN SEASON

Batsman	Scores	Season
Don Bradman (8)	156, 100, 172, 185, 132, 127*, 201, 115	1947–48
Walter Hammond (7)	145, 225, 251, 200, 119, 177, 114	1928–29
Don Bradman (7)	131, 133*, 132*, 112, 340*, 175, 123	1928–29
Don Bradman (7)	135, 226, 219, 112, 167, 167, 299*	1931–32
Don Bradman (7)	101, 246, 107, 113, 104*, 144, 102	1937–38
Mark Taylor (7)	199, 164, 108, 101, 101*, 127, 100	1989–90
Matthew Hayden (7)	125, 173*, 165, 116, 121*, 126, 155	1993–94

Hayden also proved a powerful force in domestic limited-overs cricket averaging over 50 in each of his first

Matthew Hayden—the first Australian batsman to score 1,000 first-class runs in his first four seasons, a record that earned him his first Test cap, against South Africa at Johannesburg in 1993–94

two seasons. He made an unbeaten half-century on his debut in 1992–93 and a not out hundred in his second match.

Season	M	NO	Runs	HS	100s	50s	Avge
1992–93	4	2	250	121*	1	2	125.00
1993–94	3	0	157	110	1	0	52.33

•

Fred Geeson, a medium-paced bowler who played for Leicestershire, is the holder of a most unusual first-class batting record. In 1899 he had three innings of 32 in a row, against Derbyshire and Warwickshire—the highest-ever score made in three *successive* first-class innings.

•

Batting against Surrey at The Oval in 1976, Zaheer Abbas scored a mammoth 372 runs for Gloucestershire without being dismissed—216 not out and 156 not out. Later in the season he repeated the feat of a double-century and a century in the same match, and went on to complete four such doubles, a world record.

216* & 156* — Gloucestershire v Surrey at The Oval in 1976
230* & 104* — Gloucestershire v Kent at Canterbury in 1976
205* & 108* — Gloucestershire v Sussex in Cheltenham in 1977
215* & 150* — Gloucestershire v Somerset at Bath in 1981

•

'Sunny Jim' Mackay, who played in just 16 matches for New South Wales, once reeled off six centuries and a ninety in eight innings. In his last knock of the 1904–05 season, Mackay scored 131 and then made 203, 90, 194, 105 & 102 not out and 4 & 136 in his next seven outings

the following summer. His double of 105 & 102* against South Australia at the SCG was the first example of a NSW batsman scoring two first-class hundreds in the same match. The 1905–06 season brought Mackay 902 runs, average 112.75, but was not enough to win him a spot in the Australian Test side.

Later in the season, Algy Gehrs matched Mackay's feat, becoming the first South Australian to score a century in each innings, carrying his bat for 148 not out and then scoring an unbeaten 100, batting at No. 4, against Western Australia at Fremantle. West Australian opener Harry Howard also carried his bat, for 47, in this match and like Gehrs batted down the order in the second innings, scoring an unbeaten 6. These two openers provide the only instance in Australian first-class cricket of rival batsmen carrying their bats in the same match.

•

A case of batting to remember, or bowling to forget? In 1993 Lancashire's Glen Chapple recorded the fastest century of all time during the County Championship match against Glamorgan at Old Trafford. Scored off joke bowling, his maiden first-class hundred was reached from 27 balls in 21 minutes. Glamorgan's attempts to contrive a finish saw fielders deliberately let balls go to the boundary—Viv Richards even tried to kick one over the rope. Chapple ended up scoring 109 not out with 10 fours and nine sixes. He hit 34 runs (6,6,4,6,6,6) off Phil Cottey's second over and 32 off his third.

	FASTEST CENTURIES IN FIRST-CLASS CRICKET	
Mins	*Batsman and Score*	*Match*
35	Percy Fender (113*)	Surrey v Northamptonshire at Northampton in 1920
40	Gilbert Jessop (101)	Gloucestershire v Yorkshire at Harrogate in 1897
40	Ahsan-ul-Haq (100*)	Muslims v Sikhs at Lahore in 1923–24
42	Gilbert Jessop (191)	Gentlemen of South v Players of South at Hastings in 1907
43	'Monkey' Hornby (106)	Lancashire v Somerset at Manchester in 1905
43	David Hookes (107)	South Australia v Victoria at Adelaide in 1982–83

	FASTEST FIRST-CLASS CENTURIES SCORED IN CONTRIVED CIRCUMSTANCES	
21	Glen Chapple (109*)	Lancashire v Glamorgan at Manchester in 1993
26	Tom Moody (103*)	Warwickshire v Glamorgan at Swansea in 1990
35	Steve O'Shaughnessy (105)	Lancashire v Leicestershire at Manchester in 1983
37	Chris Old (107)	Yorkshire v Warwickshire at Birmingham in 1977
41	Nigel Popplewell (143*)	Somerset v Gloucestershire at Bath in 1983
46	Graeme Fowler (100)	Lancashire v Leicestershire at Manchester in 1983

•

Gilbert Jessop, one of the biggest hitters of the ball in cricket history, was also one of the fastest scorers, recording a first-class century in 60 minutes or less on no

Gilbert Jessop

fewer than 14 occasions in his illustrious career. He twice scored a fifty in 15 minutes and for over 80 years was the holder of the record for the fastest double-century in first-class cricket. Batting for Gloucestershire against Sussex at Hove in 1903 he reached 200 in 120 minutes, a record equalled by Clive Lloyd in 1976 and then broken by Bombay's Ravi Shastri in 1984–85.

FAST FIFTIES

Mins	Score	Match
15	61	Gloucestershire v Somerset at Bristol in 1904
15	92	Gloucestershire v Hampshire at Cheltenham in 1907

FAST CENTURIES

40	101	Gloucestershire v Yorkshire at Harrogate in 1897
42	191	Gentlemen of South v Players of South at Hastings in 1907
53	139	Gloucestershire v Surrey at Bristol in 1911
55	123*	South v North at Hastings in 1900
55	126	Gloucestershire v Nottinghamshire at Nottingham in 1902
55	119	Gloucestershire v Sussex at Hastings in 1907
55	116	Lord Londesborough's XI v Kent at Scarborough in 1913
57	124	Gloucestershire v Middlesex at Lord's in 1901
59	139	Gloucestershire v Yorkshire at Bradford in 1900
60	112*	The Rest v A.E. Stoddart's XI at Hastings in 1898
60	126	Gloucestershire v Nottinghamshire at Nottingham in 1899
60	109	Gloucestershire v Middlesex at Lord's in 1900
60	169	MCC v Leicestershire at Lord's in 1901
60	165	Gloucestershire v Worcestershire at Stourbridge in 1910

FAST DOUBLE-CENTURIES

120	286	Gloucestershire v Sussex at Hove in 1903
130	234	Gloucestershire v Somerset at Bristol in 1905
135	233	The Rest v Yorkshire at Lord's in 1901
140	206	Gloucestershire v Nottinghamshire at Nottingham in 1904

In 1901 the same season that Jessop scored 200 in 135 minutes at Lord's, he combined with Australian Sammy Woods in a match at Bristol, recording a partnership of 142 against E.H. Cook's XI in just 22 minutes. The pair reached 50 in eight minutes and 100 in 16.

•

South Australia's David Hookes created history in 1976–77 when he hit a century in each innings of two consecutive first-class matches—185 & 105 v Queensland at Adelaide and 135 & 156 against New South Wales, also at Adelaide. In each of the four innings, Hookes was South Australia's top scorer, a unique feat.

•

During the 1992 Sunday League, the powerful West Australian batsman Tom Moody scored his 1,000th run in the competition for Worcestershire, completing the feat in just 18 innings, a record for any county.

•

There was some big scoring in Sydney first-grade cricket during the 1993–94 season, with three batsmen posting double-centuries in the space of a week. All were history-making innings, the most significant being one of 275 by Canterbury's wicket-keeper Sean Pope against Hawkesbury at Bensons Lane. Batting as a night-watchman, his runs came off 225 balls in 307 minutes and included 29 fours and five sixes. It was the highest innings played in Sydney club cricket since World War II and the third best of all time after Victor Trumper (335) and Harry Donnan (308). During the same round, Penrith and New South Wales batsman Trevor Bayliss also notched a double-ton—a club record 206 not out against Petersham.

The following weekend Petersham incurred the wrath of another state batsman, Randwick's Martin Haywood, who belted 204 not out, putting his name in the record books by hitting six sixes in one over off spinner Wayne Mulherin. The right-hander figured in an unbroken third wicket partnership of 321 with Andrew Millican, who made 107.

On the same day that Haywood hit the big-time, several other batsmen around the state also recorded double-centuries. On his way to posting 1,000 first-class runs for the season, the New South Wales dasher Michael Bevan scored his maiden double-century—203 not out against Western Australia. It was the first Sheffield Shield 200 at the SCG since Bob Simpson's 277 v Queensland in 1967–68.

In a sub-district match at Balmoral, Northcote batsmen Brendan Kilham and Damien Poder both made 200 against Northbridge, while Terry Baldwin playing for Bowraville on the North Coast smashed 210 not out against Taylors Arm.

Sri Lanka's Aravinda de Silva

When Aravinda de Silva scored 68 against South Africa at Moratuwa in 1993–94, it was his 59th innings in Test cricket—his career to that point, duck-free. His first run in the second innings at the Tyronne Fernando Stadium took from Clive Lloyd the record for the most Test innings from debut without making a duck.

•

Playing for South Australia in 1970–71, the South African batsman Barry Richards became the first and only batsman since Don Bradman to score 1,500 runs in a season at a century average. Helped by his big knock of 356 against Western Australia at Perth, Richards made a total of 1,538 runs, average 109.85.

Richards and Bradman are the only batsmen to complete 1,000 runs in the Sheffield Shield at an average of over 100. In 62 Shield appearances Bradman clocked 8,926 runs at 110.19; Richards in eight matches in 1970–71 scored 1,145 runs at 104.90.

In 1925 Orange Free State's Len Tuckett finished the year on a high note, sharing a 115-run last-wicket partnership with L.G. Fuller against Western Province at Bloemfontein. In the second innings, he celebrated the new year in unique fashion with another century 10th wicket stand, one of 129 with F. Caufield, who was appearing in his first first-class match.

•

Opening the West Indies batting in the second Test at Lord's in 1963, Conrad Hunte hit the first three balls of the match to the boundary. In the previous Test he made 182, then the highest Test innings against England at Old Trafford.

•

After dismissing a New Zealand Emerging Players XI for just 93 at Napier, the touring 1993–94 Pakistanis then rattled up a mighty eight declared for 485. A most unusual aspect of this innings was that three batsmen retired halfway through. Perhaps bored with the mediocre bowling attack or wanting to give others a go, Saeed Anwar gave up when on 114, Basit Ali retired on reaching 100 while Inzaman-ul-Haq retired with his score on 65.

•

In a minor match in South Africa in 1901–02, A.C. Richards hit a pair of centuries in a display that totally outclassed all his team-mates. In the first innings he scored 101 not out—next highest score 2; and 185 in the second innings—next highest score 6.

•

BARRY RICHARDS' ALL-TIME BEST TEST XI
1 Len Hutton
2 Colin Milburn
3 Don Bradman (c)
4 Graeme Pollock
5 Garry Sobers
6 Ian Botham
7 Alan Knott
8 Andy Roberts
9 Dennis Lillee
10 Harold Larwood
11 Bishen Bedi

1,000 RUNS AT A CENTURY AVERAGE IN AN AUSTRALIAN SEASON

Batsman	Season	M	I	NO	Runs	100s	HS	Avge
Don Bradman (NSW)	1929–30	11	16	2	1,586	5	452*	113.28
Barry Richards (SA)	1970–71	10	16	2	1,538	6	356	109.85
Don Bradman (SA)	1939–40	9	15	3	1,475	5	267	122.91
Don Bradman (NSW/A)	1931–32	10	13	1	1,403	7	299*	116.91
Don Bradman (SA/A)	1947–48	9	12	2	1,296	8	201	129.60
Bill Ponsford (Vic)	1926–27	6	10	0	1,229	6	352	122.90
Bill Ponsford (Vic)	1927–28	6	8	0	1,217	4	437	152.12
Don Bradman (NSW)	1933–34	7	11	2	1,192	5	253	132.44
Don Bradman (SA)	1935–36	8	9	0	1,173	4	369	130.33
Matthew Hayden (Qld)	1993–94	6	12	3	1,136	7	173*	126.22
Graham Yallop (Vic/A)	1983–84	8	11	1	1,132	5	268	113.20
Bill Brown (Qld/A)	1938–39	7	11	1	1,057	3	215	105.70

When Jimmy Cook carried his bat for 120 and 131 against Nottinghamshire in 1989, each of his unbeaten hundreds represented over 50% of Somerset's total in each innings (186 & 218).

•

Ron Headley, who would go on to play for the West Indies, forged a unique partnership with Peter Stimpson in the English County Championship in 1971. They produced four century opening partnerships in their first two matches together for Worcestershire, the first time this had happened in English first-class cricket. In their first outing, the two opened with 125 and 147 v Northamptonshire at Worcester and against Warwickshire at Birmingham, 102 and an unbeaten 128.

•

In the opening match of the 1993–94 season, the occasional West Australian opening pair of Geoff Marsh and Mark McPhee carved a special niche in cricket history when they became the first duo to record four 100-run first-wicket partnerships in the domestic limited-overs arena. In 1990–91 they opened the innings four times and on each occasion reached 50, going on to the century mark thrice. McPhee then found himself out of favour for a couple of seasons, but on his return to the side in 1993–94 smashed 97 against South Australia, sharing with Marsh an opening stand of 120—their fourth 100-run partnership in five consecutive innings together.

The South African and Somerset batsman Jimmy Cook

Geoff Marsh

Mark McPhee

When A. Campbell scored 117 not out and 118 in Sydney in 1897–98, he became the first schoolboy in the world to produce two centuries in the same match.

•

On his Test debut for Australia at Perth in 1983–84, Wayne Phillips' score of 159 was 20 runs greater than Pakistan's 11 batsmen managed in the first innings. His feat of outscoring the opposition on debut is unique amongst Australian batsmen.

•

When Mark Taylor and Michael Slater opened the innings with 128 in the first Test at Manchester in 1993, they became the first New South Wales pair to open for Australia since Rick McCosker and Ian Davis at Leeds in 1977—156 Tests ago. They were also the first opening pair from any one state since Western Australia's Graeme Wood and Bruce Laird went in first against Pakistan at Lahore in 1982–83.

The marriage of Taylor and Slater at the top of the order proved to be a happy one, with the pair passing the 50-mark four times in the six Tests against England. They averaged 67.70 for the first wicket with a best stand of 260 in the second Test at Lord's. During their double-century partnership both openers scored centuries, the first time this had happened in a Test match at Lord's. Five Tests later, Taylor and Slater missed out by just one run in becoming the first opening pair to score centuries at Perth. In the first Test of the 1993–94 Trans-Tasman series against New Zealand, Taylor made an unbeaten 142 in the second innings, while his partner was dismissed for 99.

Jack Hobbs and Herbert Sutcliffe, the England opening pair, who on two occasions both hit centuries in the same Test innings

---

CENTURIES BY PAIRS OF OPENING BATSMEN IN A TEST INNINGS

Batsman and scores	*Match*
F.S. Jackson (118) and Tom Hayward (137)	England v Australia at The Oval in 1899
Jack Hobbs (178) and Wilfred Rhodes (179)	England v Australia at Melbourne in 1911–12
Jack Hobbs (154) and Herbert Sutcliffe (176)	England v Australia at Melbourne in 1924–25
Jack Hobbs (100) and Herbert Sutcliffe (161)	England v Australia at The Oval in 1926
'Stewie' Dempster (136) and John Mills (117)	New Zealand v England at Wellington in 1929–30
Bruce Mitchell (123) and 'Jack' Siedle (141)	South Africa v England at Cape Town in 1930–31
Jim Christy (103) and Bruce Mitchell (113)	South Africa v New Zealand at Christchurch in 1931–32
Bill Brown (121) and Jack Fingleton (112)	Australia v South Africa at Cape Town in 1935–36
Vijay Merchant (114) and Mushtaq Ali (112)	India v England at Manchester in 1936
Charlie Barnett (126) and Len Hutton (100)	England v Australia at Nottingham in 1938
George Carew (107) and Andy Ganteaume (112)	West Indies v England at Port-of-Spain in 1947–48
Allan Rae (109) and Jeffrey Stollmeyer (160)	West Indies v India at Madras in 1948–49
Len Hutton (158) and Cyril Washbrook (195)	England v South Africa at Johannesburg in 1948–49
Arthur Morris (111) and Jack Moroney (118)	Australia v South Africa at Johannesburg in 1949–50
Colin McDonald (110) and Arthur Morris (111)	Australia v West Indies at Port-of-Spain in 1954–55
Vinoo Mankad (231) and Pankaj Roy (173)	India v New Zealand at Madras in 1955–56
Geoff Pullar (175) and Colin Cowdrey (155)	England v South Africa at The Oval in 1960
Bill Lawry (106) and Bob Simpson (311)	Australia v England at Manchester in 1964
Bill Lawry (210) and Bob Simpson (201)	Australia v West Indies at Bridgetown in 1964–65
Bob Simpson (225) and Bill Lawry (119)	Australia v England at Adelaide in 1965–66
Bob Simpson (109) and Bill Lawry (100)	Australia v India at Melbourne in 1967–68
Glenn Turner (259) and Terry Jarvis (182)	New Zealand v West Indies at Georgetown in 1971–72
Roy Fredericks (109) and Gordon Greenidge (115)	West Indies v England at Leeds in 1976
Gordon Greenidge (154*) and Desmond Haynes (135)	West Indies v India at Antigua in 1982–83
Graeme Fowler (105) and Chris Tavaré (109)	England v New Zealand at The Oval in 1983
Gordon Greenidge (120*) and Desmond Haynes (103*)	West Indies v Australia at Georgetown in 1983–84
Sunil Gavaskar (172) and Kris Srikkanth (116)	India v Australia at Sydney in 1985–86
Geoff Marsh (138) and Mark Taylor (209)	Australia v England at Nottingham in 1989
Desmond Haynes (167) and Gordon Greenidge (149)	West Indies v England at Antigua in 1989–90
Mark Taylor (111) and Michael Slater (152)	Australia v England at Lord's in 1993

HIGHEST SCORES ON FIRST-CLASS DEBUT

260	Amol Muzumdar	Bombay v Haryana at Faridabad in 1993–94
240	Eric Marx	Transvaal v Griqualand West at Johannesburg in 1920–21
232*	Sam Loxton	Victoria v Queensland at Melbourne in 1946–47
230	Gundappa Viswanath	Mysore v Andhra at Vijayawada in 1967–68
227	Tom Marsden	Sheffield and Leicester v Nottingham at Sheffield in 1826

Bombay's Amol Muzumdar, 19, broke a 73-year-old world record in 1993–94 when he scored 260 against Haryana at Faridabad, the highest innings by a batsman on his first-class debut.

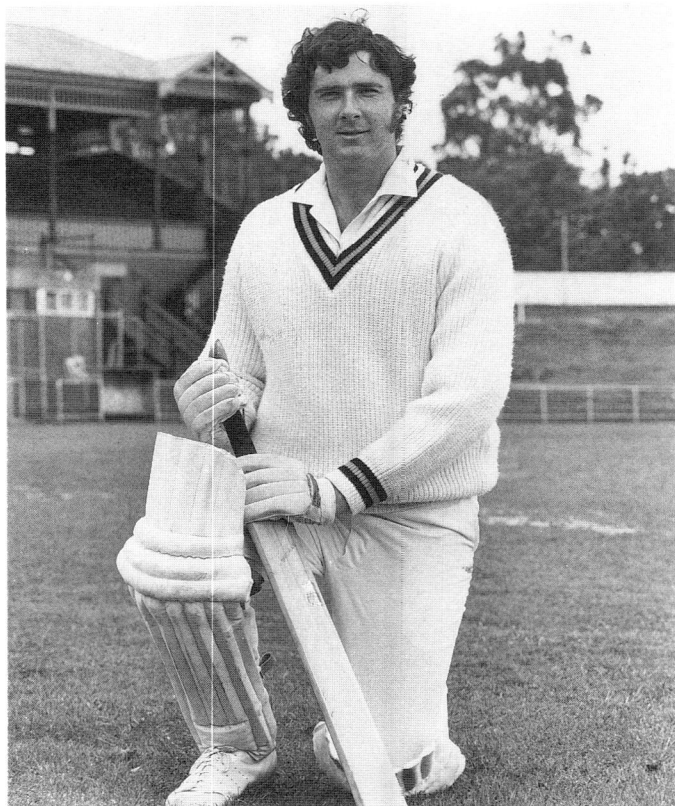

Graham Yallop, who scored 1,000 first-class runs for Victoria and Australia between October and December 1983

In 1927–28 Victoria's Bill Ponsford became the first Australian batsman to score 1,000 first-class runs in a season by the end of the calendar year. What made his performance all the more meritorious was that all of his runs were scored during December, a unique accomplishment. In 1962–63 Bob Simpson became the next Australian batsman to top the 1,000-run mark by the end of the year, and repeated the feat the following season.

On his way to a whirlwind 111 against Ireland in 1993, Allan Border hit five successive sixes off a single over sent down by spinner Angus Dunlop (1–0–32–0). The first six landed on the clubhouse roof, the second over the roof and out of the ground, the third over the sightscreen, the fourth over the club roof and the fifth over the fence. Two of the balls hit out of the ground were never recovered. Border raced to his century in just 31 minutes off 46 balls, his second fifty was scored in 13 minutes off 14 balls and all-up he hit eight sixes and 10 fours. Border scored more in half-an-hour than Ireland did in an afternoon. Australia declared after piling on 361 runs for the loss of three wickets and beat Ireland (89) by a whopping 272 runs, the biggest defeat in Irish cricket history.

Steve Waugh proved to be the perfect No. 6 batsman in Test cricket with five of his first six centuries not outs. And four of his first seven were in excess of 150. His maiden hundred in Test cricket was 177 not out against England at Leeds in 1989, which was followed by an undefeated 152 in his next innings at Lord's.

177* v England	Leeds	1989
152* v England	Lord's	1989
134* v Sri Lanka	Hobart	1989–90
100 v West Indies	Sydney	1992–93
157* v England	Leeds	1993
147* v New Zealand	Brisbane	1993–94
164 v South Africa	Adelaide	1993–94

After finishing second to Allan Border in the batting averages against New Zealand in 1992–93, Waugh then proceeded to come out on top in the following four Test series, against England, New Zealand and two against South Africa.

Series	M	I	NO	Runs	HS	Avge
England 1993	6	9	4	416	157*	83.20
New Zealand 1993–94	3	3	2	216	147*	216.00
South Africa 1993–94	1	2	0	165	164	82.50
South Africa 1993–94	3	4	1	195	86	65.00

1,000 RUNS IN AN AUSTRALIAN SEASON BY THE END OF DECEMBER

Batsman	Season	M	I	NO	Runs	100s	HS	Avge
Bill Ponsford	1927–28	4	5	0	1,146	4	437	229.20
Herbert Sutcliffe	1932–33	8	10	1	1,004	5	194	111.56
Bob Simpson	1962–63	9	15	1	1,042	5	205	75.14
Bob Simpson	1963–64	7	12	1	1,078	4	359	98.00
Geoff Boycott	1970–71	9	16	1	1,051	4	173	70.06
David Hookes	1982–83	10	18	1	1,163	3	146	68.41
Graham Yallop	1983–84	7	10	1	1,102	5	268	124.44
Allan Border	1985–86	10	17	2	1,172	6	194	78.13

Allan Border

Steve Waugh

Peter Sleep

Graeme Fowler

Mark Taylor

While playing league cricket for Middleton in England in 1992, former Australian all-rounder Peter Sleep was invited to play for a World XI against the touring Pakistanis at Scarborough. He responded by scoring a century in his only first-class innings of the summer—a career-best 182. And in his only first-class innings the following English season, he repeated the feat in the same fixture, scoring 151 against the Zimbabweans.

•

In 1987–88 Tasmania's Danny Buckingham became the first batsman to score a first-class century with the aid of a runner on two occasions. His score of 112 against New South Wales at Devonport followed his 150 not out against Western Australia at Perth in 1986–87. Graeme Fowler provides the only instance of a batsman scoring a hundred in each innings of a match with the assistance of a runner—126 and 128 not out for Lancashire against Warwickshire at Southport in 1982.

•

Hot on the heels of making a pair against New South Wales in 1902–03, Victorian wicket-keeper Tom Hastings made history when, in his next match, he became the first No. 11 batsman in the world to score a first-class century. In the Sheffield Shield match against South Australia at Melbourne, Hastings (106 not out) and Mathew Ellis (118) batting at No. 9, both scored centuries in a last wicket partnership of 211.

When Mark Taylor scored 170 in the Boxing Day Test match against South Africa in 1993–94 he became the first batsman in Test history to record a century on his debut against four different countries. He'd previously made hundreds in his first Test against England, Sri Lanka and Pakistan. Taylor also became the first Australian, and only the second after New Zealand's Martin Crowe, to score centuries against seven different countries at Test level. It was the sixth time in his career that he'd made a hundred in the first Test of a series. He also reached the milestone of 1,000 Test runs in the calendar year, and with Mark Waugh he posted a record 169-run stand for the fourth wicket in Tests against South Africa, passing the 4,000-run landmark in his 50th Test.

•

South Africa's Hansie Cronje created havoc against the 1993–94 Australians plundering close to 600 runs at a century average in the five lead-up matches to the Test series. In four successive one-day internationals he scored 112, 97, 45 and 50 not out, and then hit 44 and a career-best 251 for Orange Free State. His double-century is one of the highest individual scores by any batsman in the fourth innings of a first-class match and the second-best by a South African against Australia, after Graeme Pollock's 274 at Durban in 1969–70. He then took his sparkling form into the Test matches with knocks of 21 and 122 in the historic first Test at Johannesburg.

•

	FIRST-CLASS CENTURIES BY NUMBER 11 BATSMEN	
163	Peter Smith	Essex v Derbyshire at Chesterfield in 1947
126	Bill Smith	MCC v Barbados at Bridgetown in 1912–13
121	Shute Banerjee	India v Surrey at The Oval in 1946
115*	Graham Stevenson	Yorkshire v Warwickshire at Birmingham in 1982
112*	Arthur Fielder	Kent v Worcestershire at Stourbridge in 1909
109*	Maqsood Kundi	Muslim Commercial Bank v National Bank at Lahore in 1981–82
106*	Tom Hastings	Victoria v South Australia at Melbourne in 1902–03
101	Arthur Gilligan	Cambridge University v Sussex at Hove in 1919
100*	Ahsan-ul-Haq	Muslims v Sikhs at Lahore in 1923–24

5 Wide World of Sports

Gil Langley, the Australian Test wicket-keeper of the 1950s, was a star footballer who represented South Australia 15 times. He also played in the 1943 VFL grand final for Essendon, which went down to Richmond by five points.

•

Ted Dexter was a talented golfer who came close one year to playing in the British Open. He missed entrance to the main draw of one of golf's majors by just one putt. In 1983 he appeared in the English Amateur Championship at the Wentworth course and in the same year won the Oxford and Cambridge Presidents' Putter tournament.

•

Former England captain Tony Greig won the celebrity race at the Adelaide Grand Prix in 1985.

•

During the calendar year of 1993, New Zealand's Jeff Wilson gained international selection in both cricket and rugby union. In March the teenage all-rounder made his cricket debut in the first one-day international against Australia at Dunedin, and seven months later made his first appearance for the All Blacks in a Test against Scotland. His first rugby match was a memorable one, with him scoring a hat-trick of tries in New Zealand's 51 points to 15 demolition of the Scots at Muirfield.

•

Alison Inverarity, the daughter of former Australian Test batsman John, finished eighth in the high jump event at the 1992 Barcelona Olympic Games.

•

One of Allan Border's sporting dreams came true in 1992 when he went to the Masters Golf Championship at the magnificent Augusta course in the United States. The Australian skipper enjoyed a better view of the course layout than most, when he caddied for Wayne Grady in a par-three tournament just before the main event. Another cricketer who caddied for Grady was former Australian batsman Greg Ritchie at the 1993 Australian PGA.

> It was something special with an atmosphere like a Test match at Lord's, or the tennis at Wimbledon.
> —Allan Border, on the US PGA

Graham Thorpe, who scored a century on his Test debut in 1993, played soccer for an England Under-18 Schools side.

•

On 2 February 1974 Chris Old was representing England in the first Test against the West Indies at Port-of-Spain while his brother, Alan, was playing in a rugby Test for England v Ireland.

•

'Picker' Newton, one of Tasmania's top tennis players, was also a leading state cricketer. Newton won eight major tennis championships, including consecutive singles titles in 1924 and 1925, and three state doubles competitions. He was also a more than handy cricketer, scoring over 1,000 first-class runs and taking 66 wickets.

•

Towards the end of the 1935–36 tour of South Africa, the Australian team agreed to oppose Transvaal at baseball rather than another game of cricket. The tourists were able to field a pretty good team with a few of them having experience at either national or state level—Len Darling, a third baseman, had represented Australia, Vic Richardson had played for South Australia, Ben Barnett for Victoria, while Leo O'Brien was a Victorian first-grade player and Clarrie Grimmett a club player. The Australians, who took to the field in uniforms supplied by the Wanderers Baseball Club, won the game 12–3.

Clarrie Grimmett (left, back row) with the East Torrens Baseball Club in 1925

'Johnny Won't Hit Today' Douglas—England Test captain and Olympic boxing champion

'Snowy' Baker, one of Australia's most gifted all-round sportsmen, played first-grade cricket for Sydney University, and gained international recognition at the 1908 Olympic Games in London when he took on, but lost to, future England Test captain Johnny Douglas in the final of the middleweight boxing championship.

•

Lew Hoad, the former Australian Wimbledon tennis champion, was appointed president of the Costa de Sol Cricket Association in 1987.

•

A West Australian rugby player and national BMX champion was the star performer with both bat and ball in the final of Perth's grade competition in 1993–94. Sixteen-year-old Tama Canning, representing Fremantle, took 10 wickets in the match, including a first innings haul of 7 for 72, and also scored an unbeaten 51. His extraordinary all-round performance was not enough though, with Midland-Guilford taking the premiership by four wickets.

•

Rod Marsh's brother Graham Marsh is a well-known professional golfer. In 1993–94 Rod's son Paul showed a talent for the game when he took out a championship at the Glenelg course in Adelaide.

South Australian batsman Norrie Claxton also represented his state at Aussie Rules football and baseball. He was also an A-grade hockey player and a champion cyclist. In 1934 he donated the Claxton Shield, the trophy for Australia's national baseball competition.

•

Before finally turning to cricket, Shane Warne was an aspiring half-forward with the St Kilda AFL club. He played two seasons of Under-19 football and appeared in one seniors reserve match in 1988.

•

The big-hitting England batsman Robin Smith was offered a trial with the New York Mets baseball team in 1990.

•

While on tour of Sri Lanka in 1993–94, South Africa's Allan Donald got his first-ever hole-in-one on a par four at the Royal Colombo golf course.

•

Mike Walford, who played cricket and rugby for Oxford University, captained Somerset in 1946 and led England's hockey team at the 1948 Olympic Games.

•

West Indies batsman Brian Lara played junior soccer and table tennis for Trinidad and Tobago.

•

Stuart Trott, a grandson of 'Harry' Trott who captained Australia's cricket side in the late 1890s, played in over 200 games for the St Kilda and Hawthorn AFL clubs.

•

Clem Hill, one of Australia's greatest left-handers, later became a handicapper for the Victorian Amateur Turf Club. His duties for the VATC included weighing Caulfield Cup runners.

•

South Africa's Hansie Cronje once took part in a charity decathlon event, finishing second to former world champion Daley Thompson.

•

When a member of the Jamaican Youth Team, Michael Holding opened the bowling with Seymour Newman who, like his partner, was very fast. Newman's speed won him a track and field scholarship in the United States and fame as an 800-metre world champion and finalist at the 1976 Olympic Games. Holding was also handy at athletics— he still holds the Under-12 high jump record at his school, one of 4 feet 11¼ inches.

•

Two footballing cricketers—Peter Sterling...

...and Paul Vautin

Famous cricketers and famous footballers came together at the Gabba in 1993–94 for a one-day tribute match to Allan Border. Three of the four footy codes supplied players—AFL's Dermott Brereton, rugby league's Wally Lewis, Allan Langer, Peter Sterling and Paul Vautin, and rugby international Tim Horan.

Old cricketing foes and friends, like Richard Hadlee, Mike Procter, Jeff Thomson and Greg Chappell also turned out in front of a sell-out 15,000-strong crowd. Thanks to some generous bowling, Border's XI (255) was able to defeat the International XI (251) by one wicket off the last ball of the match.

- Langer, a former Queensland Under-16 cricket representative, was the first bowler to capture a wicket in the match, clean-bowling the former South African batsman Barry Richards for 17. Langer, named Man of the Match, finished with the impressive figures of 2 for 44 and was the top-scoring footballer with an innings of 32 off 37 balls for A.B's XI.
- Brereton, who made five representing the International XI, got off the mark with a boundary off Border.
- Vautin completed the first rugby league tackle on a cricket field when he downed Sterling, as the former Parramatta half-back attempted to take a quick single.
- Two former Queensland captains combined to get rid of Sterling. He was caught by Border off the bowling of Lewis for 6.
- The footballing dismissal of the day saw Horan caught by Vautin off Langer. It was a tremendous one-handed catch in the outfield, which Tony Greig in the Channel 9 commentary box thought should be included in the 'Classic Catches' competition—it eventually was. Sterling declared 'It was the greatest fluke in cricket history'. Horan, who played Queensland Schools Cricket in 1987, made 21.
- Brereton claimed the wicket of Chappell for 13 in his first over.
- Sterling earned the prized wicket of the day, dismissing Border for 46, and deputising for Rod Marsh effected a neat stumping to dismiss Lewis (17) off the bowling of David Boon.
- Vautin batted without gloves scoring 9 before he was bowled by Boon.
- Michelle Lock, an Australian runner who made the semi-finals at the Barcelona Olympic Games, acted as a runner for Joel Garner.

•

Neil Hawke, the fast bowler who played in 27 Tests during the 1960s, was an accomplished Australian Rules footballer. A full-forward, he was the leading goal kicker in the 1959 West Australian Football League, booting 114 for the East Perth club.

•

After Andrew Stoddart had finished England's 1887–88 cricket tour of Australia he stayed behind to join an England rugby union party.

•

After his cricket-playing days, former Australian Test spinner John Gleeson sent down a different type of ball, becoming a club champion at lawn bowls in the New South Wales city of Tamworth.

Australian Test all-rounder Brendon Julian represented a West Australian under-16 rugby union side as a five-eighth.

•

Spencer Gore, a Surrey cricketer and the first Wimbledon singles champion in 1877, was unable to successfully defend his tennis title the following year, losing to another first-class cricketer, Frank Hadow from Middlesex. The two combatants had two weeks earlier played together on the cricket field for the Old Harrovians Club. R.J. Hartley, another Old Harrovian cricketer, won the third Wimbledon championship in 1879.

•

In 1933–34 Horace Lindrum, the champion Australian snooker player and a nephew of Walter, scored an unbeaten century and took 5 for 10 in a match at Swan Hill in Victoria. He set some kind of local record when he hit one bowler for three consecutive sixes onto a nearby road and sent another smashing through the window of a grain shed.

I find making a break of a thousand in billiards comparatively easy. One of these days when Bradman is in the mood he will find it just as easy to score a thousand runs in one innings.
—**Walter Lindrum**

England soccer star Gary Lineker scored a century (103) at Lord's in 1992 playing for Cross Arrows against the Stock Exchange.

•

Les Stillman, who represented both Victoria and South Australia at cricket during the 1970s, also played Australian Rules football, for Essendon and Footscray.

•

Test cricket's 72nd venue, the Babu Stadium in Lucknow, opened in 1994, is named after K.D. 'Babu' Singh—India's gold medal-winning hockey captain at the 1948 Olympics.

•

Apart from playing cricket for Barbados, the great West Indies all-rounder Garry Sobers also represented the island at golf, soccer, basketball and, believe it or not, dominoes.

•

In 1972 Jeff Thomson received a life ban from playing soccer after allegedly hitting a referee. The incident took place during a Protestant Churches Soccer Association match while he was playing for St Paul's Bankstown, and although the ban was lifted in 1978, it was later reimposed.

•

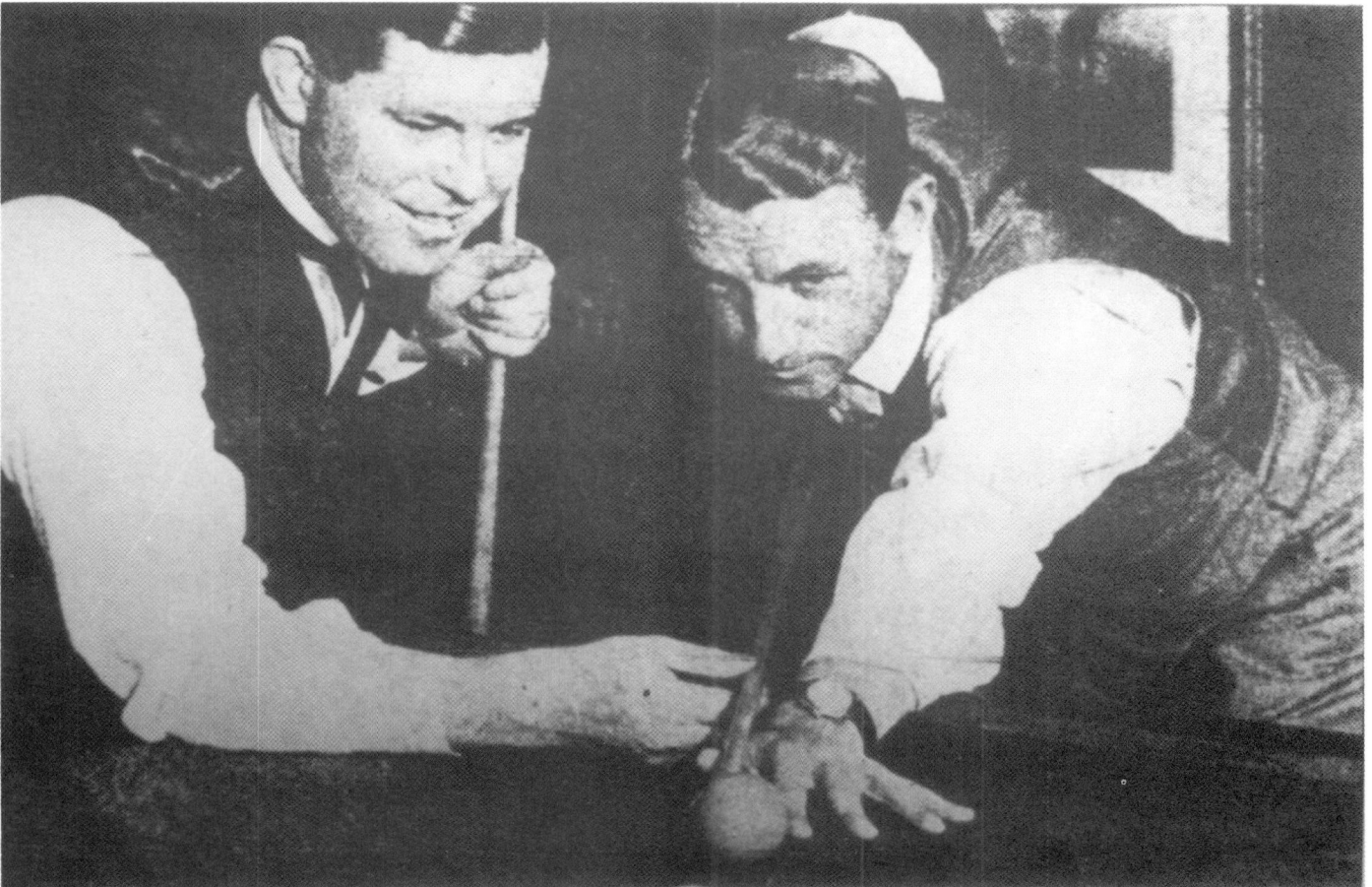

Two undisputed world champions—Walter Lindrum and Don Bradman. Writer Neville Cardus once described Bradman as the 'Lindrum of cricket', while Lindrum was sometimes known as the 'Bradman of billiards'.

Australian Test, State-of-Origin and Canberra Raiders rugby league star Ricky Stuart

The second overseas team—after the 1868 Australian Aborigines—to tour England, was a group of American baseball players in 1874, on a promotional trip to publicise America's number-one sport. The touring party, which consisted of 11 members of the Philadelphia Athletes Club and 11 from Boston, played a series of baseball matches and seven cricket matches, winning four of them—the other three were drawn. Their first match was against the MCC at Lord's.

12 GENTLEMEN OF MCC v 18 OF AMERICA
Lord's, August 1874
Match Drawn

MCC

C. Courtenay	b McBride	0
A. Lubbock	b H. Wright	24
J. Round	b McBride	0
A.C. Lucas	c Schafer b McBride	12
G.E. Bird	c McVey b H. Wright	15
V.E. Walker	b H. Wright	27
A. Anstruther	c Batten b G. Wright	0
F.P.U. Pickering	b H. Wright	9
E. Lubbock	b G. Wright	0
R.A. Fitzgerald	c Hall b G. Wright	4
W.M. Rose	b G. Wright	0
A. Appleby	not out	0
Extras		14
		105

Bowling figures
H. Wright 52-32-43-4, McBride 37-19-34-3, G. Wright 16-9-14-4

AMERICA

H. Wright	b Rose	2
J.D. McBride	b Rose	5
A.G. Spalding	b Appleby	23
W. Anson	c Fitzgerald b Rose	2
R.C. Barnes	b Pickering	5
G. Wright	b Rose	12
E.B. Sutton	b Pickering	3
W. Fisher	run out	3
A.J. Leonard	b Rose	13
S. Wright	c A. Lubbock b E. Lubbock	0
C.A. McVey	b Pickering	10
J. O'Rourke	b E. Lubbock	4
J. Sensenderfer	b Picking	0
T. Batten	c Appleby b Pickering	4
J. McMullen	b Pickering	5
G. Hall	c Round b Pickering	5
H.C. Schafer	c A. Lubbock b Pickering	5
G. Beales	not out	1
Extras		5
		107

Bowling figures
Pickering 15.3-4-23-8, Appleby 15-4-26-1, Rose 12-3-35-5, E. Lubbock 8-4-13-2

•

The Canberra Raiders rugby league side contains a number of big cricket fans, including Ricky Stuart, Bradley Clyde, Laurie Daley and Steve Walters, who each year take on the local media in a 20-overs match at a suburban football ground. In one match—played using indoor cricket rules—the Green Machine embarrassed the journalists by amassing well over 200 and then bowling them out for just 4. In their next match the media XI were forced to recruit some ring-ins to bolster their chances, namely ACT cricket representatives Darryle Macdonald

and Peter Solway. The move proved to be a worthless exercise, though, with the Raiders again taking victory, and again by a sizeable margin.

RICKY STUART'S ALL-TIME BEST TEST XI
1 Gordon Greenidge
2 Sunil Gavaskar
3 Viv Richards
4 Greg Chappell
5 Allan Border
6 Ian Botham
7 Imran Khan
8 Rod Marsh (c)
9 Dennis Lillee
10 Shane Warne
11 Michael Holding

•

Darren Webber, who has represented South Australia at both cricket and javelin throwing

Before gaining his big break in first-class cricket, South Africa's Fanie de Villiers played rugby union and was a nationally ranked javelin thrower. Another to throw the javelin competitively was South Australian batsman Darren Webber, who excelled at the sport while at school and represented his state.

•

One of the security guards hired to protect the Australian cricket team in South Africa in 1993–94 was Pierre Coetzer, a former heavyweight boxing champion and world top 10 contender.

●

THE FAVOURITE SPORT STARS OF SOME MODERN-DAY TEST CRICKETERS

Curtly Ambrose—Boris Becker
David Boon—Ray Floyd, Joe Frazier
Ian Botham—John McEnroe
Martin Crowe—Michael Jordan, Nick Faldo
Tony Dodemaide—Stefan Edberg, Steffi Graf
Allan Donald—Serge Blanco, Gary Lineker
Graham Gooch—Bobby Charlton

David Gower—Seve Ballesteros, Greg Norman
Ian Healy—Steffi Graf, Mal Meninga, Wayne Grady
Merv Hughes—John McEnroe, Pat Cash, Dermott Brereton, Michelle Timms
Imran Khan—Mohammad Ali
Dean Jones—Jimmy Connors, Jack Nicklaus
Kapil Dev—John McEnroe, Diego Maradona
Dennis Lillee—Muhammad Ali
Malcolm Marshall—Jim Courier, Stefan Edberg
Damien Martyn—Michael Jordan, Greg Norman
Tom Moody—John McEnroe, Michael Jordan, Carl Lewis
Derek Pringle—David Campese, John McEnroe
Richie Richardson—Steffi Graf, Michael Jordan
Jack Russell—Steve Davis, Nigel Mansell
Robin Smith—Stefan Edberg, Ian Woosnam
Alec Stewart—Steffi Graf, Gary Lineker
Dilip Vengsarkar—Bjorn Borg
Mark Waugh—Terry Lamb, Greg Norman

6 Cricket and Politics

The first mention of cricket in Parliament was in the House of Commons in 1803, when William Pitt briefly referred to the game when introducing his Defence Bill.

•

One of the oldest 'wandering' clubs in world cricket, second only to I Zingari, is England's Lords and Commons XI which played its first match in 1850. Lords and Commons, still going strong today, is essentially comprised of current and former MPs from both houses of Parliament, sons of peers and staff members.

•

Two former Test players contested India's general election in 1991. Chetan Chauhan, the opening batsman, won a seat in Parliament for the Hindu BJP Party with a majority of over 50,000. The former Indian Test captain Mansur Ali Khan Pataudi, representing the Congress Party, was not so lucky, and failed in the constituency of Bhopal.

•

In preparation for the 1987 World Cup, England and the West Indies both had a warm-up match against a Lahore Club XI, a side that included Punjab's Chief Minister Nawaz Sharif. Sharif, who later became Pakistan's Prime Minister, scored a duck in the match against the West Indies and one against England.

•

'Doc' Evatt, the former ALP leader and deputy Prime Minister, was a member of the SCG Trust and a vice-president of the New South Wales Cricket Association. An occasional writer on the game, he had three articles published in *Wisden*—in the 1935, 1938 and 1949 editions.

Evatt was always fond of commemorating worthy events on the cricket field. In 1940 he presented Arthur Morris with a new cricket bat after the young opener scored two centuries on his first-class debut for New South Wales, and in 1947 sent Don Bradman a congratulatory telegram on his success as captain in the then just-completed Test series against England.

•

Ric Charlesworth, who made over 2,000 runs in the Sheffield Shield for Western Australia, held the federal seat of Perth for the ALP for 10 years until his retirement in 1993.

•

Former Pakistan fast bowler Sarfraz Nawaz was elected to the Punjab Provincial Assembly in 1985, winning his seat by 6,000 votes in a constituency of 100,000. Two years later, Sarfraz was attacked by a group of youths outside his home in Lahore after threatening to make certain sensational disclosures in Parliament.

•

Ted Dexter once stood as a candidate, unsuccessfully, in a British general election. In 1964 the then England captain, who'd never previously been a member of the Conservative Party, contested the seat of Cardiff South-East against the future Prime Minister, James Callaghan.

•

Lords and Commons undertook a tour of Barbados in 1989 and played against a side captained by the island's Tourism Minister, the former West Indies fast bowler Wes Hall. They also played against a Barbadian Parliamentarians' XI at Kensington Oval, the only game they won on the four-match tour.

•

Robert Mugabe

Cricket? It civilises people and creates good gentlemen. I want everyone to play cricket in Zimbabwe. I want ours to be a nation of gentlemen.

—Robert Mugabe, President of Zimbabwe

John Major, a member of the Surrey County Cricket Club, hits out at The Oval

Despite protestations that he hit the ball in the meat of the bat, British Prime Minister John Major was once given out lbw for a golden duck in a school match, an event that remains his worst cricketing memory. But his finest moment was also at school, when he once took 7 wickets for 9, including a hat-trick—a performance that won him a newspaper award as Best Young Cricketer of the Year.

> The first English XI to play abroad was in the 1850s, when they came to the United States. I understand that you beat us once, so we have not been back.
>
> —John Major, to former U.S. President George Bush

•

Evan Willis, the son of the Federal Treasurer Ralph Willis, figured in a history-making cricket grand final in Melbourne in 1993–94. His team, Williamstown, took out an Under-12 final defeating Port Colts who were dismissed for just 7—probably one of the lowest-ever totals in a final in any class of cricket.

•

John Udal, who played first-class cricket for the MCC, later spent a considerable amount of time and effort in developing the standard of cricket in Fiji, where he was Attorney-General. In 1894–95 a Fijian team that included Udal undertook a first-class tour of New Zealand. He also promoted the game in the Leeward Islands when Chief Justice.

•

Sir Grantley Adams, the founder of the Barbados Labour Party and Prime Minister of the West Indies Federation between 1958 and 1962, once said that if South Americans were encouraged to play cricket there would probably be fewer revolutions in Latin America.

•

To celebrate the independence of Barbados in 1966, 200 cricketers threw, in relay-style, a cricket ball through the city of Bridgetown. The ball contained a goodwill message from the island's cricketers to the Prime Minister, Errol Barrow.

•

When the Maharashtra Chief Minister's XI took on the Governor's XI at Poona in 1963–64, all but one of the 22 players had a bowl. At the time, this was a record number for a first-class match.

•

Dirk Wellham failed by the narrowest of margins in 1987 in his quest to become a New South Wales MP. Wellham—at the time the captain of New South Wales—lost by one in the vote for preselection as the Liberal Party candidate for the seat of Carlingford.

> The fact that the PM had never picked me in his XI had nothing to do with my joining the Liberal Party.
>
> —Dirk Wellham

•

In 1985 India's then Prime Minister, Rajiv Ghandi, passed a special law exempting Ravi Shastri from paying import duty on a $40,000 car he'd won as Player of the Series in the World Championship of Cricket tournament played in Australia.

•

In 1993 former Pakistan captain Imran Khan turned down an offer to serve as a minister in Pakistan's caretaker government. The proposal, from the interim Prime Minister Moeen Qureshi, was for Imran to join the Cabinet until the country's general election.

The very first ball sent down in the inaugural Prime Minister's XI match in Canberra in 1951–52 resulted in a wicket. West Indies fast bowler John Trim had former Australian Test batsman and match captain Jack Fingleton caught in the slips for a duck. His dismissal was a little unexpected as the Prime Minister, Bob Menzies, and the captains had decided that no batsman would be given out before scoring. It seems, though, that the umpire—former Australian fast bowler Ernie McCormick—was either unaware of the agreement, or forgot, and instinctively gave Fingleton out. Menzies was so moved by what had happened, he wrote a poem to commemorate Fingleton's duck.

> **What, Fingleton,**
> **Not even a singleton,**
> **A fruitless journey—**
> **Thanks to some pretty slow thinking by Ernie.**
> —Bob Menzies

PRIME MINISTER'S XI FIRSTS

First duck
Jack Fingleton v West Indies 1951–52
First fifty
Martin Donnelly (72) v West Indies 1951–52
First century
Peter May (101) for MCC 1954–55
First century opening stand
Glenn Bishop and Mike Veletta (109) v England 1986–87
First five-wicket haul
Wilf Ferguson (7–94) for West Indies 1951–52
First stumping
Kevin Gibb v MCC 1954–55

F.S. Jackson, who captained England five times and scored 1,415 Test runs, was an MP from 1915 to 1926. When he was due to deliver his maiden parliamentary speech, the Speaker handed him a note that said: 'I have dropped you down the batting order—it's a sticky wicket'. A little later, his debut in the House of Commons arrived when the Speaker sent another note declaring: 'Get your pads on— you're in next'. Jackson was Chairman of the Unionist (Conservative) Party for two years and in 1927 was appointed Governor of Bengal, where he claimed he made 'the quickest duck of his life' as he avoided five bullets from the gun of a young woman in an assassination attempt.

His father-in-law held the same seat as he did in Yorkshire, while his father W.L. Jackson was also a politician, holding the posts of Financial Secretary to the Treasury and Chief Secretary for Ireland in the government of the Marquess of Salisbury.

•

Joe Darling, who led Australia in five Test series—his last against F.S. Jackson's England side in 1905—followed in his father's footsteps by entering politics, becoming in 1920 an independent member of the Tasmanian Legislative Assembly. His father, John Darling, had been in the South Australian Parliament where he introduced a bill granting the state cricket association a lease for an area of land that is now the Adelaide Oval.

•

Bob Menzies tosses the coin at the beginning of the first Prime Minister's XI match at Canberra in 1951–52. With him are the captains Jack Fingleton and the West Indies' John Goddard.

•

Lord (N.M.V.) Rothschild, who played for Northamptonshire (1929–31), was an all-rounder of considerable talent in many areas of public life. Between 1971 and 1974 he was Director-General of Central Policy Review in the Cabinet Office under Prime Minister Edward Heath. In his first-class cricket career, Lord Rothschild scored 282 runs at 15.66, with a highest score of 63 against Kent.

•

The first batsman to record two first-class double-centuries in the West Indies domestic competition was a member of Parliament. Guyana's Sports Minister, the former Test opener Roy Fredericks, made a comeback to first-class cricket after a two-year absence in 1982–83 and scored 103 and 217 in his only two innings. His previous double-hundred was one of 250 against Barbados at Bridgetown in 1974–75.

•

During the 1992–93 Under-19 National Cricket Championship, one of the tournament's most successful bowlers was Mark Hatton, the son of the Northern Territory's Aboriginal Affairs Minister, Steve Hatton. The young spinner finished the series as the joint leading wicket-taker with 15 scalps at 28.20, including a best innings return of 7 for 83 against Tasmania.

•

Two great-grandfathers of 'Gubby' Allen, the former England Test captain, were MPs in the first New South Wales Legislative Council. George Allen was elected Mayor of Sydney in 1845 and later became a member of Parliament where he served as Chairman of Committees. His son, George Wigram Allen—Gubby's grandfather—also entered state politics, attaining the positions of Justice Minister and Speaker of the House. Gubby's father married into a family that had similar links with politics in New South Wales—his wife's grandfather, John Lamb, was a member of the state's first Legislative Council.

•

In 1977 a Test match involving England in Pakistan was brought to a halt when Benazir Bhutto, the wife of the country's deposed Prime Minister—in gaol on a murder charge—made an appearance at the ground in Lahore. A politically motivated riot took place on the third day of the match which resulted in police firing tear gas to disperse the crowd, estimated at around 35,000.

•

Ian McLachlan, who won the federal seat of Barker for the Liberal Party in 1990, played first-class cricket for South Australia and Cambridge University. Twelfth man for Australia in the fourth Test against England in 1962–63, McLachlan made 3,743 runs at first-class level with a highest score of 188 not out on his debut against Queensland at Adelaide in 1960–61.

IAN McLACHLAN'S ALL-TIME BEST TEST XI

1 Jack Hobbs
2 Sunil Gavaskar
3 Don Bradman (c)
4 Graeme Pollock
5 Garry Sobers
6 Ray Lindwall
7 Wasim Akram
8 Don Tallon
9 Curtly Ambrose
10 Bill O'Reilly
11 Jim Laker

Ian McLachlan

In a 1980 by-election in South Africa, former Test all-rounder Eddie Barlow was defeated by John Wiley, a future cabinet minister who had previously played first-class cricket for Western Province and Cambridge University.

•

Former England captain Len Hutton declined an offer from the East Bradford branch of the Conservative Party in 1956 to be their parliamentary candidate.

•

THE 'BODYLINE' SERIES—
WHAT THE POLITICIANS SAID

It looks as though we are leading two opposing armies.
—Joe Lyons, Australian Prime Minister

No politics ever introduced in the British Empire caused me so much trouble as this damn bodyline bowling.
—Jimmy Thomas, British Secretary of State for the Dominions

Bravo, the Ashes are won. But they are secondary to the great fighting spirit and good sportsmanship shown by both sides.
—Ramsay MacDonald, British Prime Minister

The British cabinet outside 10 Downing Street during their discussions with the MCC on the 'Bodyline' Test series of 1932–33, undoubtedly one of the most politically sensitive sporting events of all time. Following the third Test at Adelaide when Douglas Jardine's bodyline bowling strategy came to the fore, the MCC was summoned by the British Prime Minister to attend a conference. So crucial were the events, the PM's meeting displaced Hitler from the front pages.

The MCC team of 1932–33 led by Douglas Jardine (centre, front row)

Don Chipp

Don Chipp, the leader of the Australian Democrats from 1978 until 1986, once appeared in a Prime Minister's XI match at the invitation of Bob Menzies. Batting with Don Bradman, Chipp, the then federal member for the Victorian seat of Higinbotham, scored 8 against the touring England side in 1962–63.

Chipp is one of just four parliamentarians to have played in the PM's XI matches. Menzies included two in his first match in 1951–52—Tasmanian MP Bill Falkinder and Social Services Minister Athol Townley. The other MP to get a game was Mac Holten, a former Victorian Country XI captain who played in the match against the 1960–61 West Indians.

DON CHIPP'S ALL-TIME BEST TEST XI
1 Geoff Boycott
2 Sid Barnes
3 Don Bradman
4 Lindsay Hassett
5 Garry Sobers
6 Viv Richards
7 Keith Miller
8 Alan Knott
9 Richie Benaud (c)
10 Dennis Lillee
11 Harold Larwood

•

Bob Menzies had the great fortune of being able to attend conferences in London that just happened to coincide with

the Lord's Test match. One year, Menzies politely questioned a proposed meeting that had been scheduled for January by Britain's Prime Minister Sir Anthony Eden. Menzies suggested that the meeting might perhaps be held in June, and wired London to see if there was anybody on the PM's staff who had a copy of the year's cricket calendar. 'They instantly fixed the conference for June— the day after the Lord's Test Match.' 'That,' said Menzies, 'was civilisation at its best. It goes to show how important it is for a country like Great Britain to have a Prime Minister who understands cricket.'

•

Bob Hawke, who played first-grade cricket in Canberra, was a member of the University team in Perth that took out the club premiership in 1951–52. During his time at Oxford he was able to continue his love for the game, serving under the leadership of Colin Cowdrey. Back in those days, another of Hawke's great loves was drinking, and it was during a minor match for University College v Millfield School that he discovered a new beverage, Kummel. The future Prime Minister was in no condition to bat, lasting just one ball. On his return to the clubhouse the scorer enquired as to the wicket-taker's name. Millfield's principal, Jack Myers, replied, 'Bowler's name—K-U-M-M-E-L'.

•

Michael Mates, the British MP behind Michael Heseltine's leadership challenge to Margaret Thatcher in 1990, once had his jaw broken in a parliamentary cricket match. Appearing for Lords and Commons in 1978, the MP was hit in the face by a ball from West Indian Wanderers bowler Brian Mustill. In 1985 Mates became the first member of Parliament to score a century for Lords and Commons.

'ENGLAND CRUSHED AGAIN'		
D.J. Mellor	leg over wicket, b de Sancha	0
N. Lamont	c in Threshers, b Onanugu	0
M. Mates	c Redhanded, b Nadir	0
M. Heseltine	retired hurt	0
D. Hurd	run out of ideas	0
J. Major (c)	not out yet but will be soon	0
Total		0
		Private Eye, 1993

•

Graham Allen, the member for Nottingham North, made the record books in 1992 when he scored 101 not out against Old Westminsters, the first century by a Labour MP in the 140-year history of Lords and Commons cricket. Two matches later, another first was recorded when Conservative MP Cheryl Gillan became the club's first woman player.

•

Lord Dunglass, who played for Middlesex and later entered Parliament, was a member of the first England side to undertake a tour of South America, in 1926–27. Dunglass, who as Sir Alec Douglas-Home became Britain's Prime Minister in 1963, played in one of the 'Test' matches against Argentina, that was watched by the country's President, Marcelo Alvear.

Dunglass was the Unionist MP for South Lanark between 1931 and 1945, Conservative MP for Lanark, 1950–51, and the member for Kinross and West Perthshire between 1963 and 1974. Prime Minister for a short period in 1963–64, he was then Opposition Leader until 1965.

THE FIRST-CLASS CAREER RECORD OF LORD DUNGLASS
Middlesex & Oxford University—1924–26

Batting

M	I	NO	Runs	HS	Avge
10	15	6	147	37*	16.33

Bowling

Runs	W	BB	Avge
363	12	3–43	30.25

•

The thorny question of cricket was raised in Federal Parliament in 1992, when some cricket-loving senators referred to a slip-up in the ABC's Test match coverage. Due to a 'technical hitch', the cricket commentary on Canberra's 2CN was abruptly terminated to go to the news with just one over to go on the final day of the Brisbane Test match against the West Indies. 'Those who might have been listening to the cricket on the ABC would have been dismayed, if not stunned, to learn that with just four balls to go they decided to follow the practice they had adopted all afternoon, and at six minutes past six they switched to news items. Most of Australia would have missed out on whether the last two wickets have been obtained by Australia.'—Nick Bolkus, Administrative Services Minister.

•

Lord Dunglass (Douglas-Home)

> Both politics and cricket have an unusual capacity to humble those who pursue them, not least in the ease and speed of the transition from fame to oblivion.
>
> —Bob Hawke

•

Brian Sedgemore, an English Labour MP, admitted to watching Test cricket on a miniature television set during boring speeches in the House of Commons. He found, though, that the reception was poor, and once moved for an urgent debate to improve the chamber's structure before the next Test.

•

Sir Edmund Barton, Australia's first Prime Minister, was a first-class cricket umpire who officiated in a famous match between New South Wales and an England XI, at the SCG in 1878–79. This was the game in which the other umpire, Englishman George Coulthard, ruled the local hero Billy Murdoch run out, a decision that saw an invasion of the ground by upset spectators. During the break in play, Barton threatened to give the match to England if New South Wales didn't resume the game immediately. However, attempts to clear the field of spectators proved fruitless and play was abandoned for the day.

William Bridgeman, who was Britain's Home Secretary in 1922 and long-standing MP for the seat of Oswestry, appeared in 13 first-class matches for Cambridge University. He had a top score of 162 not out in first-class cricket and played his final match in 1894, for the MCC.

•

Sir Brooke Watson, a Lord Mayor of London who lost a leg in a shark attack, staged a rather bizarre cricket match at Walworth in 1796, captaining a team of one-legged players against a one-armed eleven.

•

In 1993–94, the leader of the Australian Democrats Cheryl Kernot offered her services to Paul Keating as a 'third' umpire for the Prime Minister's XI match against South Africa. Senator Kernot, a qualified cricket coach and umpire, had hoped to adjudicate on possible dismissals via video replays, but, as such a set-up was unavailable at Manuka Oval, her request was rejected. The Senator had made a previous unsuccessful 'appeal' a couple of years earlier to stand in one of Bob Hawke's matches.

Before turning to politics, Senator Kernot had umpired lower grade men's matches in Sydney and coached schoolboy cricket teams in Queensland. Two of her students, Chris Smart and Peter Anderson, went on to play first-class cricket.

A Canberra monument in honour of Sir Edmund Barton, Australia's first Prime Minister and a first-class cricket umpire

Federal politician and cricket umpire Cheryl Kernot

Australian Prime Minister Paul Keating with the PM's XI side that defeated the touring West Indians at Canberra in 1992–93

It was a case of déjà vu for the 1993–94 South Africans when they lost to the Prime Minister's XI at Manuka by four runs, the same margin of loss when they last played in the series 30 years earlier in 1963–64. Chasing 157 runs for victory, the South Africans suffered a late-order collapse in the final overs to be all out for 152.

Prime Minister Keating likened the match's exciting finale to his election victory earlier in the year. 'We took the last four wickets at the election—four wickets in the last week, and in this game we took the last four wickets in the last half-hour.'

> I have known the Prime Minister since he was about 27 and although he is not a great follower of cricket he always plays a straight bat.
> —Joan Child, former Speaker of the House of Representatives

Learie Constantine, the gifted West Indies all-rounder, was one of the early members of the Trinidad and Tobago political party, the People's National Movement. In 1956 Constantine was elected chairman of the party that was led by the islands' future Prime Minister Eric Williams. He won the seat of Tunapuna in the general election held later that year, and with the PNM in power was appointed Works and Transport Minister. It was a position Constantine held until Trinidad's independence in 1962, when he became the nation's High Commissioner in England.

> In the 1950s we went to learn, now we go to teach.
> —Trinidad and Tobago Prime Minister Eric Williams, in 1962 on the success of the West Indies cricket team

In 1992 India's leading run-scorer in Test cricket, Sunil Gavaskar, was nominated to the Upper House of the country's national parliament. He was the first cricketer afforded such an honour.

Geoffrey Rippon, a former British Conservative Party minister, is the son of Arthur Rippon, and nephew of Albert Rippon, twins who both played first-class cricket for Somerset between 1914 and 1937.

Sam Loxton, who holds the Australian record for the highest score on his first-class debut—232 not out for Victoria v Queensland in 1946–47—later dedicated 24 years of his life to state politics. He was the member for the seat of Prahran in the Victorian parliament, and for 17 years was Liberal Party whip in the governments of Henry Bolte and Dick Hamer.

When the Lords and Commons XI played the MCC at St Paul's School in Barnes in 1992 they lost nine wickets, but one batsman had to retire 'due to an appointment with the Prime Minister'. The MCC won the match by 57 runs.

In 1993 John Major radically restructured the New Year honours list which saw, for the first time, ordinary Britons receiving awards at the expense of military leaders and civil servants. In his quest to make Britain a more classless society, he invited the public to nominate worthy recipients and was inundated with thousands of ideas. Of the 70 award-winners the Prime Minister eventually chose, one was the England women's cricket captain Karen Smithies.

Aiden Crawley, England's 12th man in the Lord's Test against South Africa in 1929, had an unusual political career in which he was both a Conservative and a Labour MP. Between 1945 and 1951 the former Kent batsman represented Buckingham for the Labour Party, and West Derbyshire for the Conservatives from 1962 to 1967.

In a Lords and Commons match against an Egyptian touring team at The Oval in 1951, Crawley took an all-lbw hat-trick. Another first-class cricketing politician starred in the same match—Lord Dunglass, later Prime Minister, scored 24 as an opener and took 1 for 4 with the only two balls he bowled.

Sir W. Smithers (Conservative, Orpington)
... on a point of order, said he had asked permission to put down a motion on the Order Paper to commemorate the centenary of W.G. Grace, but the Speaker had not allowed him to do so. He bowed to that ruling, but he could not let the centenary of the greatest cricketer of all time pass without his name being mentioned in this House. (Cheers)
The Speaker
The honourable member certainly wrote to me and asked me if he might put a motion on the Order Paper to that effect, but I declined to give it my leave. It seems to me that if we put such motions on the Order Paper we might start with W.G. Grace, and we might go on to Bradman, and I do not know where we would end. (Cheers and laughter) We put motions on the Order Paper to deal with parliamentary matters. However much we might admire the cricket record of W.G. Grace, I do not think it would be in order to put it on the Order Paper.
Sir W. Smithers
(Pointing to the government front bench) At least he knew how to play the game! (Laughter)
Mr A. Crawley (Labour, Buckingham)
Lest it be thought that the commemoration of W.G. Grace is a party matter, I arise to say, that had the motion been allowed, I should have been pleased to second it.
                                    —British Parliament, 20 July 1948

•

Ian Botham's 64-year-old mother stood as a Conservative candidate in a local council election in Somerset in 1991.

•

Aucher Warner, who later became Solicitor-General and Attorney-General of Trinidad, was the captain of the first West Indies team to visit England, in 1900. Aucher was the brother of England Test player 'Plum' Warner. Their father was also a leading politician in Trinidad.

•

One of the first official duties of Sir John Leahy as Britain's new High Commissioner to Australia in 1984 was to deliver his Letter of Introduction from Margaret Thatcher to Bob Hawke. Sir John chose a very pleasant location to discharge his business—a Canberra cricket ground, where the Prime Minister was engaged in a match against the press gallery. This was the day that Hawke ended up in hospital after being hit in the face by a ball from a Melbourne journalist, Gary O'Neill.

A LETTER FROM THE BRITISH HIGH COMMISSIONER TO THE SECRETARY OF STATE FOR FOREIGN AND COMMONWEALTH AFFAIRS, SIR GEOFFREY HOWE

Sir,

1. In accordance with the instructions contained in the dispatch dated 14 September, I delivered my Letter of Introduction to the Prime Minister of Australia on 14 October. This was my second day in Australia and a Sunday. Mr Hawke was dressed in white flannels and an open-neck shirt; I more formally in grey flannels and a blue blazer. I drank beer from a can; he does not do that any more.

2. The occasion was a cricket match between Mr Hawke's selection from his staff and a team drawn from the Parliamentary press gallery. It was also the last occasion when I was likely to be able to see him until after the general election in seven weeks' time, because he was almost immediately setting out on the campaign trail. The assignation was cleverly thought up by the Deputy High Commissioner, Charles Cullimore, and readily agreed to by Mr Hawke himself.

3. When we arrived at the small ground where the match was being played, Mr Hawke was already padded up waiting on his own in front of the pavilion to bat next. We went straight up to him and introduced ourselves. Naturally he had half an eye on what was going on in the middle, but otherwise the conversation flowed freely, if not profoundly, and he was as relaxed as any 54-year-old Prime Minister would be, with a cricketing reputation to live up to and the TV cameramen all waiting to see him get out first ball.

Some of these same vultures turned their attention to the two of us as we talked and I thought it would somehow not be in keeping with the dignity of the Prime Minister's letter if I made a show of handing it over to him then. There was also the practical consideration that Mr Hawke could not easily have read it or given it to anyone before going out to the wicket. With Mr Hawke's agreement I therefore passed it shortly afterwards to Mr Hawke's Private Secretary, who, I regret to report, treated it with even less respect by stuffing it into the back pocket of his somewhat off-white flannels. I feared it might be lost in the wash, but fortunately it survived.

4. I stayed to watch Mr Hawke bat. This he did to great effect—he was 12th man for Oxford when Colin Cowdrey was captain—until, after scoring a brisk 27 runs, he was hit in the eye in attempting an ambitious hook and had to retire hurt. I can only hope that he will not attribute any of the blame for this to my having shaken his hand for a few minutes before. Anyway I enjoyed our first meeting and have subsequently heard that he did too.

5. This may seem a somewhat unorthodox way to have delivered my Letter of Introduction to the Prime Minister of Australia. But I believe that it provides an apt illustration of the nature of the relationship between Britain and Australia. We should try to keep it that way.

I am, Sir,
Yours faithfully
John Leahy.

•

Alfred Lyttelton, who appeared in four Test matches for England in the 1880s, later entered Parliament and became Colonial Secretary in 1903 in the government of his brother-in-law Arthur Balfour.

•

Tony Street, a former federal Liberal Party minister, was a fair cricketer in his day and twice played for a Victorian Country XI against South Africa, in 1952–53 and 1963–64. At the MCG in 1985–86, Street representing the Crusaders against the Politicians, finished the one-day match as the best bowler with four wickets, one of his victims being the then Prime Minister, Bob Hawke, who scored 31.

•

Gil Langley, one of Australia's Test wicket-keepers during the 1950s, had a lengthy political career, holding the South Australian seat of Unley for the Labor Party between 1962 and 1982. Among the many posts he held was Speaker of the House of Assembly from 1977 to 1979.

•

Channel 9's ad hoc coverage of Australia's historic Test series in South Africa in 1993–94 was brought up for discussion in the New South Wales Parliament. Upper House MP Ian Macdonald called on the Broadcasting Authority and the Trade Practices Commission to investigate Channel 9's licence for failing to show the series live in its entirety.

•

The West Indies' Wes Hall and England's Frank Tyson, two of Test cricket's finest fast bowlers, both played against and *for* the Prime Minister's XI in Canberra. Tyson played for the MCC against the PM's XI in 1954–55 and 1958–59, and then at the invitation of Bob Menzies opened his bowling attack against South Africa in 1963–64. Hall first played at Manuka for the West Indies in 1960–61 and then for the Prime Minister in 1965–66 against the MCC.

Gil Langley, an Australian cricketer and state politician

England openers John Morris and Wayne Larkins exit the Bradman Pavilion at Manuka Oval in Canberra to do battle with the Prime Minister's XI in 1990–91

Prime Minister and cricket enthusiast Ben Chifley with Australian Test cricketers Bert Oldfield and Clarrie Grimmett

Three men with strong ties to both cricket and politics at a gathering in 1963—Frank Worrell (left), one of the West Indies' finest Test cricketers and a Jamaican senator; British Prime Minister Harold Macmillan (centre) whose grandson Mark Faber played for Sussex in 1975; and England's Ted Dexter, who stood for the Conservative Party in the 1964 general election

On the day that the African National Congress became an official political party for the first time, its leader Nelson Mandela was a guest at Australia's first cricket match on South African soil for 24 years. Mandela, a lifelong cricket lover, met the 1993-94 Australian team during the lunch break of their first match, a one-dayer against Nicky Oppenheimer's XI.

•

Jack Fingleton, who played in the 1932-33 'Bodyline' series, later became a leading political journalist in Canberra, and earned a rare distinction upon his retirement in 1978 when both houses of Federal Parliament acknowledged his distinguished career. In 1943 Fingleton had become a press secretary to former Prime Minister Billy Hughes and was able to claim close friendships with other prime ministers, including Bob Menzies and Ben Chifley.

One of the more remarkable epilogues to the 'Bodyline' saga was the part that Chifley and Fingleton played in helping Harold Larwood emigrate to Australia. When Larwood and his family arrived in Sydney in 1950, Fingleton had arranged their accommodation at a hotel in Kingsford—it was later revealed that Chifley had paid half the hotel bill, an amount of £16 a week.

•

The great West Indies captain Frank Worrell was one of the few men to have been both a Test cricketer and a politician concurrently. Worrell, whose Test career spanned the years 1948 to 1963, joined the Jamaican Legislative Council as a senator in 1962. Two years later Worrell resigned from the Senate to take up a job offer from Trinidad's Prime Minister Eric Williams as a consultant on community development.

•

The Rt Hon. James Prior, a former British cabinet minister, played cricket at school, appearing in the same eleven as future England Test batsman Peter May.

•

Cricket was discussed at the Constitutional Convention at Boston in 1789, when an objection was raised to using the title 'President' for the leader of the United States, because cricket clubs had presidents.

•

William Ward, who was MP for the City of London and regarded as one of England's best batsmen, hit 278 for the MCC v Norfolk at Lord's in 1820, the world's first recorded double-century and a ground record for 105 years. Five years later, the ground became his, when he handed over to Thomas Lord a cheque for £5,000 on hearing of his financial problems which had led to speculation that the site was to be sold to a building developer. Had Ward not stepped in, it's almost certain that Lord's would have been lost forever.

> Me be an umpire? I'd rather face Bronwyn Bishop.
> —*Sun-Herald* headline above John Benaud column, 1994

> Without cricket there can be no summer in this land.
> —British MP Roy Hattersley

•

Brian Booth, the former Australian Test captain, stood as a Liberal Party candidate for the Sydney-based electorate of St George in the 1974 federal election. His main opponent was Science Minister Bill Morrison, who won the seat by 6,000 votes.

•

In 1993 a Welsh MP, miffed at England selectors continually overlooking Glamorgan players for Test matches, petitioned Westminster to have the Glamorgan-Australia match recognised as the seventh Test of the Ashes series. What became of his idea is unknown, but coincidentally, two Welsh players—Matthew Maynard and Steve Watkin—were called up for the England squad following his outcry.

•

Larry Gomes, the popular West Indies Test batsman, stood as the National Alliance for Reconstruction Party's candidate for the seat of Arima in Trinidad's general election in 1991.

•

After casting his vote in the 1990 general election, New Zealand's incoming Prime Minister Jim Bolger had a bat in a children's cricket match. A left-hander, he 'hit the headlines' in more ways than one, accidentally hitting one of the assembled media with one of his shots before being run out by his partner, a young girl.

•

EUROPEAN CRICKET IN THE FUTURE?
Taking into account, firstly, the need for deeper European relations with Australia, and secondly, the excessive recent success of Australia's cricket team, I'm introducing a proposal to the European Council of Ministers to change the European rules of cricket. I'm proposing that in Europe the 22 yard pitch—anachronistic—must be replaced with a 20 metre pitch; only a softball should be used, based on European health and safety requirements. You'll clearly have to have ten-ball overs in view of metrication and each side will have to have 12-person teams—one player for each of our member states. And to appeal in Europe, bowlers will obviously have to use Esperanto in order to avoid the ubiquitous use of the English language. Finally, blue or pink sunglasses used by the fielding side will have to contain a substantial European content.
> —Sir Leon Brittan, European Union Trade Commissioner and former Thatcher Cabinet Minister, in an address to the National Press Club, Canberra in 1994

•

Clement Adlee (left), a future British Prime Minister, and Edwin Stockton make their way to the wicket to open the innings in a friendly match at The Oval in 1923

•

The former South African Test captain Clive van Ryneveld became a member of Parliament upon his retirement from first-class cricket in 1963, representing the seat of East London for the Progressive Party.

•

England's Prime Minister John Major was elected a member of the MCC in 1991 after the club unanimously agreed to bring forward his application. The candidates' list for membership at the time was some 9,000 with a waiting time of approximately 18 years.

•

The first women's cricket club was the White Heather, formed in Yorkshire in 1887. One of the club's most noted players was Lucy Risdale, who married Stanley Baldwin, the British Prime Minister.

•

Responding to two back-to-back polls in 1994 on who voters wanted to lead Tasmania, the Premier, Ray Groom, stated that even David Boon or Shane Warne could have come out on top. In an ABC Television poll, Groom was the preferred Premier by just 14% of the voters, behind former Federal Minister Michael Hodgman and former state leader Robin Grey. But according to Groom,

Tasmania's batting star David Boon or even Warne, who consistently turns from left to right, would have had a strong chance of winning a similar poll. He told Parliament: 'If David Boon or Shane Warne—though he's not even Tasmanian—was in such a poll, you'd see the same sort of pattern'.

•

New South Wales Liberal Senator Michael Baume, who was Shadow Sports Minister from 1990 to 1993, was a member of the Turner Cricket Club in Canberra that won the local grade premiership in 1953–54. In the grand final against Kingston, played at Manuka Oval, Baume, who went in as an opening batsman, scored 6 in Turner's match-winning total of 269.

New South Wales Liberal Senator Michael Baume gets throttled by Tasmanian MP Michael Hodgman after being hit by a ball during a 'friendly' cricket match

•

Just 10 days after announcing his retirement from international cricket in 1994, Javed Miandad reversed his decision, after the intervention of Pakistan's Prime Minister, Benazir Bhutto. Javed, the third-highest run-scorer in Test cricket, had called it quits after failing to gain selection for the Australasia Cup in Sharjah, but was urged by the Prime Minister to reconsider. 'I cannot say no to the Prime Minister and I decided to take back the retirement. The Prime Minister asked me to make the world record. I will now present myself for selection.'

When Allan Border retired from international cricket in 1994 both houses of Federal Parliament interrupted normal proceedings to salute the long-standing Australian captain. The Prime Minister, Paul Keating, moved a motion during Question Time paying tribute to Border, one that was supported by the then Opposition Leader John Hewson. In the Senate, Sports Minister John Faulkner raised Border's retirement as 'a matter of public importance'.

> **Australians have to pay tribute to a man who has become an Australian legend. He displayed tenacity, courage and devotion to his task to a degree few Australians have matched.**
> **—Prime Minister Paul Keating**
>
> **If ever an Australian sportsman has negotiated the peaks and troughs of fame, despair, success and failure with unfailing grit and determination, it has been Allan Border.**
> **—Shadow Industrial Relations Minister John Howard**
>
> **We can't bring back knighthoods, but, if ever there was a good case for bringing them back, then it's for Allan Border.**
> **—Queensland Premier Wayne Goss**

•

In 1993 former England Test spinner Phil Edmonds took 8 for 14 against Eton Ramblers in a guest appearance for the Lords and Commons XI. He also had to open the batting as some of the regular players were still in Parliament.

•

In 1968–69 Aftab Gul, a student lawyer, became the first cricketer to appear in a first-class match while on bail for alleged political offences. He made his Test debut in the first Test against England at Lahore and it's been suggested that, considering his strong support as a student leader, Pakistan's selectors had no choice but to pick him. In 1983 Pakistan martial law authorities stormed his home and allegedly seized two Soviet surface-to-air missiles. Aftab, a founding member of the banned Pakistan Peoples Party, once led by former Prime Minister Z. Ali Bhutto, later applied for political asylum in Britain claiming that if he returned home he'd face the death sentence.

•

William Milton, who appeared in South Africa's first three Tests, later became Parliamentary Secretary to Cecil Rhodes and administrator of Southern Rhodesia.

•

On becoming Test cricket's leading wicket-taker in 1994, Kapil Dev received an unprecedented honour from the government of Prime Minister Narasimha Rao. The PM and various other cabinet ministers were among guests at a ceremony in New Delhi to mark Kapil's achievement, the first time the government had honoured an Indian sportsman by organising a special function.

One of Kapil Dev's biggest fans, the Indian Prime Minister P.V. Narasimha Rao

Bob Hawke

Bob Hawke once had his life saved by a South African Test cricketer. Employed as a part-time gardener at Perth

Federal Defence Minister, Senator Robert Ray

John Hewson—Federal Opposition Leader, 1990–94

John Howard—Federal Opposition Leader, 1985–89

Nick Greiner—New South Wales Premier, 1988–92

University in 1952, Hawke was carting some manure when his horse bolted and crushed him against a post, ripping open his leg. Bleeding profusely, he staggered towards the university cricket oval where the touring South Africans were practising, and collapsed on the ground. Springbok batsman Roy McLean then rushed to the future PM's aid, wrapping his hands around the wound to stop the flow of blood. In hospital, a doctor told Hawke that if it had not been for what McLean had done, he would have almost certainly died.

•

In 1972 Britain's Prime Minister, Edward Heath, became the first honorary patron of the Brussels Cricket Club.

•

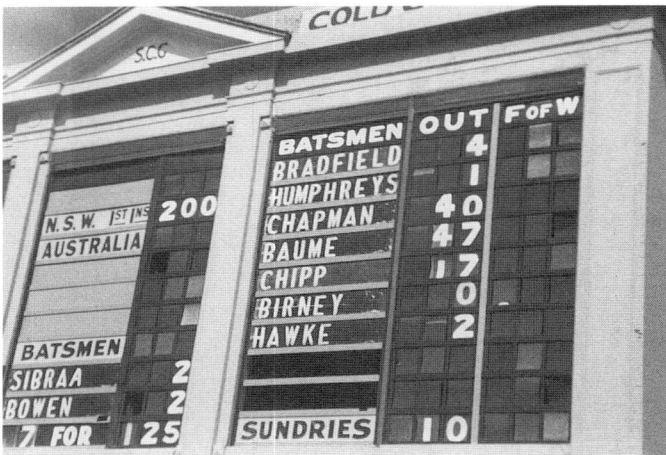

Federal Parliament v NSW Parliament at the Sydney Cricket Ground—some of the famous politicians whose names appear on the old SCG scoreboard include Lionel Bowen, Bob Hawke, Don Chipp, Michael Baume and Kerry Sibraa

•

ROBERT RAY'S ALL-TIME BEST TEST XI

1 Jack Hobbs
2 Bill Ponsford
3 Don Bradman (c)
4 George Headley
5 Viv Richards
6 Garry Sobers
7 Keith Miller
8 Alan Knott
9 Andy Roberts
10 Dennis Lillee
11 Bill O'Reilly

JOHN HEWSON'S ALL-TIME BEST TEST XI

1 Sunil Gavaskar
2 Gordon Greenidge
3 Don Bradman (c)
4 Viv Richards
5 Greg Chappell
6 Garry Sobers
7 Imran Khan
8 Alan Knott
9 Bill O'Reilly
10 Ray Lindwall
11 Dennis Lillee

JOHN HOWARD'S ALL-TIME BEST TEST XI

1 Jack Hobbs
2 Bill Ponsford
3 Don Bradman (c)
4 Allan Border
5 Garry Sobers
6 Ian Botham
7 Don Tallon
8 Ray Lindwall
9 Hedley Verity
10 Bill O'Reilly
11 Harold Larwood

LIONEL BOWEN'S ALL-TIME BEST TEST XI

1 Walter Hammond
2 Michael Slater
3 Don Bradman (c)
4 Stan McCabe
5 Viv Richards
6 Richard Hadlee
7 Bert Oldfield
8 Hedley Verity
9 Ray Lindwall
10 Bill O'Reilly
11 Harold Larwood

NICK GREINER'S ALL-TIME BEST TEST XI

1 Bob Simpson
2 Sunil Gavaskar
3 Greg Chappell
4 Garry Sobers (c)
5 Viv Richards
6 Allan Border
7 Godfrey Evans
8 Richie Benaud
9 Richard Hadlee
10 Dennis Lillee
11 Lance Gibbs

7 Old Troopers

Scoring a century in competitive club cricket when aged over 50 is a feat not many batsmen can claim, but an English pensioner Jack Hyams has more than 25 to his credit. In 1991 the 71-year-old Hyams scored 114 not out for Cockfosters Veterans, his 58th century in successive seasons. It was his 169th century in what's believed to be a world record total of over 112,000 runs. He claims his achievement of a century in seven successive decades is also a record.

•

India's first Test captain, C.K. Nayudu, who played first-class cricket over six decades, made his debut in 1916–17 and played in his last first-class match in 1963–64 at the age of 68.

•

A cricketer by the name of Reg Moss holds two unusual first-class records, both of which were achieved in his final match. In 1925 he made his first-class debut for Worcestershire at Gloucester at the age of 57, becoming the oldest player in the English County Championship. Moss, though, had played first-class cricket before. His penultimate match was way back in 1893 for Liverpool and District against the touring Australians and his 32 years between appearances is a record in first-class cricket.

•

When Frank Tarrant, the former Victorian and Middlesex all-rounder, mounted an Australian tour of India in 1935–36, five of the party were over the age of 45—Tarrant (55), 'Dainty' Ironmonger (53), Charles Macartney (49), Jack Ryder (46) and 'Nana' Ellis (45). On the last day of the match against the Madras President's XI, Tarrant was 55 years and 55 days old—he remains Australia's oldest first-class cricketer.

•

In 1979 a 74-year-old bowler, Lionel Deamer, became the oldest cricketer on record to claim a hat-trick. He took his three successive wickets when playing for the Lloyd's Bank Cricket Club against Earlswood.

•

George Cox was 52 when he took 17 for 106 against Warwickshire at Horsham in 1926. The Sussex slow bowler claimed a career-best 9 for 50 during the match, and remains the oldest county cricketer to take 15 wickets in a first-class match in England.

Sydney Barnes

Sydney Barnes, the England fast bowler who took 189 wickets in just 27 Tests, continued playing minor county and league cricket well into his sixties. Aged 56, he collected 76 wickets at 8.21 for Staffordshire. In his last Test series he took a record 49 wickets against South Africa in 1913–14, at the age of 40.

•

The sight of a streaker on a cricket field is so commonplace these days that such an event raises sometimes nothing more than a yawn. But in 1992 heads did turn when a streaker appeared on the Beaconsfield ground during the Buckinghamshire–Sussex match in the NatWest Bank Trophy competition. The streaker in question was a 71-year-old man dressed only in socks.

•

OLDEST BATSMEN TO SCORE A TEST CENTURY

Age	Batsman	Score	Match
46 years & 82 days	Jack Hobbs	142	England v Australia at Melbourne in 1928–29
45 years & 240 days	Jack Hobbs	159	England v West Indies at The Oval in 1928
45 years & 151 days	'Patsy' Hendren	132	England v Australia at Manchester in 1934

The oldest Australian to score a Test century is Warren Bardsley (43 years and 201 days)—193* v England at Lord's in 1926

OLDEST BATSMAN TO SCORE A CENTURY AND A DOUBLE-CENTURY FOR SURREY
Jack Hobbs

Age	Score	Match
51 years & 161 days	116	Surrey v Lancashire at Manchester in 1934
50 years & 165 days	221	Surrey v West Indies at The Oval in 1933

Jack Hobbs, who played first-class cricket when over the age of 50, is the oldest batsman to score a century in a Test match. He was 46 when he made 142 against Australia at Melbourne in 1928–29. In county cricket, Hobbs is the oldest player to score both a century and a double-century for Surrey.

•

As part of England's Test Cricket Centenary celebrations in 1980, an oldies match between England and Australia was played at The Oval. On aggregate the Old Australians were 96 years the younger and beat Old England by seven wickets. Bob Simpson, at the age of 44, top-scored for the visitors with 75, while a 43-year-old John Edrich made 61 for Old England.

•

When W.G. Grace appeared in his last Test match, at Nottingham in 1899, he became at the age of 50 years and 320 days the oldest Test captain on record. Coincidentally, Wilfred Rhodes made his debut in this match, and eventually became the oldest Test player ever—he was 52 years and 165 days old on the last day of his last Test, against the West Indies at Kingston in 1929–30.

•

At the age of 103, John Durant, bowling for the first time in his life, opened the attack for G.W. Ayres XI v Weybridge, and took a wicket with his second delivery.

•

The oldest Australian batsman to score a first-class hundred is Jack Ryder. He made 115 for the Australians against Southern Punjab at Amritsar in 1935–36 aged 46 years and 152 days. Two other Australians made centuries at the age of 49, but both were playing for teams in England—Billy Murdoch for The Gentlemen v The Players at The Oval in 1904, and Bill Alley for Somerset v Kent at Weston-Super-Mare in 1968.

•

W.G. Grace, the first batsman to complete 1,000 first-class runs during the month of May, was also the oldest. In 1895 Grace, in consecutive innings, scored 13, 103, 18, 25, 288, 52, 257, 73 not out, 18 and 169 for a total of 1,016 runs at 112.88. He was 47. Grace scored 26 centuries in minor county cricket in his fifties and appeared in his last first-class match at the ripe old age of 60.

8 Whoops!

In 1990 David Gower had a lucky escape when his car sank in Switzerland's frozen Lake St Moritz. He'd been following tyre-marks thinking it was safe to continue when his car crashed through the ice and sank. Gower managed to walk away, but there was no sign of the car when he returned the next morning. A few weeks later, former England Test players Peter Walker and Jonathan Agnew played in an annual 'cricket-on-the-ice' match on the lake, with Gower's car still lying underneath, somewhere near square leg.

•

Frustrated at being run out in a one-day match against the 1993 Australians at Lord's, Middlesex captain Mike Gatting smashed his bat through a window in the dressing room, the shattered glass badly gashing his right arm. It was an injury that required 25 stitches and forced him out of selection for the upcoming three one-day internationals.

•

Former England Test captain Ted Dexter once broke a leg when he was run over by his own car. On another occasion he crashed a plane that had on board the former South African fast bowler Peter Pollock.

•

In a match played in Tasmania during the 1897–98 season, a batsman, who was most probably a smoker, went to the crease with a box of matches in his pocket. During his innings he was hit by a ball with such intensity it ignited the matches, inflicting severe burns.

•

During the 1993–94 season Pakistan's famous spin bowler Abdul Qadir spent three days in a coma after being hit in the head by a ball during net practice.

•

In 1986 a Torquay club cricketer, Martyn Goulding, sustained a fractured foot bone when hit by a ball, travelling at 75 mph, dispatched from a bowling machine. Lying on the ground in agony, he was then struck by another ball from the machine, which gave him two broken ribs.

•

England's Derek Pringle was once forced to miss a Test match after hurting his back writing a letter.

The accident-prone Bruce French

While on tour of Pakistan in 1987–88, the English wicket-keeper Bruce French recorded a hat-trick of accidents in the one day, the first of which required hospital treatment. During net practice, French was hit in the face by a wayward ball. Outside the local hospital he was hit by a car and, inside, hit his head on a light getting out of bed after receiving four stitches to his face for his original injury.

On England's tour of the West Indies in 1985–86, French was bitten by a dog while jogging. He missed most of the 1988 season due to a finger injury, and the following year broke the same finger again!

•

Ian Greig

Greg Matthews

Ian Greig, who made his England Test debut in 1982, fell from grace after an indifferent performance in his two matches against Pakistan. But the following year he suffered another, and perhaps more painfull, fall. After scoring 42 for Sussex against Kent at Hove, he broke his ankle after plunging 18 feet, trying to climb into his flat when his front door key had broken in the lock.

•

Rowan Lyle, a fast bowler with the South African side Eastern Province, made history during the 1993–94 Castle Cup competition when he came out to bat in a match against Transvaal on crutches. Lyle, Eastern Province's No. 11 batsman, had broken a toe during the match but managed to hobble to the wicket, his foot in plaster, accompanied by a runner and another player carrying his bat. Upon arrival at the crease the umpires ordered his crutches be sent back to the pavilion, which forced him to hop around to avoid further damaging his toe. Batting with captain Eldine Baptiste, he survived three deliveries without scoring, sharing a valuable final-wicket partnership of 23. With the innings complete, Lyle was then required to return to the dressing-rooms minus his crutches. It's thought the time taken to leave the field was a record for a batsman in first-class cricket!

•

Former Australian Test player Greg Matthews found himself in hospital on the eve of a Sheffield Shield match in 1993–94 following an incident at a Perth nightclub. Matthews was found unconscious by singer Jon Stevens on the footpath outside the Hip-E Club after the all-rounder had been forcibly removed early in the morning. Matthews underwent a brain scan at Royal Perth Hospital after vomiting blood and complaining of severe headaches.

•

'Dickie' Bird was attacked by a bird at an aviary exhibition in Birmingham in 1994. The Test umpire suffered a bloody nose after being bitten by a cockatoo.

•

It had to happen, and it did, in 1993–94, when Channel 9's Tony Greig lost a key in a cricket pitch. Prior to the start of the Australia–South Africa one-day international at Perth, Greig stuck Mike Procter's hotel room key in a crack on the WACA strip as part of his famous 'pitch report'. But so deep was the crack, he was unable to retrieve the key and that's where it stayed.

During the same season in the West Indies, play in the match between Jamaica and Guyana at Kingston was held up for a short time when a glove ended up in the pitch. While using a heavy roller, the groundsman accidentally dropped a glove, which was rolled into the strip leaving an indentation that took 30 minutes to repair.

•

On his way home from the 1986 Test tour of England, New Zealand batsman Trevor Franklin suffered multiple leg fractures after being hit by a motorised baggage trolley at Gatwick Airport.

Standing in only his second Test match, New Zealand umpire Dick Shortt perpetrated a major gaffe when he allowed Kiwi spinner John Sparling to bowl an 11-ball over against England at Auckland in 1962–63. Umpires in New Zealand have a history of similar errors. At Wellington in 1973–74, Brian Hastings was dismissed for 101 off the ninth ball of an eight-ball over sent down by Australia's Geoff Dymock. And at Auckland 20 years later, Steve Dunne lost count of the number of balls in an over five times during the first two days of the first Test against Pakistan in 1993–94. Standing at the bowlers' end, he allowed two seven-ball overs and a five-ball over from Ata-ur-Rehman, and on one occasion oversaw an eight-ball over.

9 Bowling to Remember

The 1991–92 Ranji Trophy produced some remarkable spells of bowling in terms of overs, with one stint by Hyderabad's Arshad Ayub equalling a first-class record set by West Indian bowler Sonny Ramadhin in 1957. Bowling against Madhya Pradesh (535) at Secunderabad, Ayub sent down 98 overs in the first innings of the match, a record in first-class cricket outside Tests. Earlier in the season, two bowlers—R.K. Chauhan and S.S. Lahore—appearing for Madhya Pradesh also made the record books when they sent down nearly 173 overs between them in the first innings against Railways (417) at Gwalior. Chauhan sent down 92 overs, Lahore 80.5, the greatest number of six-ball overs by two bowlers in the same innings of a first-class match.

•

Clive Rice and Garth Le Roux made history in 1986 when they both claimed a hat-trick in the *same* first-class match, for South Africa in an unofficial Test against Australia at Johannesburg.

•

While representing South Australia in 1990–91, paceman Colin Miller pulled off one of the most outstanding spells of bowling in all first-class cricket. In the Sheffield Shield match against New South Wales in Sydney, Miller captured five wickets in eight balls and six in 10. During the innings he took three wickets in four balls *twice*, a unique performance in Australian first-class cricket.

Three seasons later playing *against* South Australia, Miller produced another fiery burst of pace bowling taking 4 for 5 in 22 balls in a Sheffield Shield match at Hobart.

Colin Miller

During the summer of 1962–63 Alan Davidson twice dismissed a batsman with the first ball of a first-class match—Western Australia's Kevin Gartrell at Perth, and South Australia's Les Favell at Sydney. Victoria's Alan 'Froggy' Thomson performed a similar feat in 1969–70, accounting for New South Wales batsmen Bruce Francis and Alan Turner, at Melbourne and Sydney respectively.

•

The first wicket in the Test career of New Zealander Danny Morrison was that of Allan Border at Brisbane in 1987–88. In the subsequent 10 Test matches in which the two opposed each other, Morrison claimed the Australian captain's wicket on another seven occasions, including five in a row between 1989–90 (Perth) and 1992–93 (Auckland).

•

Australia's Jimmy Matthews who uniquely took a hat-trick in each innings of a Test match in 1912, claimed another two hat-tricks in his first-class career. His total of four is an Australian record, one that's shared by the great fast bowler Fred Spofforth. In all first-class cricket the record belongs to the Kent and England leg-break bowler Doug Wright, who achieved the hat-trick seven times.

MOST HAT-TRICKS IN AUSTRALIAN FIRST-CLASS CRICKET

Bowler	Match
Fred Spofforth (4)	Australians v MCC at Lord's in 1878
	Australians v Players at The Oval in 1878
	Australia v England at Melbourne in 1878–79
	Australians v South of England at The Oval in 1884
Jimmy Matthews (4)	Victoria v Tasmania at Launceston in 1908–09
	Australia v South Africa (1st inns) at Manchester in 1912
	Australia v South Africa (2nd inns) at Manchester in 1912
	Australians v Philadelphians at Germantown in 1912–13
George Giffen (3)	Australians v Lancashire at Manchester in 1884
	South Australia v Vernon's XI at Adelaide in 1887–88
	Australians v England XI at Wembley Park in 1896

•

During the opening round of matches in the 1990–91 Ranji Trophy, a bowler by the name of D.S. Mishra performed a feat with the ball that had been achieved only once before in the history of first-class cricket. Bowling for Railways against Madhya Pradesh at Delhi, Mishra took a wicket with his first ball in *both* innings of what was his maiden first-class match. The only other bowler to have previously chalked up such a double was Rudi Webster, for Scotland v the MCC at Greenock in 1961.

•

Ron Davis, a fast bowler from Sydney, had the distinction of once dismissing three of the Waugh brothers in the same innings of a club match. In round three of the 1993–94 season, Davis dismissed Steve for a duck, Mark for 8 and Dean for 1 in the first innings of the match between Fairfield and Bankstown.

•

During the calendar year of 1888, two Australian bowlers took over 200 wickets in first-class matches—Charlie Turner claimed 365, one for each day of the year, while his comrade-in-arms, J.J. Ferris accounted for 234. The feat of taking 200 first-class wickets in a calendar year is a relatively rare one—the deed has been achieved by Australians just nine times, the last in 1930.

200 FIRST-CLASS WICKETS BY AUSTRALIAN BOWLERS IN A CALENDAR YEAR

Bowler	Year	Wkts	M	5wi	10wm	BB	Avge
Charlie Turner	1888	365	47	40	16	9–15	12.49
Albert Trott	1899	281	37	29	11	8–64	16.48
J.J. Ferris	1888	234	45	18	3	8–41	15.52
Clarrie Grimmett	1930	228	38	25	6	10–37	18.16
Arthur Mailey	1921	221	41	14	4	10–66	21.39
Fred Spofforth	1884	212	33	22	10	8–62	13.04
Albert Trott	1900	211	33	22	5	10–42	23.33
J.J. Ferris	1890	210	34	17	6	8–84	14.54
'Ted' McDonald	1925	205	35	19	8	8–86	18.67

On each occasion the bowler concerned took the majority of his wickets while on tour with the Australians, with the exception of Albert Trott, who took most of his wickets while playing county cricket for Middlesex.

•

In a 1992 World Cup warm-up match between Pakistan and the ACT in Canberra, Greg Irvine conceded only one scoring stroke from his allotted 10 overs. Salim Malik hit the first ball of Irvine's second over for three. He then conceded four wides and finished the match with the impressive figures of 10–6–7–2.

•

Rodney Hogg and Terry Alderman are the only bowlers in Test history to take 40 wickets in their debut international series. Hogg took 41 wickets at 12.85 in the six-Test series against England in 1978–79, while Alderman earned 42 wickets at 21.26 in six Tests in England in 1981. An additional two Tests against Pakistan in 1978–79 increased the number of wickets taken by Hogg to 51, a unique performance by a bowler in his first season of Test cricket.

MOST WICKETS IN FIRST TEST SERIES

Bowler and Test series	Wicket hauls
Terry Alderman (42) v England 1981	4–68 & 5–62 at Nottingham
	1–79 & 1–42 at Lord's
	3–59 & 6–135 at Leeds
	5–42 & 3–65 at Birmingham
	4–88 & 5–109 at Manchester
	3–84 & 2–60 at The Oval
Rodney Hogg (41) v England 1978–79	6–74 & 1–35 at Brisbane
	5–65 & 5–57 at Perth
	5–30 & 5–36 at Melbourne
	2–36 & 4–67 at Sydney
	4–26 & 3–59 at Adelaide
	1–42 at Sydney
Arthur Mailey (36) v England 1920–21	3–95 & 3–105 at Sydney
	5–160 & 5–142 at Adelaide
	4–115 & 9–121 at Melbourne
	2–89 & 5–119 at Sydney

•

Terry Alderman (below), Rodney Hogg (above left) and Arthur Mailey (above right), who each claimed over 35 wickets in their debut Test series for Australia

England's bowling line-up against Australia at Nottingham in 1993 was one of their most inexperienced on record, yet surprisingly proved to be one of their best attacks in a long time. Its opening pair of Martin McCague and Mark Ilott were both making their Test debuts while the other two—Andy Caddick, with an average of 237.00, and spinner Peter Such—had four Test appearances and nine wickets between them. The foursome combined reasonably well and, although the match was drawn, it ended England's seven-match losing streak. The last time England went into a Test with two debutant opening bowlers was at Lahore in 1961–62, when the colourful pair of 'Butch' White and Alan Brown took the new ball in a match England won by five wickets.

•

In the final of the 1993 Hero Cup one-day tournament in Calcutta, Indian spinner Anil Kumble pencilled his name in the record books by taking six wickets against the West Indies, all without assistance from the field. He bowled five of them and picked up an lbw for four runs in the space of just 26 deliveries. His 6 for 12 off 6.1 overs was the best-ever performance by a spinner in one-day international cricket.

•

Spinner Pat Pocock, who appeared in 25 Tests for England, produced one of cricket's greatest spells of bowling in 1972, when playing for Surrey at Eastbourne. Sussex, 1 for 187 and chasing 205 for victory, was reduced to 9 for 202 after Pocock tore through the line-up taking a world-record seven wickets in 11 balls, including a hat-trick and five wickets in the final over. Before his onslaught, Pocock's figures were 0 for 63 off 14 overs—he finished the innings with 7 for 67 off 16.

•

George Lohmann, who opened the bowling in the first Test at Port Elizabeth in 1895–96, took 15 for 45 in the match including a hat-trick. In the first innings he bowled seven of the South Africans, and hit the stumps five times in the second, a performance that contributed to a record number of batsmen to be bowled in a match. In the three-Test series Lohmann took a staggering 35 wickets at just 5.80. Match-by-match his figures were 7–38 & 8–7, 9–28 & 3–43 and 7–42 & 1–45. In his brief Test career Lohmann got 112 wickets in 18 matches at the record low average of 10.75. His strike rate of a wicket every 34.11 balls is also a Test record.

MOST BATSMEN BOWLED IN A TEST
23/40   South Africa (14) v England (9) at Port Elizabeth in 1895–96

FEWEST BATSMEN BOWLED IN A TEST
0/36   Australia (0) v India (0) at Perth in 1991–92

Lohmann's two eight-wicket hauls in the 1895–96 series represented the best performances by any bowler in Test cricket during the decade, and with another eight wickets in an innings in 1886–87, his name figures prominently in the list of the leading wicket-takers in Test history.

BEST BOWLING IN A TEST INNINGS, DECADE BY DECADE

Analysis	Bowler	Match
		1870s
7-55	Tom Emmett	England v Australia at Melbourne in 1876–77
7-62	Fred Spofforth	Australia v England at Melbourne in 1878–79
		1880s
8-11	Johnny Briggs	England v South Africa at Cape Town in 1888–89
8-35	George Lohmann	England v Australia at Sydney in 1886–87
		1890s
9-28	George Lohmann	England v South Africa at Johannesburg in 1895–96
8-7	George Lohmann	England v South Africa at Port Elizabeth in 1895–96
		1900s
8-31	Frank Laver	Australia v England at Manchester in 1909
8-59	'Charlie' Blythe	England v South Africa at Leeds in 1907
		1910s
9-103	Sydney Barnes	England v South Africa at Johannesburg in 1913–14
8-29	Sydney Barnes	England v South Africa at The Oval in 1912
		1920s
9-121	Arthur Mailey	Australia v England at Melbourne in 1920–21
8-126	Jack White	England v Australia at Adelaide in 1928–29
		1930s
8-43	Hedley Verity	England v Australia at Lord's in 1934
7-40	Clarrie Grimmett	Australia v South Africa at Johannesburg in 1935–36
		1940s
7-38	Ray Lindwall	Australia v India at Adelaide in 1947–48
7-49	Alec Bedser	England v India at Lord's in 1946
		1950s
10-53	Jim Laker	England v Australia at Manchester in 1956 (2nd inns)
9-37	Jim Laker	England v Australia at Manchester in 1956 (1st inns)
		1960s
8-38	Lance Gibbs	West Indies v India at Bridgetown in 1961–62
8-53	'Goofy' Lawrence	South Africa v New Zealand at Johannesburg in 1961–62
		1970s
9-86	Sarfraz Nawaz	Pakistan v Australia at Melbourne in 1978–79
9-95	Jack Noreiga	West Indies v India at Port-of-Spain in 1970–71
		1980s
9-52	Richard Hadlee	New Zealand v Australia at Brisbane in 1985–86
9-56	Abdul Qadir	Pakistan v England at Lahore in 1987–88

•

After going wicketless on his first-class debut in 1894–95, Tom McKibbin, a slow-medium bowler from New South Wales, took his 100th wicket in his 13th match. Along the way, he took 12 or more wickets in a match four times, becoming in 1896–97 the first NSW bowler to gain 15 wickets in a Sheffield Shield match, against South Australia at Adelaide. In six first-class matches in 1895–96, McKibbin captured 46 wickets at 23.86. The following season he took 44 wickets, average 14.88, in just four matches.

•

Bowling in a schools match in New Zealand in 1967–68, 14-year-old Stephen Fleming took a triple hat-trick. He took nine wickets in nine balls for Marlborough College against Bohally Intermediate at Blenheim, dismissing the last batsman in the first innings and obtaining a wicket with each ball of his first over in the second innings. Another schoolboy, Paul Hugo, also took nine wickets in successive balls, for Smithfield against Aliwal North at Johannesburg in the 1930–31 season.

Lance Gibbs, whose 8 for 38 against India at Bridgetown in 1961–62 was the best bowling analysis in a Test match during the decade

•

Richard Hadlee, the first bowler to take 400 Test wickets, had the odd experience in 1993–94 of playing in a one-day match against his own country. To open their tour of Australia, the New Zealanders took on the Australian Cricket Board Chairman's XI at Lilac Hill and faced not only an opening attack of Dennis Lillee and Jeff Thomson, but also their own Sir Richard Hadlee. From 23 overs the trio claimed five wickets for 56, Lillee taking 2 for 25, Thomson 2 for 13 and Hadlee 1 for 18.

RICHARD HADLEE'S ALL-TIME BEST TEST XI
1 Geoff Boycott
2 Sunil Gavaskar
3 Viv Richards
4 Greg Chappell
5 David Gower
6 Allan Border (c)
7 Imran Khan
8 Alan Knott
9 Michael Holding
10 Dennis Lillee
11 Derek Underwood

•

A Victorian bowler was on a hat-trick in a minor match in 1942–43 when his next delivery hit the wicket-keeper after missing the stumps. It then rebounded onto the batsman, who was out of his crease, and deflected onto the stumps. The hat-trick was avoided as the batsman was ruled run out.

•

The Jamaican-born fast bowler Cleveland Lindo only played in two first-class matches, once for Nottinghamshire in 1960 and then three years later for Somerset, when he took an innings haul of 8 for 88 against the Pakistan Eaglets at Taunton.

•

It seems that the England medium-pace bowler Alec Bedser definitely had the edge over Australian batsman Arthur Morris. In the 21 Tests in which they played against each other, Bedser took his wicket on 18 occasions. Bedser got him five times in 1950–51 and another three times in the first three Tests of 1953. Then at Manchester, Morris exacted sweet revenge when he was given the ball for one over towards the end of England's innings and bowled Bedser for 8.

•

Pakistan's Waqar Younis took seven or more wickets in his first four Tests against New Zealand, 38 in all. In the three-match series in 1990–91 he took 7 for 79 at Karachi, 10 for 106 at Lahore, 12 for 130 at Faisalabad and then 9 for 81 in the one-off Test at Hamilton in 1992–93. Boasting one of Test cricket's best strike rates, Waqar had a sensational first-up encounter with Zimbabwe in 1993–94. In his first series against the new African Test nation, Waqar took 27 wickets in three matches—7–91 & 6–44 at Karachi, 5–88 & 4–50 at Rawalpindi and 5–100 at Lahore. At the end of his 25th Test match for Pakistan, at Rawalpindi, Waqar had a phenomenal 143 wickets to his credit, with five wickets in an innings 15 times. He made it to the 150-wicket milestone in his 27th Test, at Auckland in 1993–94.

•

Dennis Lillee, who dismissed Pakistan's Abdul Qadir with his final delivery in Test cricket in 1983–84, took a wicket with his first delivery on his return to first-class cricket, for Tasmania in 1987–88.

•

Australia's Charlie Turner ended his Test career in 1894–95 in fine style, reaching the milestone of 100 Test wickets in the last of his 17 Test match appearances. Turner was the first Australian to take 100 Test wickets and the number of matches he needed to acquire the milestone is a record for a fast bowler.

FEWEST TEST MATCHES TO REACH 100 WICKETS
(Australians only)

T	Bowler	Test debut	100th wicket
17	Charlie Turner	1886–87	1894–95
17	Clarrie Grimmett	1924–25	1930–31
20	Bill O'Reilly	1931–32	1936–37
20	Bill Johnston	1947–48	1951–52
23	Graham McKenzie	1961	1964–65
23	Jeff Thomson	1972–73	1977–78
23	Shane Warne	1991–92	1993–94

•

Peter McPhee

On his first-class debut for Tasmania in 1989–90, Peter McPhee took the wicket of Mark Taylor with his very first ball, and followed it up by dismissing Mark O'Neill with the first ball of his next spell, an extremely rare double in first-class cricket.

•

Shane Warne's magic ball that dismissed Mike Gatting at Manchester in 1993 was the first instance of a player *bowling* an opponent with his first delivery in 116 years of Anglo–Australian Test cricket. Four others before him had claimed a wicket with their first ball in an Ashes Test, including the Australians Arthur Coningham (Melbourne 1894–95) and Ernie McCormick (Brisbane 1936–37), but Warne's feat of hitting the stumps first-up was unique.

Gatting's wicket was the first of an eventual 34 wickets for Warne in the '93 series—a record by an Australian spinner in England, beating Clarrie Grimmett's 29 in 1930. Tim May also had a profitable series taking 21 wickets, and in partnership the two spinners claimed 55 scalps between them in the six-Test series, a new record, eclipsing the 53 taken by Bill O'Reilly (28) and Grimmett (25) in 1934.

MOST TEST WICKETS BY AUSTRALIAN SPINNERS IN ENGLAND

Bowler	Year	T	W	BB	Avge
Shane Warne	1993	6	34	5–82	25.79
Clarrie Grimmett	1930	5	29	6–167	31.89
Bill O'Reilly	1934	5	28	7–54	24.92
Hugh Trumble	1902	3	26	8–65	14.26
Clarrie Grimmett	1934	5	25	5–64	26.72
Bill O'Reilly	1938	4	22	5–56	27.72
Tim May	1993	5	21	5–89	28.19

1993 was Shane Warne's year, with him taking 72 Test wickets, a record number for a spin bowler. When he took his 56th, in the second Test against New Zealand at Hobart, he claimed the record held previously by Arthur Mailey and Richie Benaud. Even though he only twice achieved five wickets in an innings during the year, he claimed a bag of four wickets four times in a row, followed by two successive three-wicket hauls.

His best match performance during 1993 was a career-best 9 for 67 against New Zealand in Hobart. He improved on those figures just three Tests later, claiming two five-wicket hauls in his bag of 12 wickets for 128 in the first Test of 1994, against South Africa at Sydney. It was his first 10-wicket haul in first-class cricket and along the way passed the milestone of 50 first-class wickets in the '93–94 season in just nine matches.

SHANE WARNE'S RECORD YEAR OF TEST CRICKET— 72 WICKETS IN THE CALENDAR YEAR OF 1993

41–6–116–1 v West Indies at Sydney
2–0–11–0 & 6–2–18–1 v West Indies at Adelaide
12–0–51–0 v West Indies at Perth
22–12–23–3 & 26–7–63–4 v New Zealand at Christchurch
29–9–59–2 & 40–25–49–2 v New Zealand at Wellington
15–12–8–4 & 27–8–54–2 v New Zealand at Auckland
24–10–51–4 & 49–26–86–4 v England at Manchester
35–12–57–4 & 48.5–17–102–4 v England at Lord's
40–17–74–3 & 50–21–108–3 v England at Nottingham
23–9–43–1 & 40–16–63–0 v England at Leeds
21–7–63–1 & 49–23–82–5 v England at Edgbaston
20–5–70–2 & 40–15–78–3 v England at The Oval
37.1–6–90–1 & 13–6–23–0 v New Zealand at Perth
18–5–36–3 & 19.5–9–31–6 v New Zealand at Hobart
28.3–12–66–4 & 35–11–59–4 v New Zealand at Brisbane
31–8–63–1 v South Africa at Melbourne

MOST TEST WICKETS BY A SPIN BOWLER IN A CALENDAR YEAR

Bowler	Year	T	W	5wi	10wm	BB	Avge
Shane Warne (Australia)	1993	16	72	2	0	6–31	23.56
Arthur Mailey (Australia)	1921	10	55	4	2	9–121	28.49
Richie Benaud (Australia)	1959	9	55	4	0	5–76	18.74
Hugh Trumble (Australia)	1902	8	53	4	2	8–65	18.75
Vinoo Mankad (India)	1952	10	53	5	2	8–52	22.07
B.S.Chandrasekhar (India)	1976	11	52	3	0	6–94	28.03

MOST TEST WICKETS BY ANY BOWLER IN A CALENDAR YEAR

Bowler	Year	T	W	5wi	10wm	BB	Avge
Dennis Lillee (Australia)	1981	13	85	5	2	7–83	20.95
Joel Garner (West Indies)	1984	15	77	4	0	6–60	20.81
Kapil Dev (India)	1983	18	75	5	1	9–83	23.17
Kapil Dev (India)	1979	18	74	5	0	6–63	23.24
Malcolm Marshall (WI)	1984	13	73	9	1	7–53	20.15
Shane Warne (Australia)	1993	16	72	2	0	6–31	23.56
Graham McKenzie (Aust)	1964	14	71	4	1	7–153	24.46

•

On a sticky Brisbane pitch in 1947–48, India, in its first Test match with Australia, was dismissed for 58 and 98. The main destroyer was Ernie Toshack, a slow-medium, left-arm bowler who came away with match figures of 11 for 31, including a first innings haul of 5 for 2—the most economical five-wicket analysis in the history of Test cricket.

Another bag of five for not many runs was achieved by Tim May in 1992–93. May induced a West Indies collapse at Adelaide, producing his best Test figures of 5 for 9 off 6.5 overs.

Tim May

Andrew Newell, a New South Wales medium-pace off-break bowler, had a bumper season in 1893–94 taking 60 wickets for the Glebe club at the record low average of 5.43. In first-class matches he claimed 25 wickets at 19.56 with a 10-wicket haul in the Sheffield Shield match against South Australia in Adelaide.

•

Victoria's Tony Dodemaide returned the impressive figures of 11–7–9–6—a record for Sussex in its nine-wicket victory over Ireland at Downpatrick in the 1990 NatWest Bank Trophy.

•

In a match for Manly B against the Bank of New South Wales in 1896–97, F. Walsh took a hat-trick with the first deliveries of his opening over, and then took another hat-trick with the first three balls of his last over. He finished the game with 9 for 3 in five overs.

•

What a difference a day makes. On the 1993 Ashes tour, New South Wales bowler Wayne Holdsworth was down and out after being hit for 113 runs off 20 overs on the first day of the match against Derbyshire. He bounced back in a big way the following morning, taking the first hat-trick of his career and four wickets for four to finish the innings with 5 for 117 off 22 overs. His hat-trick was the first by a New South Wales bowler since Dave Gilbert's in 1984–85 and the first by an Australian in England in over 80 years.

HAT-TRICKS FOR AND AGAINST AUSTRALIA IN ENGLAND

Australian hat-tricks	Match
Fred Spofforth	Australians v MCC at Lord's in 1878
Fred Spofforth	Australians v Players at The Oval in 1878
'Joey' Palmer	Australians v Sussex at Hove in 1882
George Giffen	Australians v Lancashire at Manchester in 1884
Fred Spofforth	Australians v South of England at The Oval in 1884
George Giffen	Australians v England XI at Wembley Park in 1896
Tom McKibbin	Australians v Lancashire at Liverpool in 1896
Hugh Trumble	Australians v Gloucestershire at Cheltenham in 1896
Bert Hopkins	Australians v Cambridge University at Cambridge in 1902
Jimmy Matthews	Australia v South Africa (1st inns) at Manchester in 1912
Jimmy Matthews	Australia v South Africa (2nd inns) at Manchester in 1912
Wayne Holdsworth	Australians v Derbyshire at Derby in 1993

English hat-tricks	Match
Walter Humphries	Sussex v Australians at Hove in 1880
Walter Humphries	Sussex v Australians at Hove in 1884
Jack Hearne	England v Australia at Leeds in 1899
George Wilson	Worcestershire v Australians at Worcester in 1905
John Newman	Hampshire v Australians at Southampton in 1909
Henry Enthoven	Middlesex v Australians at Lord's in 1934
Bob Woolmer	MCC v Australians at Lords in 1975
Winston Benjamin	Leicestershire v Australians at Leicester in 1989

Wayne Holdsworth

A seventeen-year-old English schoolboy, Alex Kelly, earned a place in the record books in 1994 when he clean-bowled ten batsmen in an innings without conceding a run. He finished the match for Bishop Auckland v Newton Aycliffe with the history-making figures of 4.3–4–0–10.

•

A bowler by the name of W. Clarke once took *five* hat-tricks in the same match. Appearing for St Augustine's College against the Ashford Church Choir in England in 1912, Clarke took three hat-tricks in the first innings and two in the second.

•

Clarrie Grimmett, with 1,424 victims, and George Giffen, with 1,022, are the only Australian bowlers to take 1,000 first-class wickets without the luxury of playing county cricket in England.

•

In his limited appearances for South Africa, Mike Procter took 41 wickets in just seven matches at 15.02, the lowest average of any bowler taking 25 Test wickets this century. In his first Test series, against Australia in 1966–67, he claimed 15 wickets at 17.53, and 26 at 13.57 against Australia in 1969–70. His average is the fourth-lowest in Test history after George Lohmann (10.75), J.J. Ferris (12.70) and Albert Trott (15.00).

10 That's Entertainment

Larry Hagman, the star of *I Dream of Jeannie* and *Dallas*, developed a passion for the game of cricket during his formative years as an actor in London in the 1950s. Hagman, a young unknown back then, was a frequent visitor at The Oval and Lord's.

•

Two Gentlemen Sharing, a 1969 British film about inter-racial couples, featured a cameo appearance by West Indies all-rounder Garry Sobers. He was engaged to 'double' for one of the film's stars Hal Frederick, a black American actor who played the part of a West Indian cricketing law student. England fast bowler John Snow also featured in the film, in a small part where he bowled to Frederick.

•

It's believed that Wolfgang Amadeus Mozart was taught the finer points of cricket while in England in 1765. He and his family, on their first visit to the country, were invited to the home of Horatio Mann, one of the game's greatest patrons. He staged many significant matches at Bourne House near Canterbury, and it was here that the nine-year-old Mozart just may have been introduced to the great game.

•

Basil Foster, one of seven brothers who played first-class cricket for Worcestershire, was a leading stage actor in London, and a member of The Thespids XI, a theatrical cricket club that also included its founder C. Aubrey Smith and fellow actors Gerald du Maurier, H.B. Warner and Nigel Bruce. In 11 seasons of first-class cricket (1902–13), Foster scored 753 runs in 34 matches with a top score of 86.

•

The big adventure film *The Four Feathers*, made in 1939, featured two former England Test captains. Archie MacLaren, the famous Lancashire batsman, was in Los Angeles when he picked up a few days work as an extra in the film, his work secured by the cricketing actor C. Aubrey Smith, who played the part of General Burroughs.

•

> I have always fantasised about cricket. Even now, on sleepless nights, I can dismiss the entire Australian XI for a few runs.
> —Actor Donald Pleasance

•

Mark Greatbatch as W.G. Grace in a scene shot for the New Zealand film *The End of the Golden Weather*

Mark Greatbatch, the New Zealand batsman who hit a century on his Test debut in 1988, made his acting debut for a New Zealand film company in 1992. Greatbatch appeared as W.G. Grace in a daydream sequence in *The End of the Golden Weather*, although the entire scene was later edited from the film.

•

David Boon, as David Byrne, with *The Late Show*'s Santo Cilauro

Former Australian fast bowler Mike Whitney displayed a hidden talent in 1993 when he appeared on ABC Television's *The Late Show*. As part of a comedy routine called 'Musical Mix-Ups', Whitney 'sang' the Whitney Houston hit 'I Will Always Love You'. Later in the series, David Boon got in on the act performing 'Once in a Lifetime', in a parody of David Byrne, the lead singer of Talking Heads. Max Walker was also on the show, singing Cyndi Lauper's 'Girls Just Want to Have Fun'.

•

Say, when do they begin?
    —Groucho Marx, watching a cricket match at Lord's

•

The actress Dame Peggy Ashcroft was a great lover of the game, so much so that, during a Royal Shakespeare Company performance of *The War of the Roses*, she hid a small radio in her costume to hear the latest Test score. In 1963 Ashcroft wore a different costume when she appeared in a charity cricket match between the Houses of York and Lancaster. Captaining the Lancastrians against the opposition skippered by actor Donald Sinden, she batted with Cyril Washbrook and scored 16 before being dismissed by Len Hutton.

•

Yorkshire supporter John Alderton, who appeared in the hit TV shows *Upstairs Downstairs* and *No Honestly*, has often been mistaken for Graham Gooch, even by players. When Alderton appeared in a charity match, former England Test batsman Bill Edrich was convinced all through the game he was playing with Gooch, that was, until Alderton started batting—then he realised his mistake. If asked for a Gooch autograph, Alderton always obliges.

•

Charlie Chaplin never forgot the time he went to see a match between Nottinghamshire and Surrey, but witnessed no play because it rained. He could never get over the fact that after paying half-a-crown to get it, there were no refunds if play was called off because of bad weather. 'I had to go to America and see baseball, where at least if they didn't play, you got your money back or the chance of coming again.'

•

Vic Lewis has two passions in life—show business and cricket. A successful musician, Lewis formed his own orchestra in 1947 and later became an agent responsible for artists such as The Beatles and Shirley Bassey. In 1952 he founded the Show Business Cricket Team, and possesses a cricket tie collection which numbers around 3,000.

•

Actor Peter O'Toole gets a few tips from Imran Khan

Peter O'Toole, of *Lawrence of Arabia* fame, is a qualified cricket coach. He also runs his own cricket team, The Lazarusians, which is made up of actors, script writers and stage-hands. In 1992 the team went on its first overseas trip, to France, and beat a French XI, which earlier in the year had defeated the MCC.

•

In 1888 a game of cricket was played in London between men and women employed in the theatre. It was the second match between the two sexes—the first had been won by the gentlemen, even though they'd been handicapped using broomsticks. In the return game, the women were given further advantage, with the men again using brooms as bats, but also having to bat and field left-handed. This time the women of the stage were victorious, scoring 60 to the men's 23.

•

'Plucka Duck', one of the popular characters on Channel 9's *Hey! Hey! It's Saturday*, was the unofficial mascot for the 1993 Australian touring team in England. Every time a batsman made a duck he became the guardian of a Plucka doll until another batsman made nought. Some of the Plucka carers included David Boon, Brendon Julian and Merv Hughes.

•

Tim Rice and Andrew Lloyd Webber, famed for their stage hits such as *Jesus Christ Superstar* and *Evita*, wrote a half-hour musical called *Cricket*. The show, that includes music from *Aspects of Love*, has enjoyed just a handful of private performances, including one in 1986 for the Queen at Windsor Castle.

> Cricket has been one of the most important themes in my life. I've had plenty of enthusiasms, but the willow and leather have always been a stable factor for me.
>
> —Tim Rice

•

The *Monty Python* and *Fawlty Towers* star John Cleese has a cricketing claim to fame—he once dismissed the great Denis Compton. Cleese was a pupil at Clifton College, as was Compton's son, and the England batsman was invited there to play in a social match in 1958. Cleese, normally a fast bowler, was in the team as a spinner and was lucky enough to have as his school coach the former England bowler Reg Sinfield, who gave him a few tips on how to bowl to Compton. It worked, and Cleese got the wicket although when the match scorecard appeared in a newspaper, the dismissal read: *D.C.S. Compton, c White, b Cheese.*

•

Sandeep Patil, the actor

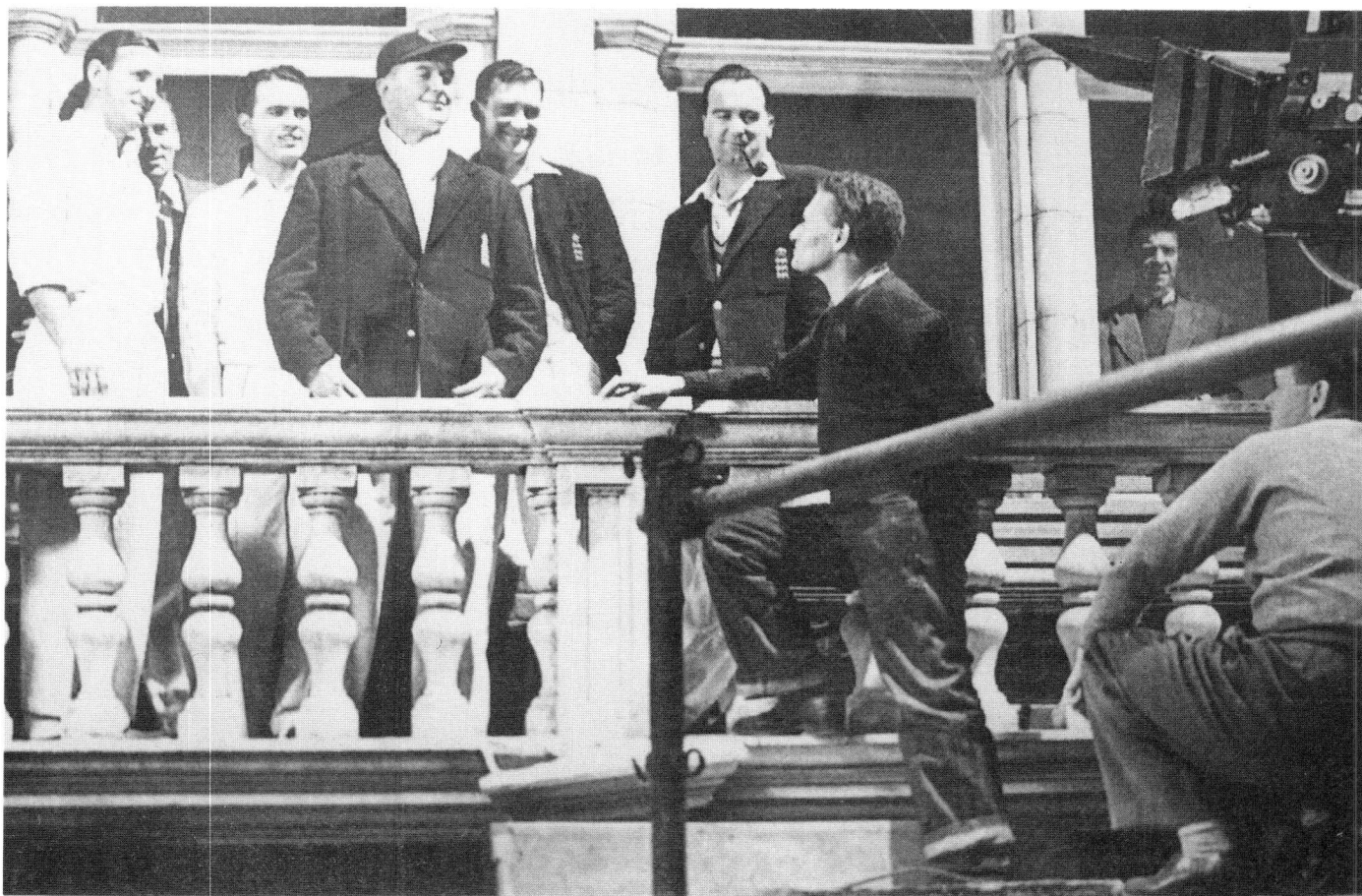

The making of the 1953 film *The Final Test*

The former Test batsman Sandeep Patil made a name for himself as an actor at home in India, appearing in a Hindu film *Once We Were Strangers*, which also starred fellow players Syed Kirmani and Balwindersingh Sandhu.

•

Terence Rattigan, the distinguished playwright and screenwriter, played for his school Harrow, opening the batting in one match against Eton at Lord's in 1929. In Rattigan's obituary published in the 1977 *Wisden*, he was described as 'an elegant stroke-player, but unsound'. The author of many successful plays, Rattigan wrote the script for the 1953 film *The Final Test*, which starred Jack Warner and Robert Morley and six England Test cricketers—Alec Bedser, Denis Compton, Godfrey Evans, Len Hutton, Jim Laker and Cyril Washbrook.

> My two favourite pastimes, watching Test cricket and going to the theatre, would both seem to have had it, and the future would be quite unlivable. I would take to drink and, happily, die of it.
> —Terence Rattigan

•

Jimmy Cutmore, who played first-class cricket for Essex during the 1920s and '30s, was known as 'The Singing Cricketer'. Cutmore had a fine tenor voice and sang professionally in clubs and theatres in London.

•

Actor David Niven was a playing member of the Hollywood Cricket Club and appeared alongside its founder C. Aubrey Smith not only in the field, but also on the screen, in the 1937 film *The Prisoner of Zenda*. Three years later Niven played the leading role in the 1940 version of *Raffles*, based on E.W. Hornung's novel *The Amateur Cracksman*.

In a match against Pasadena in 1937, Niven played alongside three England captains—'Gubby' Allen, who hit 27, C.B. Fry (12) and C. Aubrey Smith (dnb). Niven, batting at No. 5, scored 13.

•

MICHAEL PARKINSON'S ALL-TIME BEST TEST XI
1 Geoff Boycott
2 Barry Richards
3 Viv Richards
4 Greg Chappell
5 Allan Border (c)
6 Garry Sobers
7 Keith Miller
8 Godfrey Evans
9 Shane Warne
10 Michael Holding
11 Jim Laker

•

> It's a funny kind of month, October. For the really keen cricket fan, it's when you realise that your wife left you in May.
> —Denis Norden, British television writer and compere

Gary Sweet

Gary Sweet, who played the part of Don Bradman in the Channel 10 television series *Bodyline*, apparently possessed none of the batting skills required for such a demanding role. Sweet played cricket while at high school in Adelaide, and on his promotion to the first-grade side was promptly dismissed for three consecutive golden ducks.

Bodyline was a ratings winner when it first screened in 1984, attracting 53% of the audience in Melbourne. The previous record was 50% for the Royal Wedding.

> There's a certain lure about the game which takes some beating. It's hard to put a finger on it. Anyone who has played it feels it.
> —Gary Sweet

•

References to cricket in films abound. One of the best-known appears in Alfred Hitchcock's 1938 mystery-comedy *The Lady Vanishes*, which starred Michael Redgrave and Margaret Lockwood. The film, about the disappearance of an old lady, Miss Froy, on a train in Europe, marked the first appearances of two famous screen characters, Charters and Caldicott, played by Basil Radford and Naunton Wayne. Despite the drama and intrigue that surrounded them on the train, their only concern was to get home to watch a Test match at Old Trafford. Charters and Caldicott proved such a hit in the film they were recalled for a number of other appearances, including one in the 1949 movie *It's Not Cricket*.

CRICKET AT THE MOVIES

A selection of well-known feature films that contain references to cricket, either visual or audio.

British
The Lady Vanishes (1938)—Michael Redgrave, Margaret Lockwood and Dame May Whitty
Goodbye, Mr Chips (1939)—Robert Donat and Greer Garson; (1969)—Peter O'Toole and Petula Clark
The Four Feathers (1939)—John Clements, Ralph Richardson and C. Aubrey Smith
Night Train to Munich (1940)—Rex Harrison, Margaret Lockwood, Basil Radford and Naunton Wayne
Rebecca (1940)—Laurence Olivier and Joan Fontaine
The Browning Version (1951)—Michael Redgrave and Jean Kent
Reach for the Sky (1956)—Kenneth More and Muriel Pavlov
Happy is the Bride (1957)—Ian Carmichael and John Le Mesurier
This Sporting Life (1963)—Richard Harris, Rachel Roberts and Arthur Lowe
The Great Escape (1963)—Steve McQueen, James Garner and Donald Pleasance
What's New, Pussycat? (1965)—Peter Sellers, Paula Prentiss, Woody Allen and Ursula Andress
How I Won the War (1967)—Michael Crawford and John Lennon
Accident (1967)—Dirk Bogarde, Michael York and Harold Pinter
Two for the Road (1967)—Audrey Hepburn and Albert Finney
Follow That Camel (1967)—Phil Silvers, Charles Hawtrey, Kenneth Williams and Joan Sims
The Go-Between (1971)—Julie Christie, Michael Redgrave and Edward Fox
The Pink Panther Strikes Again (1976)—Peter Sellers and Herbert Lom
The Deep (1977)—Robert Shaw, Jacqueline Bissett, Nick Nolte and Eli Wallach
The Shout (1978)—Alan Bates, Susannah York and John Hurt
Chariots of Fire (1981)—Ben Cross, Nigel Havers, John Gielgud, Patrick Magee and Derek Pringle
Gandhi (1982)—Ben Kingsley, Candice Bergen, Edward Fox, John Gielgud, Trevor Howard, John Mills and Martin Sheen
Another Country (1984)—Rupert Everett and Colin Firth
The Crying Game (1992)—Forrest Whittacker, Stephen Rea and Miranda Richardson

Australian
How McDougall Topped the Score (1924)—Leslie Gordon and Dorothy May
The Flying Doctor (1936)—Charles Farrell and Mary Maguire
Alvin Rides Again (1974)—Graeme Blundell
The Getting of Wisdom (1977)—Susannah Fowle, Barry Humphries and John Waters
Break of Day (1977)—Andrew McFarlane
Newsfront (1978)—Bill Hunter and Chris Haywood
Careful, He Might Hear You (1983)—Wendy Hughes, Robyn Nevin and John Hargreaves

American
Charley's Aunt (1941)—Jack Benny and Kay Francis
Fancy Pants (1950)—Bob Hope and Lucille Ball
The Power of One (1992)—Stephen Dorff, Morgan Freeman and John Gielgud

•

During the early 1990s, two of Australia's top-rating TV dramas, the ABC's *G.P.* and Channel 7's *A Country Practice*, spawned an annual cricket match contested by rival actors. The match was always meant to be a friendly affair, but in 1993 it took on a distinctly professional look when *ACP* brought in Greg Matthews to help them and *GP* signed on Geoff Lawson. The match was played at the Wandin Valley Estate Winery and attracted a crowd of around 5,000.

•

Boris Karloff, the British actor who achieved worldwide recognition as the monster in *Frankenstein*, began his stage career producing plays at a small cricket club in England. A member of the Surrey CCC, Karloff later helped establish the Hollywood Cricket Club with C. Aubrey Smith. Perhaps his finest cricketing moment came in 1932 when he scored 12 for the Hollywood club against the touring Australians, a team that included Don Bradman, Stan McCabe and Vic Richardson. The Australians won the match comfortably, on Bradman's birthday.

THE AUSTRALIANS v HOLLYWOOD CRICKET CLUB
Los Angeles, 27 August 1932

HOLLYWOOD CRICKET CLUB

Roberts	st Carter b Smith	13
Greaves	c Carney b McCabe	2
Maynard	b McCabe	0
Whitley	b Ives	20
Hoyle	b Smith	3
Thomas	c Kippax b Ives	0
Hall	b Smith	6
Karloff	b Ives	12
Wright	c Richardson b Ives	0
Harper	b Ives	0
Smith	c Richardson b Smith	24
Kinnell	b Smith	1
Harper	b Smith	5
Du Domaine	b Smith	6
Finlayson	b Ives	0
Moore	b Smith	4
Brown	c Ives b Smith	0
Cross	not out	1
Extras		17
		114

Bowling figures
McCabe 2–7, Ives 6–59, Smith 9–31

THE AUSTRALIANS

Richardson	c Thomas b Harper	42
McCabe	c Wright b Harper	26
Bradman	not out	52
Kippax	not out	23
Extras		1
	2 for	144

Bowling figures
Roberts 0–32, Du Domaine 0–37, Wright 0–6, Haper 2–57, Whitley 0–1

•

TONY BARBER'S ALL-TIME BEST TEST XI
1 Len Hutton
2 Garry Sobers
3 Don Bradman (c)
4 Greg Chappell
5 Viv Richards
6 Rod Marsh
7 Ray Lindwall
8 Harold Larwood
9 Dennis Lillee
10 Wes Hall
11 Jack Iverson

•

Television and newspaper journalist Michael Parkinson has to his credit the distinction of once forcing the selectors at Yorkshire's Barnsley cricket club to drop an up-and-coming

Australian Test cricketer Vic Richardson (right) with Boris Karloff (centre) on the MGM set during the filming of *The Mask of Fu Manchu* in 1932

NSW and *G.P.* bowler Geoff Lawson

Tony Barber, radio announcer and compere of the TV quiz shows *Great Temptation, Sale of the Century* and *Jeopardy*

player by the name of Geoff Boycott, so he could be reinstated following a stint in the national service. When Parkinson played club cricket he used to open the batting with one 'Dickie' Bird, and vindicated the selectors decision to drop Boycott by scoring successive centuries.

•

John Warner, the son of former England captain 'Plum' Warner, was a contestant on the BBC Television program *Mastermind* in 1984. His specialist subject was England v Australia Test Matches 1920–38.

•

In 1992 Greg Matthews auditioned for a presenters' spot on ABC Television's *Play School.*

•

Allan Border, Shane Warne and Steve and Mark Waugh were all spotted at a big music festival in Perth in 1994 enjoying the music of Australian rock band INXS. The following day INXS were guests of the Australian cricket team at the World Series match against South Africa at the WACA. Guitarist Tim Farriss, a keen cricket follower, also enjoyed a brief stint as a commentator alongside Simon O'Donnell on Channel 9.

Aiden Crawley, the scorer of over 5,000 first-class runs for Kent and Oxford University, was a noted journalist and BBC documentary film-maker. He was also chief editor of England's ITN News and president of London Weekend TV.

•

> There are many people, who, if you told them the real reason for cricket, would look at you in horror, almost as though you had said something profane. But the fact remains that the only real reason for cricket is fun.
>
> —Ben Travers

The eminent British playwright Ben Travers, who possessed an encyclopedic memory of the game, was a member of the MCC and a vice-president of the Somerset County Cricket Club. Travers spent much of his spare time at Test matches, and in 1928–29 followed Percy Chapman's England side around Australia, the first of his many cricketing holidays down-under. The English comedian Robertson Hare, noted for his appearances in Travers' Aldwych theatre farces of the 1920s and '30s, starred in a Ben Travers play with a cricketing theme, *A Bit of a Test*, a skit on the 'Bodyline' Test series.

•

Former Australian all-rounder Simon O'Donnell in his role as a reporter on Channel 9's *Midday* show

Ben Travers (front row, third from left) with the 1930 Australian touring team

---

I have no memories of cricket, except avoiding it at all times.
—John Mortimer, scriptwriter of the TV show *Rumpole of The Bailey*

●

During a break in the filming of *The Loves of Joanna Godden* in 1946, two of its stars—Australian actors John McCallum and the famous Chips Rafferty—took part in a cricket match in Sussex securing a win for their team off the last ball. It was the annual Pelsham–Peasmarch village match, and McCallum batting at No. 7 and Rafferty at 11 required 34 runs in 16 minutes. Rafferty, an unwilling participant, actually scored a six off the first ball he hit, and with the help of a few byes and overthrows, eventually guided his side to a one-run victory with another six and a four.

●

Daryl Braithwaite, of 'Howzat?' fame, used to play cricket at school and regularly played the game in California when his group Sherbet was based in the United States.

●

Godfrey Evans, the former England wicket-keeper, once won £1,000 on the British TV quiz show *Double Your Money* after correctly answering questions on the subject of jewellery.

Brian Johnston, one of cricket's most cherished commentators, enjoyed a rich and varied career behind the microphone in his long career with the BBC that stretched from 1946 to 1994. Apart from his cricketing commitments, Johnston was involved with the Jubilee, the Coronation and the funeral of King George VI. He was the presenter of two of BBC Radio's most popular shows *Down Your Way* and *In Town Tonight*, and made numerous guest appearances on other radio and television programs.

One of Johnston's most treasured moments came in 1974 when he guest-starred on *Desert Island Discs* with Roy Plomley. The records he chose for the show were 'The Eton Boating Song' by the Eton College Musical Society, 'All The Things You Are' by Hutch, 'We'll Gather Lilacs' by Vanessa Lee and Bruce Trent, 'Double Damask' by Cicely Courtneidge, 'Strolling' by Bud Flanagan, Elgar's 'Enigma Variations' performed by the Philharmonia Orchestra, 'Tie a Yellow Ribbon Round the Old Oak Tree' by Tony Orlando and Dawn, and 'End of the Party' by Barry Alexander.

Johnston had a great affection for old-time music and comedy. Once during a break in play at a cricket match, he sang, on air, Flanagan and Allen's 'Underneath the Arches' with the English pop star and cricket fan David Essex. He wrote the words for 'The Ashes Song', recorded by the 1970–71 MCC side, using an old music hall number 'Show Me Your Winkle Tonight', and in 1994 posthumously entered the British album charts with a recording of his stage show *An Evening with Johnners*.

BRIAN JOHNSTON'S ALL-TIME BEST TEST XI

1 Len Hutton
2 Barry Richards
3 Don Bradman (c)
4 Walter Hammond
5 Viv Richards
6 Garry Sobers
7 Richie Benaud
8 Godfrey Evans
9 Ray Lindwall
10 Richard Hadlee
11 Jim Laker

•

Three ladies of stage and screen—Eartha Kitt, Phyllis Diller and Cleo Laine—enjoy the midday sun at the Hollywood Cricket Club in Los Angeles

The Hollywood Cricket Club is believed to have been the first club to allow women in its pavilion. Some of the famous female spectators and helpers at its cricket matches included Olivia de Haviland, Greer Garson, Merle Oberon and Elizabeth Taylor.

•

I have never got over the shock of seeing my first cricket ball. I simply couldn't believe that there was something so dangerous loose in what up to then had seemed a safe sort of world.
—**British actor Robert Morley**

Joe O'Gorman, an all-rounder who played for Surrey in 1927, was one half of a famous comedy act with his brother Dave. His stage commitments prevented him from pursuing a full-time cricket career, one that showed plenty of promise. A right-arm slow bowler, O'Gorman dismissed the Glamorgan opener Bill Bates at The Oval with his first delivery in first-class cricket. In another of his three County Championship matches he scored 42 not out against Essex, sharing a century partnership with Andy Sandham. He finished his brief first-class career with a batting average of 106.00.

In 1922 Joe and Dave were asked to play in a charity match for The Actors v Variety Artists at Lord's. Joe was the star, taking 7 for 32, including a hat-trick.

•

Christopher Lee, the star of countless horror films including *Dracula* and *The Curse of Frankenstein*, rates his greatest cricketing performance the time he took nine wickets for his Air Force squadron in a match played in the desert during World War II. With the bat, he once scored 149 not out while at school, but burst into tears when he returned to the pavilion having failed to reach 150.

•

In 1908 two cricket teams playing a match *on* stage was on the bill for London theatregoers at the Coliseum. *Surrey v Middlesex* was a four-a-side match, played over a week, and featured top players from each county, including the Surrey wicket-keeper Alan Marshall and Middlesex batsman 'Patsy' Hendren.

•

Cricket commentator John Arlott was the author of a hymn which appeared in the standard edition of *Hymns Ancient and Modern*.

•

Richard Attenborough, the star of films such as *The Great Escape* and *10 Rillington Place*, found himself in hospital several years ago following a mishap on the cricket field that involved a former England Test batsman. Appearing in a charity match organised by fellow thespian John Mills, Attenborough decided that, due to his lack of match practice, he should be placed in the outfield, well away from the action. Midway through the innings Denis Compton went for a huge slog that skied towards Attenborough near the boundary. He put up both hands in a valiant attempt to take the catch, but he missed it, with the ball hitting him right on the head. He collapsed to the ground unconscious and splattered with blood. Rushed to hospital, Attenborough received 22 stitches and was sidelined for two weeks on a film he was then working on.

•

The *Monty Python* pair of Michael Palin and Terry Jones wrote a cricket-flavoured play called *Underwood's Finest Hour*, in which one of the most famous No. 11 batsmen of recent times, Derek Underwood, struck a six to win a Test match for England.

The revered cricket writer Neville Cardus was also renowned for his writings on music. His first cricket piece was published in 1919 for the *Manchester Guardian*; his first music item, nine years earlier in *Musical Opinion*. He later became full-time music critic for the *Manchester Guardian*, and when he lived in Australia he wrote cricket and music pieces for the *Sydney Morning Herald* and conducted a weekly radio show, *The Enjoyment of Music*, on the ABC. Some of his music books were translated into Swedish and German, and included *A Portrait – Gustav Mahler, The Delights of Music, Ten Composers* and *Sir Thomas Beecham.*

> I could say that the Hammerclavier Sonata was the last thing that Beethoven wrote, and I'd get a couple of dozen letters, perhaps, 75 per cent from foreigners. But, if I said that Hutton made 363 at The Oval in 1938, I'd get thousands from Yorkshire alone.
>
> —Neville Cardus
>
> What made Neville Cardus unique and uniquely British was his love and loyalty to both music and cricket. Neville Cardus knew as much about a cricket bat as about a violin bow.
>
> —Yehudi Menuhin

Australian television personality and cricket lover, Bill Peach

BILL PEACH'S ALL-TIME BEST TEST XI
1 Arthur Morris
2 Len Hutton
3 Viv Richards
4 Garry Sobers
5 Don Bradman (c)
6 Keith Miller
7 Richie Benaud
8 Rod Marsh
9 Ray Lindwall
10 Dennis Lillee
11 Curtly Ambrose

Lord's Taverners, the world-famous charity group, was set up in 1950 by a group of cricket-loving actors in London. The idea for the organisation was the brainchild of Martin Boddey, an opera singer and actor, who became the Lord's Taverners No. 1 member and first chairman. John Mills was the first president, while others since have included Harry Secombe, Jimmy Edwards, Eric Morecombe, David Frost and Ronnie Corbett. Some very famous and familiar faces have been members over the years—Trevor Howard, Denholm Elliott, Laurence Olivier, Richard Burton and Ian Carmichael amongst them.

Harry Secombe—one of the *Goons*, and a former president of the Lord's Taverners

Actors from the Gilbert and Sullivan Opera Company and the 'Our Miss Gibbs' Company reenact the 'Bodyline' Test tactics of Douglas Jardine during a social match at Rushcutters Bay in Sydney in 1933

At the height of the 'Bodyline' controversy in 1932–33, Cyril Ritchard added an extra verse to an item in the Sydney production of *Our Miss Gibbs* at His Majesty's Theatre.

Now this new kind of cricket takes courage to stick it,
There's bruises and fractures galore.
After kissing their wives and insuring their lives
Batsmen fearfully walk out to score.
With a prayer and a curse, they prepare for the hearse,
Undertakers look on with broad grins,
Oh, they'd be a lot calmer in Ned Kelly's armour
When Larwood the wrecker begins.

•

British conductor and impresario Sir Thomas Beecham was a one-time captain of his school eleven.

•

BBC Television premiered a new children's drama series in 1994, *Sloggers*. It revolved around the junior Slogthwaite Cricket Club captained by Lenny Higgs, who had as his vice-captain a girl by the name of Roz Crabtree.

•

The first official Lord's Taverners match took place in 1953 against Bishop's Stortford. Included in the XI were England Test players Godfrey Evans, Jack Martin, Norman Mitchell-Innes and Denis Compton who hit 36 runs off an over. Some of the actors who played were Richard Greene of *Robin Hood* fame, John McCallum and Roger Livesey.

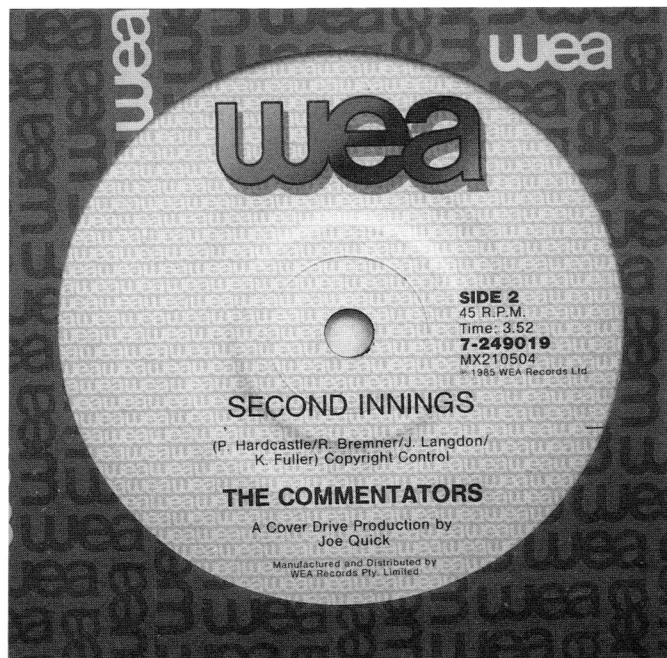

N-N-Nineteen and *Second Innings*, the 1985 single by The Commentators

The West Indies touring cricket team, which thrashed England 5–0 in 1984, gave notice of what was to come, recording a song entitled 'The West Indians are Back in Town'. The single, released by Island Records, had their leading batsman Gordon Greenidge on lead vocals, with a tribute to Clive Lloyd on the flipside featuring Joel

Garner. England's David Gower was the subject of two singles that coincided with the visit of the all-conquering West Indians—'Gower Power' by Percy Pavilion and 'N-N-Nineteen' by The Commentators, a track based on his 19-run average in the five-match Test series.

•

The celebrated British stage and screen actor Trevor Howard was so obsessed with the game he used to demand that each of his work contracts contain a clause permitting him time off during Lord's Test matches. In 1962 with the Pakistanis in town, Howard had to transfer an afternoon session of a London stage production he was in to another day to accommodate the opening day's play of the second Test match at Lord's.

TREVOR HOWARD'S ALL-TIME BEST TEST XI

1 Jack Hobbs
2 Frank Woolley
3 Don Bradman
4 Walter Hammond
5 Denis Compton
6 Graeme Pollock
7 Frank Worrell (c)
8 Keith Miller
9 Alan Davidson
10 Ray Lindwall
11 Godfrey Evans

•

Two of the keenest collectors of cricket memorabilia are the Rolling Stones' Mick Jagger and Charlie Watts. At an MCC Bicentenary auction held by Sotheby's in 1987, the Stones' drummer secured many prized items, including a blazer reputedly worn by K.S. Ranjitsinhji and a portrait of England bowler J.T. Hearne. He was not so lucky in his quest for another painting, which fetched £10,000, an item also pursued in a telephone bid by Jagger. At an auction in 1984, Watts paid £120 for a blazer belonging to former Australian fast bowler Graham McKenzie.

> I remember Mick Jagger once describing how he got interested in cricket. It was the sight of Dennis Lillee roaring up in his full glory. I had felt the same way about Lillee.
> —Imran Khan

•

Bill Yardley, the first batsman to score a first-class century in a university match in England (100 for Cambridge in 1870), was a well-known theatrical figure at the time. A drama critic and producer, he co-wrote several highly regarded pieces including *Little Jack Shepherd* and *The Passport*.

•

The first English chart hit for the US rhythm and blues band Booker T & The MGs was 'Soul Limbo' in 1969, which later became familiar as the theme for BBC TV's coverage of Test match cricket. On the flipside was an instrumental with a cricket-related title, 'Heads or Tails'.

England v Australia, Lord's Cricket Ground 1886 by George H. Barrable and Sir Robert Ponsonby Staples. Among the many people portrayed is the famous stage actress Lillie Langtry (front of painting, to the right, looking away from the game).

Kate Fitzpatrick

Australian actress Kate Fitzpatrick, like Trevor Howard, used to insist that some of her contracts contain no extra work that might interfere with cricket matches. Fitzpatrick, who made television history in 1983–84 when employed by Channel 9 as a commentator and interviewer, has also played the game and is a member of the Primary Club. In a charity match which featured the former West Indies Test player Wes Hall, Fitzpatrick was approached by the towering fast bowler who enquired as to whether she'd be opening the batting. 'No,' she replied, 'not if you're opening the bowling.' On another occasion she captained a friendly cricket match in Sydney against a team skippered by Peter O'Toole.

KATE FITZPATRICK'S ALL-TIME BEST TEST XI

1 **Sunil Gavaskar**
2 **Gordon Greenidge**
3 **Viv Richards**
4 **Don Bradman**
5 **Garry Sobers**
6 **Ian Chappell (c)**
7 **Imran Khan**
8 **Alan Knott**
9 **Dennis Lillee**
10 **Wes Hall**
11 **Abdul Qadir**

•

The Goodies' Tim Brooke-Taylor, whose cousin and uncle played first-class cricket for Derbyshire, was a fair cricketer in his youth and once captained an under-15s side for his school Winchester. He also played cricket, with John Cleese, at Cambridge University.

I love cricket. I made several centuries—in my bath.

—Tim Brooke-Taylor

•

In 1994 two of Australia's more popular cricketers—Allan Border and Mike Whitney—were immortalised in song. 'Where Would We Be Without A.B.', recorded by rock singer Doug Parkinson, was written by two avid cricket

fans—David Miller, a counter officer in the Bankruptcy Department of the Federal Court, and Yuri Worontschak, a Melbourne-based musician.

'Whit', although not commercially released, was co-written by Blues off-spinner Gavin Robertson and was premiered at a lunch in Sydney in honour of Mike Whitney's retirement from first-class cricket. Accompanied on guitar, it was sung at the luncheon by Robertson and batsman Michael Bevan.

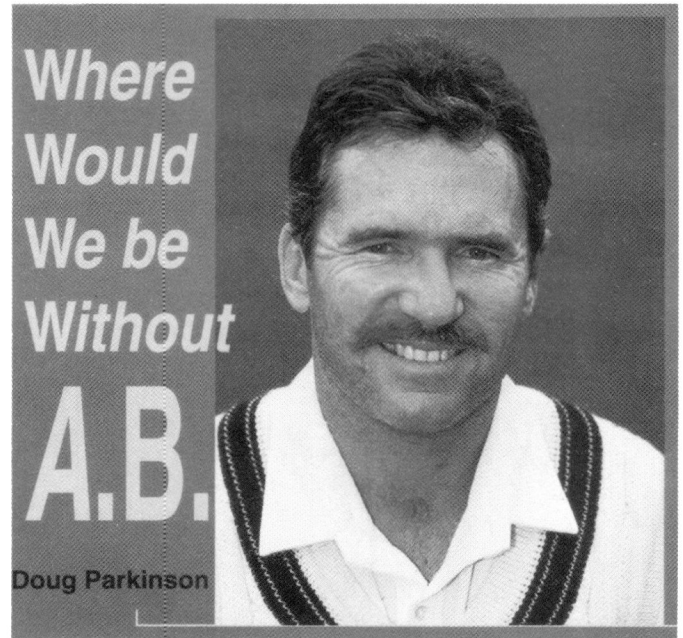

Doug Parkinson

Where would we be. . .without A.B.
He's the favourite son
Of a champion breed
Whenever he wears and green and gold
He's you and me, our A.B.

•

The Maharaja of Porbandar, who captained the Indian side on its tour of England in 1932, was a composer of orchestral music. The Maharaja was a more accomplished writer than he was a cricketer, with over 40 of his compositions published, about the same number of runs he managed to score in his first-class career.

•

The Lord's Taverners secured a famous victory in 1984 when they took on and beat Monaco. The Taverners' eleven, which included TV and radio star Terry Wogan and actor Omar Sharif, were set 226 to win by the tiny country, which had in its side Australian Test batsman Graham Yallop.

•

On the eve of their departure for the 1994 ICC Trophy in Kenya, United States fast bowler Kenrick Dennis withdrew from the team to pursue a career as a reggae singer.

•

A group of jubilant fans introduce calypso singing and dancing to the hallowed turf at Lord's in 1950 in celebration of the West Indies' first Test victory in England

Upon his retirement from first-class cricket, England's Fred Trueman took up a number of jobs in the media and entertainment world, including singing, acting, writing, broadcasting and after-dinner speeches. One of the all-time great fast bowlers, Trueman even made an appearance in an episode of the popular TV comedy *Dad's Army*.

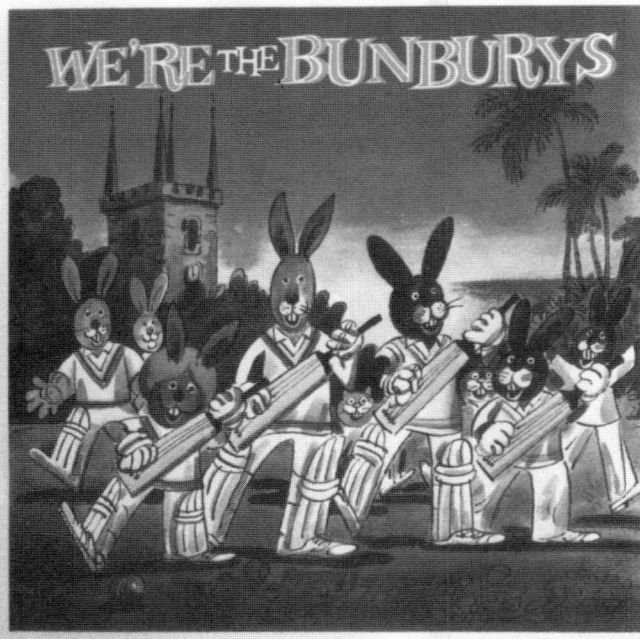

One of the more unusual 45s to come out of England in 1987 was one by David English, a part-time cricketer, actor and entrepreneur. 'Record Breakers', the B-side, was a seven-minute children's story, written and narrated by English, that told of a cricket match between cats and rabbits—The Bunburys v the Whiskertown Cats in the Bunsen & Hedges CatWest Final. The Bunburys were captained by Ian Buntham and included players such as Viv Radish, Rodney Munch and John Emberbunny. Representing the feline XI were Mike Catting, Geoff Boycatt, Imran Kitten and Jeff Thomcat. (The Bunburys, by the way, won the match by a whisker.) The other side of the single is 'We're The Bunburys', sung by the Bee Gees' Barry Gibb.

•

Cricket rates a brief mention in the 1893 Gilbert and Sullivan operetta, *Utopia Limited*—performed by the famous D'Oyly Carte Opera Company.

Oft cricket her kin, will lose or win,
She and her maids on grass and clover,
Eleven maids out, eleven maids in,
And perhaps an occasional maid over.

The D'Oyly Carte occasionally put together its own eleven, and was known as the only singing cricket team on the circuit.

•

Arthur Treloar had a very unspectacular first-class cricket career, scoring just 10 runs and taking one wicket in his only match, for Middlesex in 1872. But he later found fame and fortune with another cricket club, one that he founded and captained. The Imperial Clown Cricketers was a travelling team of players that combined both serious cricket and entertainment. Wherever they played, 'Treloar's Clowns' attracted huge crowds with their on-field

pranks—in 1876 they undertook a tour of North America. The famous Surrey batsman William Caffyn and England Test spinner Ted Peate were among first-class cricketers who occasionally turned out for this very odd club.

•

Sometimes I dream of revolution, a bloody coup d'état by the second rank—troupes of actors slaughtered by their understudies, magicians sawn in half by indefatigably smiling glamour girls, cricket teams wiped out by marauding bands of twelfth men.

—Tom Stoppard, *The Real Inspector Hound*

The Australian playwright Alex Buzo is a great lover of the game who compiled a book on cricket writing—*The Longest Game*—published in 1990. He also covered the 1992 World Cup for *The Australian* newspaper.

ALEX BUZO'S ALL-TIME BEST TEST XI

1 Barry Richards
2 Sunil Gavaskar
3 Ian Chappell
4 Viv Richards
5 Ian Botham
6 Imran Khan
7 Richard Hadlee
8 Richie Benaud (c)
9 Alan Knott
10 Dennis Lillee
11 Jim Laker

•

Frances Edmonds, the wife of former England spinner Phil Edmonds, has the dubious distinction of once being sacked as the presenter of an Australian television program. In 1986–87 she joined her husband for the Ashes tour of Australia and during her travels found herself in great demand, appearing at the National Press Club in Canberra, on radio and on television. At the invitation of Channel 10, she was asked to co-host the national breakfast show *Good Morning Australia* with Gordon Elliot, a task she accepted with some trepidation, having never undertaken such a program before. On her scheduled penultimate appearance on *GMA* she read to the nation a slightly risque limerick about Elliot, that she'd written the night before.

Our GMA anchor man, Gordon,
Kept dunking his nuts on the program.
When quite flaccid and soft
He held them aloft
Saying 'No man can cope with a hard 'un'.

That morning's show was her last.

•

Cricket's most famous on-the-field catchcry once inspired former England fast bowler Bob Willis to record a single.

However, the record company, Splash Records, went bust and his song 'How's That?' was never released.

●

New Zealand's Dayle Hadlee, who played in 26 Test matches, also played guitar in a band that recorded a single under the name Tarrega Four. Hadlee's group once won a trip to Germany after success in a local radio competition.

●

Two New South Wales bowlers tasted the glitter of big-time television in 1994, becoming 'soapie stars'. After making his farewell to first-class cricket, fast bowler Mike Whitney made his acting debut on Channel 10's long-running drama series *Neighbours*. In a role originally earmarked for Greg Matthews, Whitney played the part of a cricket coach in a show he coyly admitted beforehand that he'd never actually seen.

Although unable to visit the famous Ramsey Street set, Matthews appeared in an ABC TV 'mini-soap'—*The World of Ian*—a comedy piece aired on H.G. and Roy's *This Sporting Life*.

'Rampaging' Roy Slaven and H.G. Nelson, the irreverent hosts of the ABC's *This Sporting Life*

Mike Whitney, a TV star on Channel 10's *Neighbours*

●

It seems that Allan Border may have gained some of his invaluable leadership qualities as far back as 1967, when he was a prefect at the Mosman High School in Sydney. Two other prefects that year also went on to bigger and better things—Rob Hirst, who became the drummer for Midnight Oil, and Tom Burlinson, the actor.

●

A 1991 video of Viv Richards' biography, *Hitting Across The Line*, featured a special tribute from singer Eric Clapton.

●

There is but one fundamental change we would make to the one-day game. The conventional idea has always been that the ball is propelled towards the bat. If we unshackle this outmoded thinking and consider a game where the bat is hurled towards the ball, then this simple revolutionary inversion would lure back spectators who have drifted away in their droves to watch the dreaded Test match form of the game.

—Roy Slaven and H.G. Nelson

●

I want to play cricket. It doesn't seem to matter whether you win or lose.

—Meat Loaf, American rock singer

THE FAVOURITE MUSIC OF SOME MODERN-DAY TEST CRICKETERS

Ian Botham—Dire Straits, Supertramp, Meat Loaf
Allan Border—The Beatles
Martin Crowe—Genesis, Dire Straits
Richard Ellison—Chris Rea, Dire Straits, New Order
Neil Fairbrother—Lisa Stansfield, Simply Red, Simple Minds
Neil Foster—Van Morrison, Talking Heads, Indigo Girls
Greg Ritchie—Rolling Stones
Roger Harper—Earth, Wind and Fire
Merv Hughes—Mental as Anything
Dean Jones—Elton John
Geoff Lawson—Jackson Browne, Steely Dan
Clive Lloyd—Johnny Mathis
Devon Malcolm—Anita Baker, Gregory Isaacs
Tom Moody—Elton John, Cold Chisel, REM

Derek Pringle—Miles Davis, John Coltrane, Sonny Boy Williamson, Billy Bragg
Carl Rackemann—Petula Clark, The Beatles
Jonty Rhodes—UB40, U2, Eurythmics
Jeff Thomson—David Bowie
Courtney Walsh—Bob Marley

THE FAVOURITE FILMS AND TV SHOWS OF SOME MODERN-DAY TEST CRICKETERS

FILMS
David Boon—*Uncommon Valour*
Allan Border—*The Sting*
Ewan Chatfield—*The Guns of Navarone*
Hansie Cronje—*Last of the Mohicans, Dances with Wolves*
Martin Crowe—*One Flew Over The Cuckoo's Nest, The Deer Hunter*
Tony Dodemaide—*Caddyshack, A Few Good Men*
Gordon Greenidge—*The Jungle Book*
Ian Healy—*The Man from Snowy River*
David Hookes—*An Officer and a Gentleman*
Chris Lewis—*The Hitcher*
Gus Logie—*E.T.*
Malcolm Marshall—*Lethal Weapon*
Duleep Mendis—*The Guns of Navarone*
Mark Ramprakash—*The Sting, In the Heat of the Night*
Jonty Rhodes—*Tootsie, Dirty Rotten Scoundrels, Ghost*
Richie Richardson—*Hear No Evil See No Evil, Coming to America*
Jack Russell—*The Battle of Britain, Zulu, Oliver!*
Phil Tufnell—*Apocalypse Now, The Terminator*
Mark Waugh—*Midnight Express, Cape Fear, Mad Max, Cliffhanger, Caddyshack*
Graeme Wood—*Midnight Express*
Graham Yallop—*Raiders of the Lost Ark*

TV SHOWS
Mohammad Azharuddin—*Different Strokes*
Allan Donald—*The Young Ones*
Neil Fairbrother—*Coronation Street*
Mike Gatting—*Dr Who*
David Gower—*Rumpole of The Bailey*
David Houghton—*'Allo 'Allo*
Merv Hughes—*Bugs Bunny*
Kapil Dev—*Three's Company, The Cosby Show*
Damien Martyn—*Roseanne, Murphy Brown, Cheers*
Derek Pringle—*Twin Peaks, Fawlty Towers*
Derek Randall—*Neighbours*
Robin Smith—*Open All Hours*
Alec Stewart—*The Bill*
Shane Warne—*Get Smart, The Bold and the Beautiful, Gilligan's Island*
Tim Zoehrer—*Hey! Hey! It's Saturday, Wide World of Sports*

A COLLECTION OF CLASSIC ON-AIR CLANGERS

Yorkshire 232 all out, Hutton ill—I'm sorry, Hutton 111.
—John Snagge, BBC News

Ray Illingworth has just relieved himself at the pavilion end.
—Brian Johnston, BBC Radio

Welcome to Worcester where you've just missed seeing Barry Richards hitting one of Basil D'Oliveira's balls clean out of the ground.
—Brian Johnston, BBC Radio

He's usually a good puller—but he couldn't get it up that time.
—Richie Benaud, Channel 9

If you go in with two fast bowlers and one breaks down, you're left two short.
—Bob Massie, ABC Radio

This game will be over any time from now.
—Alan McGilvray, ABC Radio

It is important for Pakistan to take wickets if they are going to make big inroads into this Australian batting line-up.
—Max Walker, Channel 9

Glenn McGrath joins Craig McDermott and Paul Reiffel in a three-ponged prace attack.
—Tim Gavel, ABC News

In the back of Hughes' mind must be the thought that he will dance down the piss and mitch one.
—Tony Greig, Channel 9

It's been a very slow and dull day, but it hasn't been boring. It's been a good, entertaining day's cricket.
—Tony Benneworth, ABC Radio

It was close for Zaheer. Lawson threw his hands in the air and Marsh threw his head in the air.
—Jack Potter, 3UZ

Laird has been brought in to stand in the corner of the circle.
—Richie Benaud, Channel 9

Chappell just stood on his feet and smashed it to the boundary.
—Jim Maxwell, ABC Radio

Daddy, I want to go uckies.
—Hamish Maxwell, 2, to his father Jim, ABC Radio

11 Classic Catches

John Dyson is famed for one of Test cricket's classic catches—a spectacular outfield effort that brought about Sylvester Clarke's dismissal at the SCG in 1981–82. However, in the late 1970s Dyson gained even greater glory with a catch at the Sydney Showground. As part of a promotion, he and Allan Border were involved in a grape-throwing exhibition and at their first attempt broke the world record. Australia's future Test captain threw a grape a distance of 71.3 metres and Dyson caught it in his mouth, breaking the old record by 1.3 metres.

•

In the Sheffield Shield match against South Australia at Adelaide in 1986–87, Victorian wicket-keeper Michael Dimattina took six catches in the second innings, all off the bowling of Denis Hickey—a first in Australian first-class cricket.

•

In 1982–83 Bankstown's Les Andrews became the first wicket-keeper anywhere in the world to accept nine catches in a single innings. He performed the feat in the Sydney grade competition against Sydney University.

•

One of the three catches taken by wicket-keeper Alan Knott in a County Championship match at Cheltenham in 1965 was achieved in the strangest of circumstances. Gloucestershire batsman Sid Russell hit a ball from the Kent bowler Alan Dixon that ended up in his pads. Quick as a flash, Knott raced around in front of him, and as the ball fell he caught it and appealed successfully for a catch.

•

West Indies batsman Seymour Nurse was out for 74 in the second Test at Melbourne in 1968–69, caught at deep fine-leg by Keith Stackpole after the ball had rebounded off the head of Eric Freeman who was fielding at short fine-leg.

•

Although few details have survived, a fieldsman once took all 10 catches in an innings off the same bowler. Unfortunately, no name can be attached to the holder of this extraordinary record. What is known is that he performed the feat for the Islington Albion Club in England while fielding in the slips.

•

W.G. Grace

One of cricket's truly remarkable catches involved W.G. Grace and a bank clerk in 1873–74. In a match at the Adelaide Oval, a spectator, Alexander Crooks, took a catch off the great W.G. by leaning over the boundary. Much to everyone's surprise Grace, who was expecting a six to be signalled, was given out by the umpire. So impressed was the South Australian Cricket Association it made the famous part-time fieldsman its treasurer.

•

S. Santosh took five catches in an innings, all off his own bowling, in a first-class match for Kerala against Goa at Vasco Da Gama in 1985–86. In the same season a Pakistani player, Sohail Fazal, took seven catches for Lahore v Karachi on his first-class debut.

•

The only time in first-class cricket that 10 catches have been taken in an innings by 10 different fielders was in the 1967 County Championship match between Leicestershire and Northants. Jack Birkenshaw was the only Leicestershire player to miss out.

•

Ghulam Hussain took a world record 27 catches in 15 first-class matches for the Pakistan National Shipping Corporation during the 1989–90 Qaid-e-Azam Trophy when fielding as a substitute.

•

Ted Beezer, a fast bowler who played for the Lane Cove Cricket Club in Sydney, once took a running catch in his left hand when he meant to take it in his right. On another occasion in a match against Sydney University, Beezer, fielding on the boundary with his arms folded, was alerted by his captain to take a catch. He looked up, but before he could react the ball landed in his arms and stayed there.

•

Regarded as one of the most agile of fielders, South Africa's Jonty Rhodes took five stunning catches against the West Indies at Bombay in the 1993 Hero Cup, a record in one-day international cricket.

12 A Team Effort

The Test match between Australia and New Zealand at Wellington in 1945–46 produced one of the shortest contests on record. The match was over on the second afternoon with only three New Zealanders reaching double figures. The Kiwis were dismissed for 42 and 54, and in terms of balls bowled—872—it remains the shortest Test on record, and the only one completed in two days since the Second World War.

TEST MATCHES COMPLETED IN TWO DAYS

England (101 & 77) v Australia (63 & 122) at The Oval in 1882
England (53 & 62) v Australia (116 & 60) at Lord's in 1888
England (317) v Australia (80 & 100) at The Oval in 1888
England (172) v Australia (81 & 70) at Manchester in 1888
South Africa (84 & 129) v England (148 & 2–67) at Port Elizabeth in 1888–89
South Africa (47 & 43) v England (292) at Cape Town in 1888–89
England (100 & 8–95) v Australia (92 & 102) at The Oval in 1890
South Africa (93 & 30) v England (185 & 226) at Port Elizabeth in 1895–96
South Africa (115 & 117) v England (265) at Cape Town in 1895–96
England (176 & 0–14) v South Africa (95 & 93) at The Oval in 1912
Australia (448) v South Africa (265 & 95) at Manchester in 1912
England (112 & 147) v Australia (232 & 0–30) at Nottingham in 1921
Australia (8d–328) v West Indies (99 & 107) at Melbourne in 1930–31
South Africa (157 & 98) v Australia (439) at Johannesburg in 1935–36
New Zealand (42 & 54) v Australia (8d–199) at Wellington in 1945–46

•

At Perth in 1992–93, the West Indies came close to defeating Australia in record time, securing an innings victory by the lunch break on the third day. This was the earliest finish to any Test since Australia's big win at Wellington in 1945–46. While the West Indies' victory at the WACA was effortless, the preceding Test at Adelaide saw the visitors get home by just one run—the narrowest margin on record to decide a Test match.

NARROW TEST WINS BY A RUNS MARGIN

Margin	Match
1 run	West Indies v Australia at Adelaide in 1992–93
3 runs	Australia v England at Manchester in 1902
3 runs	England v Australia at Melbourne in 1982–83
5 runs	South Africa v Australia at Sydney in 1993–94

Allan Border had the misfortune of being on the losing sides in three of the four closest results in Test history, and was captain when Australia tied the first Test against India at Madras in 1986–87.

•

When Bombay played Maharashtra at Poona in 1948–49, a record 2,376 runs were scored for the loss of 38 wickets. Nine hundreds were scored in the match, with a record three batsmen recording a century in each innings—Bombay 651 (M.K. Mantri 200, U.M. Merchant 143, D.G. Phadkar 131) and 8d–714 (U.M. Merchant 156, D.G. Phadkar 160); Maharashtra 407 (M.C. Datar 143, M.R. Rege 133) and 604 (S.D. Deodhar 146, M.R. Rege 100).

•

Despite scoring 705 in the 1981–82 Ranji Trophy, Karnataka lost the match after Delhi replied with 706 and were declared the winners by virtue of a first innings lead.

•

The Australian tourists of 1938 began their English campaign with seven successive totals of over 400 in first-class matches—541 v Worcestershire at Worcester, 7d–679 v Oxford University at Oxford, 5d–590 v Leicestershire at Leicester, 5d–708 v Cambridge University at Cambridge, 502 v MCC at Lord's, 6d–406 v Northamptonshire at Northampton and 528 v Surrey at The Oval.

At Oxford, the first seven batsmen in the line-up hit half-centuries—Jack Fingleton 124, Bill Brown 72, Don Bradman 58, Stan McCabe 110, Arthur Chipperfield 53, Lindsay Hassett 146 and Mervyn Waite 54.

Bill Brown—one of seven batsmen who scored a fifty in the Australians' total of seven declared for 679 against Oxford University in 1938

In the first Test at Bridgetown in 1957–58, Pakistan was bowled out by the West Indies for 106 in the first innings, but then came back in a big way scoring 657 in the second. The difference of 551 runs between innings is a record in first-class cricket.

Variation	Team scores	Match
551	Barbados (175 & 7d–726)	v Trinidad at Bridgetown in 1926–27
551	Pakistan (106 & 8d–657)	v West Indies at Bridgetown in 1957–58
551	Middlesex (83 & 7d–634)	v Essex at Chelmsford in 1983

•

In 1927–28 New South Wales began and ended the summer with totals of over 500 that both times included four century-makers. In the first match of the season, against a New Zealand XI at Sydney, New South Wales made 571, with centuries from Jack Gregory (152), Tommy Andrews (134), Alan Kippax (119) and Archie Jackson (104). In their last match of the summer, the Blues scored 533 against Victoria, also at the SCG. The four centurions were Kippax (134), John Morgan (110), Bert Oldfield (101) batting at No. 8, and Charlie Nicholls (110) at No. 9. Four other centuries, for a total of eight, were scored in this match, an Australian record. Don Bradman scored New South Wales' fifth century (134 not out) in the second innings, while 'Stork' Hendry (138), Jack Ryder (106) and Keith Rigg (110 not out) made hundreds for Victoria.

The first-class record for most centuries in an innings is six, in a total of eight declared for 912 by the Indian side Holkar in 1945–46.

MOST CENTURIES IN AN INNINGS

6—Holkar (8d–912) v Mysore at Indore in 1945–46
K.V. Bhandarkar (142), C.T. Sarwate (101), M.M. Jagdale (164), C.K. Nayudu (101), B.B. Nimbalkar (172), R. Pratap Singh (100)
5—New South Wales (918) v South Australia at Sydney in 1900–01
Frank Iredale (118), Monty Noble (153), Syd Gregory (168), Reggie Duff (119), Les Poidevin (140*)
5—Australia (8d–758) v West Indies at Kingston in 1954–55
Colin McDonald (127), Neil Harvey (204), Keith Miller (109), Ron Archer (128), Richie Benaud (121)

Examples of four hundreds in an innings are fairly commonplace. Like New South Wales, Delhi recorded the feat twice in 1988–89. When the Indians took on Sussex at Hove in 1946 they scored 3 declared for 533, the only four batsmen to make it to the middle all making hundreds—Vijay Merchant 205, Vinoo Mankad 105, Nawab of Pataudi, Snr 110 not out and Lala Amarnath 106.

•

When Tasmania defeated New South Wales, and then South Australia, at Hobart in 1993–94, it was the first time they'd secured back-to-back victories in the Sheffield Shield. It was a winning feeling that saw the Apple Islanders gain a berth in the Shield final that season, the first time they'd done so since entering the competition in 1977–78.

•

Western Australia recorded one of the biggest ever wins in the Sheffield Shield in 1993–94, trouncing New South Wales by an innings and 253 runs inside two days at the WACA in Perth. After piling on 8 for 503—centuries from Geoff Marsh (128) and Damien Martyn (197)—they then dismissed the Blues for 73 and 177 on the second day. Only Michael Bevan was able to reach 50. Opener Richard Chee Quee was out twice, for 17 and nought, in the same session. For Western Australia, it was their biggest win in the Sheffield Shield competition; for New South Wales, their second-heaviest defeat and the first time they'd been dismissed twice on the same day.

Later in the season, the same NSW side that was so humiliated by Western Australia at the WACA surprised all when they went on to achieve their 42nd Sheffield Shield title. They contested the final without a single Test player in their ranks and made the final with 38 points on the Shield ladder, the most scored by any state in the competition's history.

•

In a one-day match in England in 1911, the Somerset Clergy team piled on a massive 453 runs in 215 minutes before declaring with nine wickets down. In reply, the Somerset Stragglers reached the target, scoring 458 for one in 122 minutes. A total of 911 runs was scored in a little under six hours, possibly the highest rate of run-scoring in a day in any class of cricket.

•

Between 1914–15 and 1923–24, South Australia lost every Sheffield Shield match they played.

•

During the 1985–86 South African season, Eastern Province B was involved in two consecutive tied first-class matches within a month—189 & 278 v Boland (211 & 256) at Grahamstown, and 279 & 292 v Natal B (367 & 5d–204) at Pietermaritzburg.

•

In a minor country match played in New South Wales in 1892–93, Sotala made 49 and 37 in a tie with Wattle Flat who also made 49 and 37.

•

In 1884–85 a team from South Australia played in New South Wales for the first time. In an extraordinary match, the Adelaide Federal XI made 192 against a Wentworth XV, which played three innings, scoring 36, 24 and 27.

•

Transvaal took out the Currie Cup title in 1923–24 in sensational style, winning all of their five matches by an innings.

•

During the 1979 Benson & Hedges Cup, Somerset made history when its captain Brian Rose declared their innings closed at 0–1 after just one over against Worcestershire. They deliberately threw away the match, losing by 10 wickets but maintaining their superior striking-rate in the competition. The match saw just two runs scored off the bat and lasted only 20 minutes, including the 10-minute innings break. Rose's ploy backfired, with the Test and County Cricket Board disqualifying Somerset from the competition for bringing the game into disrepute.

•

Victoria holds the record for both the highest and the lowest innings totals in Australian first-class cricket. They remain the only team in the world to top the 1,000-run mark, a milestone they first achieved with 1,059 against Tasmania in 1922–23. They bettered that, four seasons later, with 1,107 against New South Wales. But it was in 1903–04 that Victoria made the record books with the lowest total in Australian cricket, being dismissed for just 15 by the MCC at Melbourne.

HIGHEST INNINGS TOTALS BY AUSTRALIAN TEAMS IN FIRST-CLASS CRICKET
(Over 800)

1,107	Victoria v New South Wales at Melbourne in 1926–27
1,059	Victoria v Tasmania at Melbourne in 1922–23
918	New South Wales v South Australia at Sydney in 1900–01
843	Australians v Oxford and Cambridge Universities at Portsmouth in 1893
839	New South Wales v Tasmania at Sydney in 1898–99
7d–821	South Australia v Queensland at Adelaide in 1939–40
815	New South Wales v Victoria at Sydney in 1908–09
807	New South Wales v South Australia at Adelaide in 1899–1900
805	New South Wales v Victoria at Melbourne in 1905–06
803	Non-Smokers v Smokers at East Melbourne in 1886–87
802	New South Wales v South Australia at Sydney in 1920–21

LOWEST INNINGS TOTALS BY AUSTRALIAN TEAMS IN FIRST-CLASS CRICKET
(Under 35)

15	Victoria v MCC at Melbourne in 1903–04
18	Tasmania v Victoria at Melbourne in 1868–69
18	Australians v MCC at Lord's in 1896
23	South Australia v Victoria at East Melbourne in 1882–83
23	Australians v Yorkshire at Leeds in 1902
25	Tasmania v Victoria at Hobart in 1857–58
27	South Australia v New South Wales at Sydney in 1955–56
28	Victoria v New South Wales at Melbourne in 1855–56
31	Victoria v New South Wales at Sydney in 1906–07
32	Australian XI v G.F. Vernon's XI at Melbourne in 1887–88
33	Tasmania v Victoria at Launceston in 1857–58
34	Victoria v New South Wales at Melbourne in 1875–76

LOWEST INNINGS TOTAL IN AUSTRALIA
15 by Victoria v MCC at Melbourne in 1903–04

P.A. McAlister	st Strudwick b Rhodes	0
C.E. McLeod	c & b Arnold	0
W.W. Armstrong	c Strudwick b Rhodes	0
G.H.S. Trott	c Arnold b Rhodes	9
V.S. Ransford	c Rhodes b Arnold	0
F.J. Laver	b Rhodes	1
C.M. Baker	st Strudwick b Arnold	3
W.J. Scott	not out	1
W. Careek	c Bosanquet b Arnold	0
H.J. Fry	c Bosanquet b Rhodes	0
J.V. Saunders	absent ill	–
Extras	(b1)	1
Total		15

Fall of wickets
1/0, 2/0, 3/0, 4/0, 5/5, 6/12, 7/14, 8/15, 9/15
Bowling figures
Rhodes 6.1–3–6–5, Arnold 6–2–8–4

The Non-Smokers total of 803 at the East Melbourne Cricket Ground in 1886–87, at the time, the highest total in all first-class cricket

The first 12 Test matches completed in 1994—crammed into the months of January, February and March—all yielded results. The most significant contributor to this record sequence was India, which attained three successive victories by an innings margin over Sri Lanka.

•

Since England made its record score of 7 declared for 903 against Australia at The Oval in 1938, the only other examples of totals in excess of 900 in first-class matches have been recorded in India and Pakistan.

TOTALS OF OVER 900 SINCE 1945

7d–951   Sind v Baluchistan at Karachi in 1973–74
6d–944   Hyderabad v Andhra Pradesh at Secunderabad in 1993–94
8d–912   Holkar v Mysore at Indore in 1945–46
6d–912   Tamil Nadu v Goa at Panjum in 1988–89
6d–910   Railways v Dera Ismail Khan at Lahore in 1964–65

Hyderabad's 6 declared for 944 in 1993–94 included some big individual scores—M.V. Sridhar 366, Vivek Jaisimha 211 and Noel David 207 not out, the first instance of three batsmen scoring double-centuries in the same first-class innings

---

•

The highly successful Australian teams that went to England in 1989 and 1993 both returned home with four batsmen who exceeded 1,000 first-class runs on tour. With only 20 matches in '89 and 21 in '93, as many as four batsmen being able to reach the target was an outstanding achievement, and the best since 1964 when a record seven Australians made the thousand, from a possible 30 matches. Six other Australian touring teams have had seven batsmen scoring 1,000 runs, with the 1905 side boasting two who went on to accumulate 2,000. Three of their bowlers also claimed 100 wickets on the tour, a remarkable team effort. The 1921 Australians, one of the strongest sides of all time, included six batsmen to top the 1,000-run mark and four bowlers reaching 100 first-class wickets.

AUSTRALIAN TOURING TEAMS WITH MOST INSTANCES OF 1,000 FIRST-CLASS RUNS

1893 in England (7)   'J.J.' Lyons (1,527), 'Harry' Trott (1,437), Harry Graham (1,435), William Bruce (1,311), Alec Bannerman (1,229), George Giffen (1,220), Syd Gregory (1,162)

1896 in England (7)   Joe Darling (1,555), Syd Gregory (1,464), Frank Iredale (1,328), 'Harry' Trott (1,297), George Giffen (1,208), Clem Hill (1,196), Harry Donnan (1,009)

1899 in England (7)   Joe Darling (1,941), Monty Noble (1,608), Victor Trumper (1,556), Jack Worrall (1,202), Hugh Trumble (1,183), Syd Gregory (1,181), Frank Iredale (1,039)

1902 in England (7)   Victor Trumper (2,570), Clem Hill (1,534), Reggie Duff (1,403), Monty Noble (1,357), Joe Darling (1,112), Bert Hopkins (1,100), Warwick Armstrong (1,075)

1905 in England (7)   Monty Noble (2,084), Warwick Armstrong (2,002), Victor Trumper (1,754), Clem Hill (1,731), Joe Darling (1,696), Reggie Duff (1,395), Bert Hopkins (1,094)

1948 in England (7)   Don Bradman (2,428), Arthur Morris (1,922), Lindsay Hassett (1,563), Bill Brown (1,448), Sid Barnes (1,354), Neil Harvey (1,129), Keith Miller (1,088)

1964 in England (7)   Bob Simpson (1,714), Bill Lawry (1,601), Brian Booth (1,551), Norman O'Neill (1,369), Bob Cowper (1,286), Peter Burge (1,114), Ian Redpath (1,075)

1921 in England (6)   Charles Macartney (2,317), Warren Bardsley (2,005), Warwick Armstrong (1,213), Tommy Andrews (1,212), Jack Gregory (1,135), Johnny Taylor (1,040)

The 1905 Australians—the only team to return home with two batsmen having scored 2,000 first-class runs on tour and another five with 1,000. Three bowlers added to the team effort with 100 or more first-class wickets.

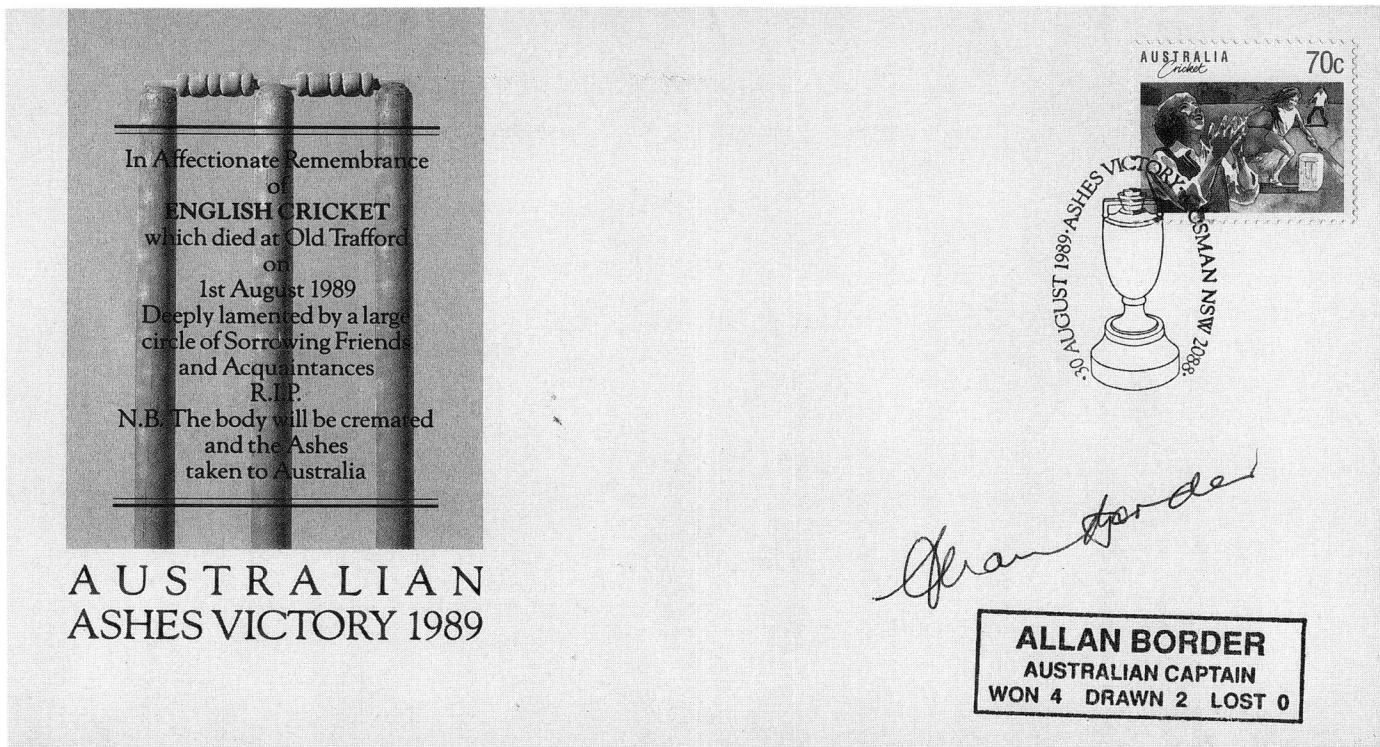

Australia Post's commemoration of the Australians' victorious tour of England in 1989

1930 in England (6)   Don Bradman (2,960), Alan Kippax (1,451), Bill Woodfull (1,434,), Bill Ponsford (1,425), Archie Jackson (1,097), Stan McCabe (1,012)

1934 in England (6)   Stan McCabe (2,078), Don Bradman (2,020), Bill Ponsford (1,784), Bill Brown (1,308), Bill Woodfull (1,268), Len Darling (1,022)

1938 in England (6)   Don Bradman (2,429), Bill Brown (1,854), 'Jack' Badcock (1,604), Lindsay Hassett (1,589), Jack Fingleton (1,141), Stan McCabe (1,124)

1953 in England (6)   Neil Harvey (2,040), Keith Miller (1,433), Arthur Morris (1,302), Lindsay Hassett (1,236), Jim De Courcy (1,214), Graham Hole (1,118)

1961 in England (6)   Bill Lawry (2,019), Norman O'Neill (1,981), Bob Simpson (1,947), Neil Harvey (1,452), Peter Burge (1,376), Brian Booth (1,279)

MOST INSTANCES OF 100 FIRST-CLASS WICKETS

1882 in England (4)   Fred Spofforth (157), 'Harry' Boyle (125), Tom Garrett (118), George Palmer (100)

1896 in England (4)   Hugh Trumble (148), Ernie Jones (121), George Giffen (117), Tom McKibbin (101)

1921 in England (4)   'Ted' McDonald (147), Arthur Mailey (137), Jack Gregory (116), Warwick Armstrong (104)

1886 in England (3)   George Giffen (159), Tom Garrett (123), George Palmer (106)

1893 in England (3)   Charlie Turner (149), George Giffen (142), Hugh Trumble (120)

1899 in England (3)   Hugh Trumble (142), Ernie Jones (135), Bill Howell (117)

1905 in England (3)   Warwick Armstrong (130), 'Tibby' Cotter (121), Frank Laver (115)

1934 in England (3)   Bill O'Reilly (109), Clarrie Grimmett (109), 'Chuck' Fleetwood-Smith (106)

•

England incurred its lowest Test total this century during the 1993–94 Wisden Trophy, being routed for 46 by the West Indies at Port-of-Spain in Trinidad. It was the lowest total in a Test match since New Zealand's record score of 26 against England in 1954–55 and their worst performance since 1886–87, when Australia bowled them out for 45 in Sydney.

The Trinidad debacle was England's 12th loss in 14 consecutive Tests, and saw their world rating drop to become, at the time, the second worst performed Test nation.

> **'TRINIDEAD AND BURIED'**
> **'SCOREBOARD OF SHAME'**
> **'A LIMP TEAM OF LILY LIVERS'**
> —**British Press reaction to England's all-out score of 46 at Trinidad in 1993–94**

ENGLAND'S ALL-TIME TEST LOWS

	Opponent	*Venue*	*Season*
45	Australia	Sydney	1886–87
46	West Indies	Port-of-Spain	1993–94
52	Australia	The Oval	1948
53	Australia	Lord's	1888
61	Australia	Melbourne	1903–04

•

When Western Australia played Queensland at Brisbane in 1993–94, nine of their players were either current or former Test players, and all but one of them occupied the top eight spots in the batting order—Mike Veletta, Geoff Marsh, Justin Langer, Damien Martyn, Tom Moody, Tim Zoehrer, Brendon Julian, Jo Angel, and at No. 11, Bruce Reid.

The following month Australia went to South Africa, and Western Australia didn't have a single player in the touring party, for the first time since 1959–60.

In 1964–65 New South Wales pulled off one of the greatest victories in the history of first-class cricket when they made the highest fourth innings total on record without losing a wicket. Set 276 runs for victory in 220 minutes by South Australia, openers Bob Simpson (142 not out) and Norman O'Neill (133 not out) got them with 52 minutes to spare.

•

On three occasions during the 1993 County Championship, a side batting first scored over 500 yet went on to lose the match. The three instances, unluckily recorded by Durham, Glamorgan and Gloucestershire, brought to only seven the number of times this had occurred in the entire history of the Championship.

TEAMS TO SCORE 500 IN FIRST INNINGS OF A COUNTY CHAMPIONSHIP MATCH AND LOSE

Totals	Match	Result
597 & 97	Essex v Derbyshire (548 & 1–149) at Chesterfield in 1904	Derbyshire by 9 wickets
528 & 3d–152	Middlesex v Essex (427 & 2–254) at Lord's in 1905	Essex by 8 wickets
7d–531 & 7d–124	Essex v Nottinghamshire (418 & 2–238) at Nottingham in 1939	Nottinghamshire by 8 wickets
4d–523 & 111	Warwickshire v Lancashire (6d–414 & 0–226) at Southport in 1982	Lancashire by 10 wickets
9d–515 & 83	Durham v Lancashire (442 & 4–157) at Manchester in 1993	Lancashire by 6 wickets
3d–562 & 109	Glamorgan v Middlesex (584 & 0–88) at Cardiff in 1993	Middlesex by 10 wickets
7d–501 & 102	Gloucestershire v Hampshire (6d–393 & 9–213) at Bristol in 1993	Hampshire by 1 wicket

In the Warwickshire-Lancashire match in 1982, Alvin Kallicharran (230*) and Geoff Humpage (254) both scored double-centuries for the losing team, a 'feat' repeated in the 1993 Glamorgan–Middlesex match—Viv Richards (224*) and Adrian Dale (214*). These are the only examples of two double-hundreds in the same County Championship innings for a team which lost the match. P.A. Perrin scored 343 not out for Essex in the 1904 match mentioned above—the highest score by a batsman in a match his team subsequently lost.

•

When Sri Lanka's Roshan Mahanama scored 151 against India at Colombo in 1992–93, it was the 2,000th century in Test match cricket, and his country's 30th. Of the first 2,000 Test hundreds scored between 1877 and 1993, England recorded 28% of them, and Australia 24%.

TEST CENTURY LANDMARKS

Century	Batsman	Score	Match
1st	Charles Bannerman	165 ret.hurt	Australia v England at Melbourne in 1876–77
50th	'Plum' Warner	132*	England v South Africa at Johannesburg in 1898–99
100th	Warren Bardsley	130	Australia v England at The Oval in 1909
500th	Neil Harvey	178	Australia v South Africa at Cape Town in 1949–50
1,000th	Ian Chappell	165	Australia v West Indies at Melbourne in 1968–69
1,500th	Greg Chappell	115	Australia v England at Adelaide in 1982–83
2,000th	Roshan Mahanama	151	Sri Lanka v India at Colombo in 1992–93

When South Africa successfully chased 155 for victory in a one-day international against Australia at Durban in 1993–94, it brought to an end a run of nine 50-over matches between the two countries in which the side batting first won.

•

Four teams took 500 runs off Northamptonshire in successive first-class innings in 1921—5 declared for 616 by Surrey at The Oval, 7 declared for 604 by Essex at Northampton, 621 by the touring Australians at Northampton and 9 declared for 545 by Essex at Leyton.

•

The lowest target in all first-class cricket for a side that lost is 42, set by Eastern Province in 1946–47. Border was the unlucky team, dismissed for just 34 in the match played at East London. Border made the record books again in 1959–60 when they were dismissed for under 20 in each innings by Natal, again at East London. None of their players made a double-figure score in either innings. Natal got them out for 16 and 18—their paltry 34 runs the lowest match aggregate on record.

•

Australia's total of 248 against South Africa at Johannesburg in 1993–94 was the country's second-highest total on record not to contain an individual half-century—the highest contribution being 45 not out by Steve Waugh. Australia's highest Test innings without a fifty is 259 in the second Test against England at Melbourne in 1876–77.

•

During the calendar year of 1993, and for the first time in its history, Australia's top seven in the batting order all scored centuries in successive Test series. Against England, Mark Taylor hit 124 and 111, Michael Slater 152, David Boon 164 not out, 101 and 107, Mark Waugh 137, Allan Border 200 not out, Steve Waugh 157 not out and Ian Healy 102 not out. And then in their next series, against New Zealand, each batsman again scored a century—Taylor 142 not out, Slater 168, Boon 106, Mark Waugh 111, Border 105, Steve Waugh 147 not out and Healy 113 not out. Nine of Australia's twelve batsmen used in the New Zealand series finished with an average of over 60—Steve Waugh (216.00), Taylor (95.33), Boon (87.33), Shane Warne (85.00), Slater (76.25), Paul Reiffel (74.00), Mark Waugh (71.67), Healy (64.50) and Border (60.33).

•

When England and Australia did battle on a sticky wicket at Brisbane in 1950–51 both sides made declarations with their score under 100. Batting first, Australia made 228, with England in reply declaring their innings closed at 7 for 68. Batting a second time, Australia declared at 7 for 32, after losing their top three batsmen for nought. Australia then bowled out England for 122, securing victory by 70 runs.

13 A Family Affair

In 1993, the year of his father's retirement from first-class cricket, Liam Botham, aged 15, appeared in his first big cricket match, for a World XI v Ian Botham's England XI at Hove. Botham junior was called in as a late replacement for New Zealander Danny Morrison in a match staged for the Leukaemia Research Fund. Earlier in the season, Liam took 4 for 63 off 18 overs on his debut for the Hampshire Second XI against Worcestershire at Southampton.

The previous season, Botham junior emulated his father by taking 5 for 64 on his debut for the England Under-15s against Wales. Back in 1977 his dad also took five wickets on his England debut—5 for 74 against Australia at Nottingham.

•

When Tasmania played Victoria at Launceston in 1913–14, brothers Robert and William Bayles and their cousin Felix Headlam all made their debuts. For the two brothers, this game would be their only taste of first-class cricket, and although Headlam took wickets with his second and fourth deliveries, he was selected on only one other occasion, again against Victoria, the following season.

•

Australian cricketer Denise Emerson, the sister of former fast bowler Terry Alderman, made history in 1984 when she tied the knot with a Sheffield Shield umpire, Ross Emerson. They met during the 1983–84 Australian Women's Cricket Championship in Sydney when Denise was representing Western Australia and Emerson was umpiring.

•

When Mudassar Nazar and Shoaib Mohammad opened Pakistan's third Test innings against New Zealand at Karachi in 1984–85, the pair emulated their fathers—Nazar Mohammad and Hanif Mohammad—who had last opened the innings for Pakistan, at Calcutta in 1952–53.

•

A seniors Yorkshire League match in 1981 had a certain avian atmosphere, with the father and son combination of John and Stephen Duck bowling to brothers Ken and Colin Swan.

•

Javed Miandad's brothers, Anwar and Bashir, also played first-class cricket for Karachi.

•

Ian and Greg Chappell

Ian and Greg Chappell are the only brothers to each take 100 catches in Test cricket. Greg accepted 122 in 87 Tests, Ian 105 in 75. Coincidentally, both finished their Test careers with an average of 1.4 catches per match.

•

One of Dirk Wellham's uncles, Wally, also played first-class cricket for New South Wales, while his father Charlie, brother Greg and a cousin, Dale, played grade cricket in Sydney.

•

Although Les Richardson made only one appearance in first-class cricket, for Tasmania in 1921–22, his contribution to the game was unique, for he produced no less than five sons who also played first-class cricket. Brian, Colin, Les, Reg and Ted Richardson all played for Tasmania, as did Les' brother Walter.

Ned Gregory, the eldest of four brothers who represented New South Wales, had two sons—Syd and Charles—who also played for the Blues, and he and Syd remain the only father and son to have played Test cricket for Australia. Ned Gregory is one of only 14 Australian

South Australian cricketers Greg Blewett (top left), Jamie Brayshaw (top right) and Daniel Marsh (above)—their fathers also played first-class cricket

Ray, Mervyn and Neil Harvey, brothers who played together in the same Victorian XI in 1947–48

Test cricketers to have a son also play first-class cricket, the most recent addition to the list Rod Marsh, whose son Daniel made his Sheffield Shield debut in 1993–94. When Daniel played his first match, for South Australia, the side also included two other sons of former first-class cricketers—Greg Blewett, whose father Bob represented South Australia, and Jamie Brayshaw, whose father Ian played for Western Australia.

AUSTRALIAN TEST CRICKETERS WITH SONS WHO PLAYED FIRST-CLASS CRICKET

Father, state and season of first-class debut	*Son, state and season of first-class debut*
Ted a'Beckett (Vic)—1927–28	Ted a'Beckett (Vic)—1966–67
Les Favell (SA)—1951–52	Allan Favell (SA)—1983–84
Ned Gregory (NSW)—1862–63	Syd Gregory (NSW)—1889–90
	Charles Gregory (NSW)—1898–99
Jeff Hammond (SA)—1969–70	Ashley Hammond (SA)—1992–93
Tom Horan (Vic)—1874–75	Jim Horan (Vic)—1900–01
	Tom Horan (Vic)—1906–07
Bill Howell (NSW)—1894–95	Bill Howell (NSW)—1932–33
'Affie' Jarvis (SA)—1877–78	Harwood Jarvis (SA)—1905–06
Bill Johnston (Vic)—1945–46	David Johnston (SA)—1978–79
Len Maddocks (Vic)—1946–47	Ian Maddocks (Vic)—1977–78
Rod Marsh (WA)—1968–69	Daniel Marsh (SA)—1993–94
Hugh Massie (NSW)—1877–78	Jack Massie (NSW)—1910–11
Ken Meuleman (WA)—1945–46	Rob Meuleman (WA)—1968–69
Norman O'Neill (NSW)—1955–56	Mark O'Neill (WA/NSW)—1979–80
Victor Trumper (NSW)—1894–95	Victor Trumper (NSW)—1940–41

THE MOST BROTHERS IN AUSTRALIAN FIRST-CLASS CRICKET

7	Arthur Hill (SA), Clem Hill (SA), Henry Hill (SA), Les Hill (SA), Percival Hill (SA), Roland Hill (SA), Stanley Hill (SA/NSW)
5	Brian Richardson (Tas), Colin Richardson (Tas), Les Richardson (Tas), Reg Richardson (Tas), Ted Richardson (Tas)
4	Arthur Gregory (NSW), Charles Gregory (NSW), Dave Gregory (NSW), Ned Gregory (NSW)
4	Mervyn Harvey (Vic), 'Mick' Harvey (Vic/Qld), Ray Harvey (Vic), Neil Harvey (Vic/NSW)

•

In 1992–93 Andy Bichel and Wade Seccombe played together for the first time in a first-class match for Queensland, against England 'A' at Caloundra. In 1964–65 their uncles—Don Bichel and Don Seccombe—played in the Queensland–South Australia Shield match at Brisbane.

•

The Raysons from Victoria provide the only example of three generations of one family playing first-class cricket in Australia. Bill Rayson appeared in six matches for the Vics in the 1920s, his son Max three times in the late '30s, while his grandson Roger played in 18 first-class matches in the '60s.

•

Brothers Keith and Roy Westbrook, who played first-class cricket for Tasmania just before the First World War, had an uncle, Norman Westbrook, and two great-uncles, Tom and Walter Westbrook, who also played for the state. Walter appeared in the first first-class match ever played in Australia, against Victoria at Launceston in 1850–51.

•

Robert Power, who represented Victoria in a couple of first-class matches in 1857–58, was the father-in-law of England Test captain Archie MacLaren.

•

Through the years entire family XI's have taken to the cricket field. Some of the most notable include the Edriches of Norfolk in the 1940s, and the Partridge family in the 1980s—one of them played first-class cricket for Gloucestershire. In 1983 the Partridges put together an eleven against a team called Birdlip and Brimpsfield, and still had six other family members on stand-by. They also provided a 12th man, an umpire and scorer.

One of the first family teams in Australia were the Leaks from South Australia. In 1893–94 the Leak family defeated a side from Basket Range which was also dominated by family members. Only two players in their eleven didn't have a relative in the side.

THE LEAK FAMILY XI v THE BASKET RANGE XI
Played at Basket Range in 1893–94

THE LEAK FAMILY

F. Leak	b Moulds	2
F.N. Leak	b Cranwell	5
F.W. Leak	retired	28
W.H. Leak	run out	4
S. Leak	c Moulds b Cranwell	10
H. Leak	b Cranwell	8
E. Leak	c Burdett b Hockham	24
E. Leak	c Moulds b Hockham	10
H. Leak	b Burdett	4
R. Leak	b Cranwell	0
D. Leak	not out	1
Extras		7
		103

BASKET RANGE

H. Beauchamp	c S. Leak b E. Leak	3
W. Moulds	c H. Leak b E. Leak	1
J. Hockham	c F. Leak b F.N. Leak	5
W. Hockham	b E. Leak	2
A. Cranwell	b E. Leak	3
F. Burdett	b E. Leak	7
J. Cranwell	c E. Leak b F.N. Leak	2
A. Beauchamp	c R. Leak b E. Leak	1
E. Cranwell	b F.N. Leak	4
W. Burdett	not out	3
J. Wye	b E. Leak	6
Extras		11
		48

•

Lebrun Constantine, the father of West Indies Test player Learie, was a member of the first West Indian team to tour England in 1900. In their fourth match, against the Gentlemen of MCC at Lord's, Lebrun became the West Indies' first century-maker in England with an innings of 113. In 1922–23 the season of his first-class debut, Learie, his father and his uncle Victor Pascall were all in the Trinidad XI that took on British Guiana at Georgetown.

•

Family history was made in the United States in 1880 when four brothers—George, Robert, Daniel and Charles

Newhall—all played in an international match against Canada in Pennsylvania. The Newhalls were one of the biggest cricketing families in North America, with six members representing the United States in matches against Canada, England and Australia between 1859 and 1912.

•

When New Zealand completed its first Test victory over England, at Wellington in 1977–78, it was the last time that the Hadlee brothers Richard and Dayle played together in the national side.

•

In 1993–94 the youngest of the Waugh brothers, Danny, made his first-grade debut for the Canterbury club in Sydney. In his first match against Sutherland, Danny played alongside his brother Dean, becoming the fourth Waugh to play for the club during the season.

•

During 1989, brothers Robin and Chris Smith both scored a first-class century on the same day, but for different teams. On 27 July Robin hit 143 in the fourth Test against Australia at Manchester, while Chris, playing for Hampshire, scored 107 against Gloucestershire at Portsmouth. For Robin it was his first Test century, for Chris his first Championship century of the season.

Warren Wishart, who made his first-class debut for Western Australia in 1993–94, is a distant relative of the England Test bowler Hedley Verity. Wishart, a left-arm spinner like Verity, is a grandson of one of Verity's cousins.

•

Two uncles and their nephews were on the Derbyshire playing staff in 1947—Harry and Charles Elliot and Tom Worthington and Fred Marsh.

•

Lou Benaud, the father of former Test cricketers Richie and John, once claimed all 20 wickets in a match. Representing the Penrith Waratah club against St Marys in 1922–23, he took 20 for 65 in a game that was played over two consecutive Saturdays on different grounds. In the first innings he took 10 for 30, with four wickets coming in four balls, and 10 for 35 in the second.

•

In 1993 Leigh Atkinson, a second cousin of former England captain Graham Gooch, took five wickets in five balls in a club match for Flackwell Heath.

•

The Nawab of Pataudi, Snr, died on 5 January 1952, the 11th birthday of his son, the Nawab of Pataudi, Jnr, who like his father went on to play Test cricket.

Robin (left) and Chris Smith—brothers who both played for Natal, Hampshire and England. Their grandfather V.L. Shearer also played first-class cricket for Natal.

Three members of New Zealand's most famous and prolific cricket family—Karen and Richard Hadlee, and Walter Hadlee, all of whom played international cricket

Lou Benaud (right) with his two sons, Richie (left) and John, both of whom went on to play Test cricket for Australia

Only once in Pakistan's first 101 Test matches did they take the field without the services of at least one of the Mohammad brothers—Hanif, Mushtaq, Sadiq and Wazir. Pakistan was Mohammad-less for the first time in its 90th Test—against England at Karachi in 1977–78.

•

During the 1980s the feat of scoring a century in a session by a player from New South Wales was achieved just twice—Steve Smith hit 116 runs against Victoria at Melbourne in 1982–83 while Mark O'Neill made 106 runs against Tasmania at Devenport in 1987–88. Smith and O'Neill are cousins, and both performed the feat in the tea-to-stumps session of each match. Norman O'Neill—Mark's father, Steve's uncle—also hit a hundred in the last session of play in a first-class match for New South Wales—108 out of 233 against Victoria at Sydney in 1957–58.

•

When Dudley Nourse scored his first century in Test cricket—231 against Australia at Johannesburg in 1935–36—it provided the first instance of a father and son scoring Test match hundreds. His father, 'Dave', had scored his only century (111) in 1921–22, and like his son it was against Australia at Johannesburg. India's Lala Amarnath is the only father with a Test 100 to have two sons—Surinder and Mohinder—to also hit a century. Lala and Surinder only scored one Test century each, but uniquely performed the feat on their Test debuts.

Brothers Peter and Pat Watts were both dismissed in identical fashion in the County Championship match between Northamptonshire and Sussex at Northampton in 1966—*P.J. Watts c Parks b Oakman 13, P.D. Watts c Parks b Oakman 13.*

•

In 1993–94 Paul Kirsten equalled the South African first-class record for most wicket-keeping dismissals in an innings when he took seven catches for Griqualand West against Western Transvaal at Potchefstroom. The record had been held by his father, Noel, who in 1959–60 dismissed seven for Border v Rhodesia at East London. The father and son double act is unique in first-class cricket.

It ended up being a big season for the Kirsten family. After Paul's record performance behind the stumps, both Gary Kirsten and his half-brother Peter were called up to represent South Africa in the Test and one-day international series in Australia. In their first match together, in the World Series Cup at Perth, Gary and Peter opened the batting against New Zealand with a first-wicket stand of 80.

•

The first time sisters played together in a Test match was in 1934–35, when *two* sets represented Australia in the second Test against England at Sydney—Esse and Rene Shevill and Margaret and Barbara Peden.

•

TEST HUNDREDS BY FATHER AND SON					
Father	*Country*	*100s*	*Son*	*Country*	*100s*
Lala Amarnath	India	1	Mohinder Amarnath	India	11
			Surinder Amarnath	India	1
Walter Hadlee	New Zealand	1	Richard Hadlee	New Zealand	2
Hanif Mohammad	Pakistan	12	Shoaib Mohammad	Pakistan	7*
Vijay Manjrekar	India	7	Sanjay Manjrekar	India	4
Nazar Mohammad	Pakistan	1	Mudassar Nazar	Pakistan	10
'Dave' Nourse	South Africa	1	Dudley Nourse	South Africa	9
Nawab of Pataudi, Snr	England	1	Nawab of Pataudi, Jnr	India	6

*Hanif and Shoaib Mohammad are the only father and son to score a double-century in Test cricket

14 Around the Grounds

Sri Lanka's capital Colombo was the first city to accommodate three *current* Test match grounds, and then four. Its first Test venue was the P. Saravanamuttu Stadium, opened in 1982. The Singhalese Sports Club Ground and the Colombo Cricket Club Ground staged their first Tests two years later. The fourth, the Khettarama Stadium, opened in 1992 and was Test cricket's 66th Test ground.

•

Dennis Lillee holds the Test record for the most wickets on one ground—82 in 14 matches at the MCG. He was the first Australian bowler to exceed 50 Test wickets at a single venue. Ian Botham, Richard Hadlee, Imran Khan and Abdul Qadir have all passed the milestone at two different Test grounds.

•

In 1992 Allan Border set an unusual record when he became the first batsman to score 1,000 Test runs on one ground without a century. During his knock of 53 not out against India in 1991–92, the Australian captain passed the 1,000-Test-run mark at the SCG, and although he'd scored 10 fifties at the time, he'd never gone on to a hundred. His two highest knocks at the ground—89 and 83—came in the same match, against England in 1982–83.

In 1993–94 Border became the highest Test run-scorer at the SCG when he overtook Greg Chappell's aggregate of 1,150 runs. With a painstaking innings of 49 against South Africa, Border rewrote the record books, but still a Test century at the famous ground eluded him.

	Ground	M	I	NO	Runs	HS	50s	Avge
A.R. Border	SCG	17	29	8	1,177	89	11	56.04

1,000 TEST RUNS ON ONE GROUND WITHOUT A CENTURY

•

Greg Chappell was the first batsman to score 1,000 Test runs at three different Test venues—the MCG, the SCG and the Gabba. His performance at his home ground in Brisbane was almost Bradmanesque, reaching his 1,000 runs in just 11 innings.

1,000 TEST RUNS AT THREE GROUNDS
G.S. Chappell

Ground	M	I	NO	Runs	HS	100s	50s	Avge
MCG	17	31	4	1,257	121	4	9	45.56
SCG	12	22	4	1,150	204	4	3	63.89
Woolloongabba	7	11	2	1,006	201	5	4	111.78

Ian Botham had a certain fondness for Lord's. In 14 Tests at the ground he claimed 69 wickets—on eight occasions he took five wickets in an innings, with a best return of 8 for 34 against Pakistan in 1978.

•

England's Herbert Sutcliffe had a love affair with the MCG, scoring a 50 in all but one of his seven Test innings played there—176 & 127 and 143 in 1924–25; 58 & 135 in 1928–29; and 52 & 33 in 1932–33. Total runs 724, average 103.42.

•

Only three batsmen in the history of first-class cricket have been able to muster 20,000 runs on the one ground—Jack Hobbs and Tom Hayward at The Oval and 'Patsy' Hendren at Lord's.

MOST FIRST-CLASS RUNS ON A SINGLE GROUND

Batsman	Teams	Ground	I	Runs	Avge
Jack Hobbs	Surrey/England	The Oval	567	27,006	52.34
'Patsy' Hendren	Middlesex/England	Lord's	602	25,737	49.21
Tom Hayward	Surrey/England	The Oval	539	22,268	45.26

•

The first cricket ground to stage a floodlit international match was the SCG during the days of Kerry Packer's World Series Cricket. It was in 1978–79 that the lights went on for the first time for the match between the Australians and the West Indians on 28 November.

•

In 1914 two County Championship matches were staged at Lord's, not involving the ground's tenants, Middlesex. Two of Surrey's matches, against Kent and Yorkshire, were played at cricket's headquarters because the authorities had taken over The Oval for military purposes.

•

In what's believed to be a unique occurrence in the annals of top-class cricket, a match in New Zealand in 1893–94 was deliberately scheduled to be contested on *two* different grounds. When New South Wales and Hawkes Bay opposed each other, the match was played on the Napier Recreation Ground on the first day and Farndon Park on the second.

•

The MCG

When Mark Taylor hit 142 not out against New Zealand at Perth in 1993–94, he became the first batsman to score a Test century on all of Australia's six international cricket grounds. His WACA hundred was his 11th in Test cricket. Remarkably each of them was scored at a different venue.

136 v England	Leeds	1989
219 v England	Nottingham	1989
164 v Sri Lanka	Brisbane	1989–90
108 v Sri Lanka	Hobart	1989–90
101 v Pakistan	Melbourne	1989–90
101* v Pakistan	Sydney	1989–90
144 v West Indies	St John's	1990–91
100 v India	Adelaide	1991–92
124 v England	Manchester	1993
111 v England	Lord's	1993
142* v New Zealand	Perth	1993–94

●

THE FAVOURITE GROUNDS OF SOME MODERN-DAY TEST CRICKETERS

David Boon—SCG
Allan Border—SCG, Lord's
Mike Brearley—Lord's
Martin Crowe—Basin Reserve (Wellington), Adelaide Oval
Allan Donald—Edgbaston, Headingley
Mike Gatting—Lord's
Sunil Gavaskar—Queen's Park Oval (Trinidad)
David Gower—SCG
Ian Healy—SCG
Kim Hughes—MCG
Merv Hughes—WACA
Imran Khan—MCG
Dean Jones—MCG, Adelaide Oval
Dennis Lillee—MCG
Rod Marsh—SCG
Malcolm Marshall—Kensington Oval (Barbados)
Dilip Vengsarkar—Brabourne Stadium (Bombay)
Wasim Bari—Adelaide Oval
Bob Willis—Lord's

15 The Young Ones

During the 1929–30 season Victoria selected Len Junor for the match against Western Australia at the MCG. At the age of 15 years 265 days he remains Australia's youngest first-class cricketer. It was during the same summer that the country's second-youngest player also made his first-class debut—'Jack' Badcock, at 15 years 313 days, made his first appearance for Tasmania against Victoria, also at the MCG.

•

Andrew Zesers, who made his first-class debut at the age of 17, was the first Australian teenager to capture 100 first-class wickets. He achieved the notable milestone two days before his 20th birthday, bowling for South Australia in the Sheffield Shield match against Tasmania at Adelaide in 1986–87.

•

In only his second Test match, Neil Harvey, at the age of 19 years 121 days, became the youngest Australian to score a Test century. He secured the milestone during the fifth Test against India at Melbourne in 1947–48 in a most unusual way—he was on 95 and reached his hundred with an all-run five.

•

Two teenagers—Michael DiVenuto (19) and Ricky Ponting (18)—built a record-breaking 207-run partnership for Tasmania in the 1993–94 Sheffield Shield. Batting against Western Australia at Hobart, DiVenuto hit 125 and Ponting 105, their partnership erasing the state's previous record for the third wicket of 183 by George Paton and Reg Hawson against Victoria at Hobart in 1908–09. Later in the season, Western Australia faced another pair of teenagers, Jimmy Maher and Martin Love, both aged 19, who also blitzed their attack. At the Gabba, Maher (122) and Love (119) both scored centuries in the second innings in a record Queensland-WA fifth-wicket partnership of 189.

•

In 1895 Charlie Townsend, fresh out of school, took 16 wickets for Gloucestershire against Notts. At the time, aged 18, he was the youngest bowler in English first-class cricket to achieve the feat, and grabbed another 10-wicket haul (15–184 v Yorkshire) during the same summer. He finished his first season of first-class cricket with 131 wickets at 13.94.

•

Majid Khan

Majid Khan, who appeared in 63 Test matches for Pakistan, made his first-class debut in 1961–62 at the age of 15 and scored 111 not out, and with the ball took 6 for 67.

•

On his first-class debut for the Gents of South XI in 1865, W.G. Grace took 8 for 40, a few weeks shy of his 17th birthday. He remains the youngest bowler in the history of English first-class cricket to take five wickets in an innings on debut, and the only teenager to take eight at his first attempt.

•

Les Poidevin, who went on to play for New South Wales and Lancashire, performed an amazing feat in 1887–88, scoring a double-century and taking 19 wickets in a schools match. He was 11 years old.

•

When Sachin Tendulkar appeared in the second Test against South Africa at Johannesburg in 1992–93 he became the youngest batsman, at 19 years 217 days, to score 1,000 Test runs. During the same match he made 111 and equalled George Headley's record of four Test hundreds before his 21st birthday. The following year Tendulkar continued to impress for a player so young, with 165 against England at Madras—his fifth Test century scored in his teens. It was during this series that Tendulkar teamed up with his old schoolmate Vinod Kambli and, in partnership, each scored over 300 runs in the three-match rubber. For the first time in Test history, two players at or under the age of 21 finished a series as the leading run-scorers with a century average each. Kambli made 317 runs at 105.67 while Tendulkar collected 302 runs at 100.67.

The young duo finished the 1993 calendar year at the top of the world Test match batting averages—Kambli 793 runs in seven Tests at 113.29, Tendulkar 640 runs in eight Tests at 91.43.

•

On his Test debut for Australia at Sydney in 1886–87, J.J. Ferris, bowling unchanged with Charlie Turner, dismissed England for 45—their lowest total in any Test match. Ferris claimed 4 for 27 and backed it up with a second innings return of 5 for 76. At the age of 19, Ferris became the first Australian teenager to take five wickets in a Test innings, and today remains the youngest to do so.

YOUNGEST AUSTRALIAN BOWLERS TO TAKE
FIVE WICKETS IN A TEST INNINGS

Years	Days	Bowler	Match details
19	269	J.J. Ferris	5–76 v England at Sydney in 1886–87
20	2	Graham McKenzie	5–37 v England at Lord's in 1961
20	75	Craig McDermott	6–70 v England at Lord's in 1985
20	95	'Tibby' Cotter	6–40 v England at Melbourne in 1903–04
21	183	Steve Waugh	5–69 v England at Perth in 1986–87

16 Batting to Forget

When David Boon copped a first-ball duck at Perth in 1993–94, it gave him the record for the most Test ducks (14) by a specialist Australian batsman, one more than Greg Chappell. For Boon, his WACA nought was his second successive golden duck, having fallen first ball in the last Test match of the 1993 Ashes series. In 1989–90 Boon went through a real horror stretch, making three Test ducks off three consecutive balls.

•

A record nine ducks were registered by Sri Lankan batsmen in the Test match against India at Chandigarh in 1990–91. Three of the Sri Lankans made pairs.

•

Eric Hollies, a match-winner with the ball, could lay no claim to fame with the bat. Although he totalled over 1,500 first-class runs he needed 616 innings to do so, in a career stretching from 1932 to 1957. In three successive seasons—1948 to 1950—Hollies went for 68 first-class innings without making it into double-figures after going for 59 innings between 1939 and 1947 with only single-digit scores. In a first-class career of 515 matches for Warwickshire, the MCC and England, Hollies scored 271 ducks, remained not out 282 times and had an average of just 5.00.

•

Boys at a Sydney secondary school suffered a double dose of humiliation in 1993–94 after being walloped on the cricket field, and then having their story exposed in a major city newspaper. After the Barker College 13B side was dismissed for just 1 (a leg bye) by Waverley College, their effort was splashed across the back page of the *Telegraph Mirror*. Several of the students required counselling after the paper printed the names of the 11 players, together with 11 ducks.

Another recent example of every player in a side making a duck occurred during the 1989–90 summer, when the Belgian Garden School in Townsville was dismissed for 1—a wide—by the Kirwan State School.

•

In consecutive Test matches against Pakistan, Dean Jones suffered the misfortune of scoring three successive ducks—0 & 0 at Lahore in 1988–89 and 0 at Melbourne in 1989–90. His failure at the MCG brought to 11 the number of noughts he'd made in Test cricket.

Mark O'Neill who, like his dad, made a duck on his first-class debut

The father and son combination of Norman and Mark O'Neill got off to the worst possible start in first-class cricket, each making a debut duck. Norman made nought in his first match for New South Wales in 1955–56, while his son scored a duck on his debut for Western Australia in 1979–80. Another father and son combination—Rod and Daniel Marsh—also made ducks in their first first-class matches.

•

On England's disastrous tour of the West Indies in 1985–86, which they lost 5–0, no batsman was able to take a first-class century off any of the Caribbean teams. Eight of the party were able to score 20 fifties between them, but none was able to go on to 100. Graham Gooch hit five fifties (53, 51, 53, 51, 51) while David Gower had the highest innings, one of 90 in the last match—the fifth Test at St John's. England's inability to record a single century in the 10 first-class matches was a new record for a touring team.

Australia suffered a similar failure in New Zealand in 1992–93. In four first-class matches on tour, the best Test score was 88 by Allan Border at Christchurch—the other highest knocks were 89 by Justin Langer and 87 not out by Ian Healy against the New Zealand Board XI at New Plymouth.

•

Alby Wright, a curator at the Adelaide Oval, who bagged a 'king pair' on his first-class debut for South Australia in 1905-06

Alby Wright, a South Australian bowler and a genuine No. 11 batsman, recorded five pairs in his first-class career with three in a row in his first three matches in 1905–06. His six consecutive ducks is a world record in first-class cricket. He ended his career in 1920–21 in similar fashion as he began it, with scores of 0 not out, 1 not out & 0 and 0.

Batsmen to have collected five consecutive first-class ducks include Baroda's Anshuman Gaekwad in 1971–72/72–73, Leicestershire's Wilfred Jelf in 1911 and Michael Buss of Sussex in 1974.

•

When India met England at Delhi in 1976–77, its spinning pair of B.S. Chandrasekhar and Bishen Bedi both made pairs. Bedi's double failure was the third of his Test career, a record that was eventually claimed by Chandra who went on to register four pairs in Test cricket.

Bedi's worst stretch with the bat was in the early 1970s when he reached double figures just once in 23 consecutive Test innings—1* & 5, 0 & 2*, 8, 2, 4* & 2, 0 & 9*, 5, 4*, 0, 0 & 0, 14 & 0, 0 & 1*, 0 & 0 and 0 & 5. Chandra's most traumatic period was against Australia in 1977–78, when in consecutive innings he scored 0 & 0, 0* & 0*, 0 & 0 and 2 & 2. Chandra ended his Test match career with 23 ducks, and four pairs, in 58 matches. Bedi made three pairs and 20 ducks, including 11 against Australia, in 67 Tests.

•

New Zealand fast bowler Danny Morrison scored four successive ducks, including a pair, in the 1993–94 Test series against Australia. He was the 10th batsman to collect four successive Test ducks. His fourth blob was his 19th in Test cricket and came in his 32nd Test—Pakistan's Wasim Bari collected 19 ducks in 81 Tests, Derek Underwood 19 in 86 Tests.

•

At Johannesburg in 1949–50, Australia gained its fourth successive innings victory against South Africa. Despite the win, Australia got off to one of its worst-ever starts to a Test match losing both openers—Arthur Morris and Jack Moroney—for ducks with the score 2 for 2. For both batsmen, their duck was dramatic. Moroney was run out in this, his first Test match, while Morris' nought was his first in 101 first-class innings.

Morris and Moroney set a lamentable record in Australia's next Test series, recording another pair of ducks against England at Brisbane in 1950–51. They remain the only pair of opening batsmen to each score ducks in the same Test innings more than once. The first example of both openers failing so miserably was in 1888 on a sticky wicket at Manchester when Australia lost its first four batsmen in the second innings for nought—Percy McDonnell, Alec Bannerman, 'Harry' Trott and George Bonnor.

AUSTRALIA v ENGLAND
Manchester 1888

Second innings

P.S. McDonnell	b Lohmann	0
A.C. Bannerman	c Grace b Peel	0
G.H.S. Trott	run out	0
G.J. Bonnor	c Grace b Peel	0
J.M. Blackham	b Lohmann	5
J.J. Lyons	b Briggs	32
S.M.J. Woods	b Lohmann	0
C.T.B. Turner	b Briggs	26
J.D. Edwards	c Grace b Peel	1
J.J. Ferris	c Abel b Peel	3
J. Worrall	not out	0
Extras	(b2, lb1)	3
		70

Fall of wickets
1/0, 2/0, 3/1, 4/7, 5/7, 6/7, 7/55, 8/56, 9/70, 10/70
Bowling figures
Peel 16–4–37–4, Lohmann 8–3–20–3, Briggs 7.1–2–10–2

DUCKS BY PAIRS OF OPENING BATSMEN IN A TEST INNINGS

Batsmen	Test match
Percy McDonnell & Alec Bannerman	Australia v England at Manchester in 1888
George Challenor & Clifford Roach	West Indies v England at Manchester in 1928
Herbert Sutcliffe & Eddie Paynter	England v New Zealand at Christchurch in 1932–33
Jack Fingleton & 'Jack' Badcock	Australia v England at Brisbane in 1936–37
Bill O'Reilly & 'Chuck' Fleetwood-Smith	Australia v England at Melbourne in 1936–37
Arthur Morris & Jack Moroney	Australia v South Africa at Johannesburg in 1949–50
Jack Moroney & Arthur Morris	Australia v England at Brisbane in 1950–51
Pankaj Roy & Datta Gaekwad	India v England at Leeds in 1952
'Jackie' McGlew & Trevor Goddard	South Africa v England at Lord's in 1955
Conrad Hunte & Rohan Kanhai	West Indies v Pakistan at Port-of-Spain in 1957–58
J.K. Holt & Conrad Hunte	West Indies v India at Kanpur in 1958–59
Noel McGregor & Graham Dowling	New Zealand v South Africa at Johannesburg in 1961–62
M.L. Jaisimha & K.S. Indrajitsinhji	India v Australia at Madras in 1964–65
Terry Jarvis & Michael Shrimpton	New Zealand v England at Auckland in 1965–66
Mike Denness & Dennis Amiss	England v Pakistan at Hyderabad in 1972–73
Sunil Gavaskar & Chetan Chauhan	India v Australia at Melbourne in 1977–78
Alvin Greenidge & Basil Williams	West Indies v India at Bombay in 1978–79
Derek Randall & Geoff Boycott	England v Australia at Perth in 1979–80
Shafiq Ahmed & Sadiq Mohammad	Pakistan v West Indies at Karachi in 1980–81
Mudassar Nazar & Rizwan-uz-Zaman	Pakistan v Australia at Perth in 1981–82
Mohsin Khan & Mudassar Nazar	Pakistan v England at Leeds in 1982
Gordon Greenidge & Desmond Haynes	West Indies v India at Port-of-Spain in 1982–83
Sidath Wettimuny & Susil Fernando	Sri Lanka v Australia at Kandy in 1982–83
Graham Gooch & Tim Robinson	England v West Indies at Kingston in 1985–86
John Wright & Bruce Edgar	New Zealand v England at Lord's in 1986
John Wright & Blair Hartland	New Zealand v England at Auckland in 1991–92
Ramiz Raja & Shakeel Ahmed	Pakistan v West Indies at St John's in 1992–93
Roshan Mahamana & Chandika Hathurusinghe	Sri Lanka v South Africa at Colombo in 1993–94

•

Australia's Alan Hurst, who collected a record six ducks against England in the 1978–79 Ashes series, finished his 12-match Test career with 10 ducks in 20 innings.

•

Keith Stackpole bowed out of Test cricket with a pair. Opening the innings for Australia at Auckland in 1973–74, he was out to the first ball of the match, bowled by Richard Hadlee. Stackpole had suffered a similar fate in an earlier match in the same season. Representing Victoria, he was out to the first ball of the match against Queensland at Brisbane. John Scholes was dismissed off the second ball.

KEITH STACKPOLE'S ALL-TIME BEST TEST XI
1 Bill Ponsford
2 Jack Hobbs
3 Don Bradman
4 Viv Richards
5 Graeme Pollock
6 Garry Sobers
7 Keith Miller
8 Richie Benaud (c)
9 Alan Knott
10 Dennis Lillee
11 Jeff Thomson

•

Mark Lavender—two first-ball ducks at Hobart in 1992–93

When Western Australia played Tasmania at Hobart in 1992–93, two of the Sandgropers contributed three first-ball ducks. Mark Lavender earned a 'king pair' in the match, while Geoff Marsh was out first ball in the second innings. In Lavender's next outing the following week, he completed a hat-trick of ducks falling for nought in the match against South Australia at Adelaide. During the summer, there was a total of 28 golden ducks in first-class matches.

•

One of cricket's biggest batting bunnies is Yorkshire's Mark Robinson who in 1990 created a world record by failing to score a run in 12 successive first-class innings while playing for Northamptonshire. At the end of the 1991 season his record with the bat read 82 matches, 81 innings, 36 not outs, 89 runs, top score 19*—average 1.97. By the end of the following summer the fast bowler managed to pass a psychological barrier by increasing his average past 2.00—after 100 first-class matches his average had rocketed to 2.37!

INSTANCES OF FIRST-CLASS CRICKETERS WITH A CAREER BATTING AVERAGE UNDER 2.00
(Qualification: 10 Matches)

	M	I	NO	Runs	HS	Avge
John Howarth (Nottinghamshire—1966–67)	13	7	3	0	0*	0.00
Peter Visser (Central Districts—1983–84/86–87)	19	17	5	11	8	0.91
G.T.O. Wilson (Worcestershire—1951–53)	13	16	7	10	4*	1.11
Mark Whitaker (Cambridge University—1965–67)	12	20	7	16	4*	1.23
John Oppenheimer (Oxford University—1989–91)	10	7	2	7	7	1.40
Paul Garlick (Cambridge University—1984)	10	15	6	13	6*	1.44
John Ellis (Yorkshire—1888–92)	11	15	6	14	4*	1.55

•

Glenn McGrath, who in 1993–94 recorded a first-ball duck in his first Test and his first one-day international

New South Wales fast bowler Glenn McGrath was out for a first-ball duck on his Test debut and his one-day international debut. He also made a duck at his first attempt with the bat in first-class cricket. During the second Test against South Africa in 1993–94, he overcame a big hoodoo at his home ground—the SCG—finally scoring his first run in five first-class appearances there. In two matches he didn't bat, made a duck in the previous year's Sheffield Shield final, and 0 and 0 not out against Victoria in '93–94.

•

In 1906–07 Charles Gregory made history with an innings of 383 for New South Wales against Queensland at Brisbane. It was a new world record for the highest score in first-class cricket and he was the first batsman to score 300 runs in a day. That innings aside, Gregory was unable to muster the same sparkling form, and made a total of just 31 runs in the remaining four matches of his first-class career. In his last five innings for New South Wales he scored 3, 3, 4 & 7 and 14.

•

Surrey batsman Monty Lynch would probably like to forget the time he played against Middlesex at Lord's in 1977—he recorded a pair before lunch. In a rain-delayed match, Surrey was skittled out for just 49, with three batsmen, including Lynch, making nought. The visitors were required to bat again shortly afterwards, following Mike Brearley's decision to declare his innings at 0 for 0 after just one ball. Surrey was dismissed second time around for 89—Lynch making two noughts before lunch on the third day.

•

When Australia played England in the second Test at Melbourne in 1884–85, three of the debutants—Roland Pope, Alfred Marr and 'Digger' Robertson—made ducks in the first innings. For each player, this was his only Test match.

•

On the opening day of the fifth Test between Australia and South Africa at Melbourne in 1931–32, two batsmen from each side were dismissed for a first ball duck—Bill Woodfull, Stan McCabe, Jim Christy and Quintin McMillan.

•

Gerald Sanderson had a rather brief, but curious, first-class career in which he batted just twice, 22 years apart. On his first-class debut, for Warwickshire in 1901, he was run out for a duck and in his second match, for Worcestershire in 1923, was run out for 16.

•

S.S. Schultz made the record books with a most unflattering batting performance during a match for Cambridge University in 1881. Playing against a Gentlemen of England XI at the Christchurch ground, he was soon back in the pavilion scoring a first-ball duck, but because of the dangerous condition of the pitch the match was abandoned and transferred to The Parks. Unluckily, Schultz was again dismissed for a golden duck—*twice* first-ball in the one innings.

South African fast bowler Cuan McCarthy ended up taking more wickets (36) in Test matches than he scored runs (28). He never made it into double-figures in his 24 innings, a Test record. McCarthy began his Test career, against England at Durban in 1948–49, with a pair and then scored 1*, 1, 0*, 3, 0 & 1*, 0 & 0*, 0* & 2*, 2*, 1* & 4*, 1* & 5, 1* & 2*, 0 & 0*, 0* and 4* & 0. His career total of 28 runs came at an average of 3.11.

PLAYERS WHO NEVER MADE A DOUBLE-FIGURE SCORE IN TEST CRICKET
(Qualification: 10 Innings)

Player	Country	T	I	NO	Runs	HS	Avge
Cuan McCarthy	South Africa	15	24	15	28	5	3.11
Dave Renneberg	Australia	8	13	7	22	9	3.66
Brendon Bracewell	New Zealand	6	12	2	24	8	2.40
Tom Dewdney	West Indies	9	12	5	17	5*	2.42

•

During the 1978 John Player League series, Sussex hit the depths of despair in its match against Surrey at The Oval, with its first six batsmen scoring one run off the bat between them. Openers John Barclay and Gehan Mendis, Imran Khan, Jeremy Groome and Paul Parker all scored ducks while Michael Buss made some amends with one. Surrey's David Thomas, in only his third one-day appearance, was the wrecker, accounting for four of the ducksters. At one stage The Oval scoreboard read 0 for 4 after 13 deliveries.

SURREY v SUSSEX
The Oval 1978

SUSSEX

J.R.T. Barclay	c Smith b Thomas	0
G.D. Mendis	run out	0
Imran Khan	c Richards b Thomas	0
J.J. Groome	c Howarth b Thomas	0
P.W.G. Parker	c Richards b Thomas	0
M.A. Buss	b Jackman	1
C.P. Phillipson	b Pocock	16
A. Long	c Jackman b Knight	33
G.G. Arnold	c & b Payne	8
J. Spencer	not out	21
R.G.L. Cheatle	not out	9
Extras	(b3, lb7, w1)	11
	(9 wickets—40 overs)	99

Fall of wickets
1/0, 2/0, 3/0, 4/0, 5/4, 6/4, 7/30, 8/53, 9/73
Bowling figures
Thomas 8–4–13–4, Jackman 8–4–15–1, Knight 8–3–18–1, Payne 8–2–32–1, Pocock 8–3–10–1

•

In the last of his two Test matches for Pakistan—at Manchester in 1954—Mohammed Ghazali made history when he was out for a pair within two hours. Coincidentally, the other instances of 'fast pairs' were also recorded at Manchester during the 1950s, by Neil Harvey and Pankaj Roy.

TEST CRICKET'S FASTEST PAIRS

Batsman	Minutes	Match
Mohammed Ghazali	120	Pakistan v England at Manchester in 1954
Neil Harvey	124	Australia v England at Manchester in 1956
Pankaj Roy	164	India v England at Manchester in 1952

Richard Chee Quee

New South Wales batsman Richard Chee Quee had an up-and-down time with the bat during the 1993–94 season, incurring a number of single-figure scores. After one innings against South Australia he stormed into the Adelaide dressing room swearing at a very audible level. So expressive was his language that a police officer turned up to investigate.

•

Picked as a specialist batsman, Sri Lanka's Marvan Atapattu made a pair at Ahmedabad in 1993–94—dismissed both times by India's off-spinner Rajesh Chauhan. For the No. 6 batsman, this was his second pair of ducks in a Test career of three matches—his six innings had yielded just one run, for an average of 0.17.

Chauhan also had a frustrating time at the crease during the Ahmedabad Test, taking 85 minutes to score his first run. His effort was an Indian first-class record and second only in Test match cricket to England's Godfrey Evans, who took 97 minutes to get off the mark at Adelaide in 1946–47.

•

Carl Rackemann took 72 minutes to score his first run in the second innings of the third Test against England at Sydney in 1990–91—an Australian first-class record. He went on to score nine in 112 minutes.

17 The Numbers Game

The number '1' played a significant part in Mosman's scorecard when they played Parramatta at the Allan Border Oval in 1993–94. Three of the top four in the batting order were dismissed for one, the next two went for 11, while the No. 7 went for one, the No. 9 for 11 and the last man for one. When Parramatta batted, one of Mosman's opening bowlers took one wicket, the other sent down 11 overs—the visitor's innings lasted 211 minutes.

The following week, in Australia's opening tour match in South Africa, four batsmen made 11 against Nicky Oppenheimer's XI—Steve Waugh, Allan Border, Merv Hughes and Glenn McGrath.

•

On its way to 4 declared for 632 in the Lord's Test of 1993, Australia reached 500 off exactly 1,000 balls.

•

When Pakistan played the West Indies at Port-of-Spain in 1992–93, a record 17 wickets fell to lbw decisions. Seventeen wickets fell on the opening day of the Test, while on the second day, 17 April, Desmond Haynes reached his 17th Test match century. The West Indies' second innings contained 17 no-balls, Waqar Younis scored 17 runs in the match and Pakistan lost its first wicket in each innings with the score on 17.

•

The first Test at Christchurch in 1992–93 was the 27th between Australia and New Zealand. For one of the Kiwi bowlers—27-year-old Danny Morrison—it was his 27th Test, and he went into the match with a highest Test score of 27 not out.

•

When a New Zealand XI took on New South Wales at Sydney in 1913–14, three of its top four batsmen—Lance Hemus, Bert Tuckwell and Robert Hickmott—all made the identical scores of 0 and 7 in each innings.

•

In a match against Northamptonshire in 1938, Warwickshire's Eric Hollies took 6 for 66 in the first innings and 6 for 66 in the second.

•

The inaugural West Indies–Sri Lanka Test match, played at Moratuwa in 1993–94, was Sri Lanka's 50th and the West Indies' 350th.

•

Phillip DeFreitas

In the first Test against Australia at Manchester in 1993, Phillip DeFreitas made 5 in the first innings and took his Test career aggregate of runs to 555 with a top score to that time of 55 not out.

•

Allan Border, the first batsman to score 150 in each innings of a Test match, was the first to take 150 Test catches, achieving the feat in his 150th Test match (v New Zealand at Brisbane in 1993–94). Two months later Border became the first player to appear in 150 consecutive Test matches, against South Africa at Adelaide.

•

When Shane Warne took his 100th Test wicket, against South Africa at Adelaide in 1993–94, the champion leggie had conceded 2,444 runs to that time in his career at an average of 24.44.

•

When Australia played the West Indies on 19 January 1982, the SCG scoreboard at one stage was dominated by the number three. At 3.33 p.m., Viv Richards was on 33 not out, Faoud Bacchus 3 not out. There were 3 extras, 3 wickets down, the last batsman out was Larry Gomes for 3, and Greg Chappell had bowling figures of 0 for 3.

•

In 1960—the season of his first-class debut—Northamptonshire's Brian Crump scored exactly 1,000 runs. Australia's Ian Johnson bowed out of Test cricket with 1,000 runs beside his name, while Allan Border scored precisely 1,000 Test runs in the calendar year of 1986.

•

Clem Hill can probably lay claim to the tag of being one of Australia's most unlucky batsmen. During the 1901–02 Test series against England he was dismissed in the nineties three times in a row, and for one score of 87, supposedly Australia's hoodoo number (13 less than 100). If one score of 87 wasn't bad enough, he then collected another in the 1907–08 Test match at the SCG. He remains the only Australian batsman to have been twice dismissed for 87 in a Test match. Hill, the first batsman to be dismissed for 99 in a Test, was also the first to be out in the 190s—191 v South Africa at Sydney in 1910–11.

AUSTRALIAN BATSMEN DISMISSED FOR 87 IN TEST CRICKET	
George Bonnor	Fourth Test v England at Sydney in 1882–83
Sammy Jones	First Test v England at Manchester in 1886
Clem Hill	Fifth Test v England at Melbourne in 1901–02
Clem Hill	First Test v England at Sydney in 1907–08
Victor Trumper	Fourth Test v South Africa at Melbourne in 1910–11
Jack Ryder	Fourth Test v England at Adelaide in 1928–29
Jack Moroney	Second Test v South Africa at Cape Town in 1949–50
Brian Booth	Fifth Test v South Africa at Sydney in 1963–64
Keith Stackpole	Sixth Test v England at Adelaide in 1970–71
John Dyson	First Test v Pakistan at Karachi in 1982–83

•

On the final day of the Australia–West Indies Test match at Brisbane in 1975–76, the Gabba scoreboard at one stage read 2 for 164—Greg Chappell 64 not out, Ian Chappell 64 not out.

•

When Don Bradman made 244 in the fifth Test at The Oval in 1934, 122 runs were scored at each end.

•

A benefit match for Syd Gregory played in Sydney in 1906–07 saw both openers for The Rest scoring the same number of runs—Charles Gregory 4 & 7, Roger Hartigan 4 & 7 not out.

•

When South Africa bowled out Australia for 111 in the second Test at Sydney in 1993–94, four batsmen in the eleven were dismissed for one—Michael Slater, Ian Healy, Shane Warne and the No. 11, Glenn McGrath.

Clem Hill

111—the 'Dreaded Nelson'—is considered England's unlucky number in cricket, but has also been a bogey number for Australia. The Sydney Test match in '93–94 was the second time Australia had been dismissed for 111 chasing a total of under 200 for a win. The previous occasion was at Headingley in 1981, when 130 runs were needed for victory. And twice Australia has been set a victory target of 111, only to be dismissed for under 100—for 97 against England at Sydney in 1886–87 and 44 v England at The Oval in 1896.

The so-called 'Dreaded Nelson' popped up again in the third Test against South Africa at Adelaide when Australia won the match, the first time in 111 Tests that they'd come from behind to draw a series.

•

At 12 minutes to 2 on the final day of the third Test at Durban in 1993–94, Australia was 4 for 212, with Allan Border not out on 12. Three other batsmen before him had been dismissed for 12—Mark Taylor, David Boon and nightwatchman Shane Warne.

18 Cricket and Royalty

Prince Christian Victor of Schleswig-Holstein, the only member of the Royal Family to have played first-class cricket, scored a double-century for the King's Royal Rifles against the Devonshire Regiment at Rawalpindhi in 1893, at the time one of the highest innings played in the sub-continent.

•

Derbyshire's William Chatterton, who played in a Test match for England in 1891–92, was employed by the Prince of Wales, later King Edward VII, as his coach. The Prince played the game occasionally at Oxford and also appeared in at least two games for the famous I Zingari club, making an inglorious duck on his debut. In 1866 he went in as an opening batsman against the Gentlemen of Norfolk and lasted just two balls.

•

Prince Philip, the Duke of Edinburgh, has twice been President of the Marylebone Cricket Club, in 1949 and 1974. His Royal Highness has also been a keen player of the game from his school days, and on one occasion when playing against The Duke of Norfolk's XI at Arundel Castle scored 21 and took four wickets for 60.

> **Cricket can be as brutal as rugby and as delicate as chess—it requires all the grace and fitness of athletics, but at the same time it requires the psychological insight and judgment of master politicians.**
>
> **—The Duke of Edinburgh**

•

Prince Frederick Louis of Wales secured an immortal place in cricket history in 1751 when he died after being hit by a cricket ball during a match at Cliveden House, his home in Buckinghamshire.

•

King Hussain of Jordan once played for the Royal Amman Cricket Club in a match against a British Embassy XI in 1971.

•

King George Tubow II of Tonga gained an appreciation of cricket while at school in New Zealand, but back home was forced to ban the game on six days of the week. It seems that his decree was made to avoid possible famine as most workers preferred the cricket field to the plantations.

The Gordonstoun School cricket team of 1938 with Prince Philip (middle, front row)

King Malietoa, from neighbouring Samoa, issued a similar decree in 1890 for the same reasons. His order stated that for a village to travel and play another village was prohibited and that for villagers to play cricket among themselves was also forbidden. Failure to abide by the rules brought a fine of up to $45 and, if not paid, a three-month gaol sentence would be imposed.

•

King George VI was a great patron of the game, who once performed the hat-trick at Windsor Castle dismissing King Edward VII, King George V and the Duke of Windsor. The ball with which he performed the deed was mounted and put on display at the Royal Naval College at Dartmouth.

•

Prince Charles

In a charity cricket match at Cranwell in 1971, Prince Charles, appearing for the Royal Air Force, went out to bat on horseback. Former England batsman Ken Barrington, representing the Lord's Taverners, dismissed the Prince for 10, who in turn got Barrington out in a bowling spell of 2 for 37 in seven overs.

•

Alan Parnaby, who scored a century on his first-class debut in 1939, later became an Aide-de-Camp to the Queen.

•

When King George V attended the second day's play of the Australia–South Africa Triangular Tournament match at Lord's in 1912, it signalled the first visit of a reigning sovereign at a Test match.

•

The first team of cricketers from Fiji to undertake a tour of Australia, in 1907–08, was captained by Prince Penaia Kadavu Levu. The Fijians played a series of non-first-class matches against New South Wales, Queensland, South Australia and Victoria.

•

Royalty meets Royalty—Don Bradman, Australia's king of the crease, enjoys an informal moment with the Queen Mother and Princess Margaret at a function organised by King George VI at Balmoral in 1948

The mother of the Hon. Luke White, who played in the third 'Victory' Test against the Australian Services team at Lord's in 1945, was a lady-in-waiting to the Queen Mother when the Duchess of York.

•

There were many highlights of the 1977 Centenary Test at the MCG—Dennis Lillee's 11 wickets, Derek Randall's Man of the Match knock of 174 and the result, the same as the first Test in 1877. Even though Lillee missed out on the best player award it was in this match that he acquired something he regards as just as valuable—the Queen's autograph. During the lunch break on the final day, the Queen met all the players on the field and it was here that Lillee gamely requested her signature. Although she was unable to oblige at the time, a photograph of the incident was later autographed by Her Majesty, an item that remains one of Lillee's most treasured mementos.

•

Lord Frederick Beauclerk, the great-grandson of Charles II, was one of the earliest administrators of the MCC and one of the best amateur all-round cricketers of his time.

•

> **Naturally, quite an effort is required in order to become familiar with cricket, and even as one learns it, it remains somewhat difficult for us to fully understand the spirit behind this typically British game!**
> **—His Serene Highness, Prince Rainier of Monaco**

Princess Anne's 13-year-old son Peter Phillips was forced to abandon a school cricket tour of New Zealand in 1991 following one of the many scandals that have afflicted the Royal family in recent years. Peter withdrew from the team following the filing of a paternity suit by an Auckland woman against Mark Phillips, the former husband of Princess Anne and father of Peter.

•

In 1893 the Crown Prince and Princess of Romania attended a cricket match between Bucharest and Braila. According to *The Times* newspaper, 'Their Royal Highnesses were enthusiastically received', more so than the cricketers.

•

The Duchess of Kent's father, Sir William Worsley, appeared in 59 first-class matches for Yorkshire, captaining the side in 1928 and 1929.

•

The Fifth Earl Spencer, President of the Northamptonshire cricket club and of the MCC in 1861, was the great-great-grandfather of Princess Diana.

•

19 What's in a Name?

India played against two players by the name of Andy Roberts in consecutive Tests in 1975–76. The New Zealand medium-pacer was the first, in the third Test at Wellington, followed by the more famous one in the first Test at Bridgetown a few weeks later.

•

S.S. Schultz, who appeared in a Test match for England in 1878–79, later anglicised his German surname to Storey.

•

Scorers and commentators alike could have been forgiven for any confusion when New South Wales played Queensland at Newcastle in 1987–88. Of the first six in the Blues batting line-up there were three players by the name of Mark—Waugh, O'Neill and Taylor—and two by the name of Steve—Small and Waugh. And taking surnames into account, apart from the two Waughs, there were also two Taylors—the other being Peter.

•

Bishen Bedi, the Indian spinner, christened his son Gavasinder after Sunil Gavaskar. Gavaskar's son was christened Rohan Jaiviswa, after the West Indian Rohan Kanhai and two Indian Test cricketers M.L. Jaisimha and Gundappa Viswanath. Bob Holland, the former Australian Test spinner, also named one of his sons Rohan after the West Indies batsman.

A SELECTION OF TEST CRICKETERS NAMED AFTER OTHER TEST CRICKETERS

ENGLAND
Neil Harvey Fairbrother—Neil Harvey (Australia)
WEST INDIES
Kenneth *Charlie Griffith* Benjamin—Charlie Griffith (West Indies)
Colin *Everton Hunte* Croft—Everton Weekes (West Indies) and Conrad Hunte (West Indies)
Hammond Furlonge—Walter Hammond (England)
SRI LANKA
Duleep Mendis—K.S. Duleepsinhji (England)

•

Richard Halliwell, who kept wicket for Middlesex between 1865 and 1871, played his first-class cricket under five different aliases—Mr Allen, H. Brown, O.N.E. More, B. Richards and R. Tessib.

•

An odd dismissal appeared in the scorebook when Nottinghamshire played Hampshire at Trent Bridge in

1993—*Mike c Terry b James*. At first glance it may have appeared the scorers had adopted a rather casual approach by just using the players' first names, but in fact, Greg Mike was caught by Paul Terry off the bowling of Kevan James.

•

In the Lord's Test match of 1965 nearly half the players had a surname beginning with the letter 'B'. For England there was Geoff Boycott, Bob Barber, Ken Barrington and Dave Brown, while for South Africa there was Eddie Barlow, Colin Bland, Ali Bacher, 'Jackie' Botten and H.D. Bromfield.

A few months earlier, Queensland had five 'B' players in the Sheffield Shield match against New South Wales at Brisbane—Peter Burge, Des Bull, Graham Bizzell, John Brown and Don Bichel. In their previous match against Western Australia, players with surnames starting with 'B' occupied places two to five in the batting order—Bull, Bill Buckle, Burge and Bizzell.

•

England's Herbert Sutcliffe named his son William Herbert Hobbs Sutcliffe, after himself and his famous opening partner Jack Hobbs.

•

During the 1970s, three players from Barbados with the same surname made the West Indies Test side as opening batsmen, but none was related. Geoff Greenidge played in five Tests, Alvin Greenidge six Tests and Gordon Greenidge 108. Another Greenidge from Barbados played first-class cricket—Witney Greenidge, an opening fast bowler—who appeared in a few matches for the island in the 1985–86 Shell Shield competition.

•

Over the past 30 years, the West Indies have had the services of three Test wicket-keepers with the surname Murray. All three—Deryck, David and Junior—are unrelated.

UNRELATED AUSTRALIAN TEST CRICKETERS WITH THE SAME SURNAME

Players		Test debut
Alexander	George (Vic)	1880
	Harry (Vic)	1932–33
Allan	Francis (Vic)	1878–79
	Peter (Qld)	1965–66

Cooper	Bransby (Vic)	1876–77
	William (Vic)	1881–82
Darling	Joe* (SA)	1894–95
	Len (Vic)	1932–33
	Rick (SA)	1977–78
Davis	Ian (NSW & Qld)	1973–74
	Simon (Vic)	1985–86
Edwards	Jack (Vic)	1888
	Ross (WA & NSW)	1972
	Wally (WA)	1974–75
Hill	Clem (SA)	1896
	Jack (Vic)	1953
Hughes	Kim (WA)	1977
	Merv (Vic)	1985–86
Johnson	Ian (Vic)	1945–46
	Len (Qld)	1947–48
Jones	Dean (Vic)	1983–84
	Ernie (SA)	1894–95
	Sammy (NSW & Qld)	1881–82
Kelly	James (NSW)	1896
	Thomas (Vic)	1876–77
McDonald	Colin (Vic)	1951–52
	'Ted' (Tas & Vic)	1920–21
Marsh	Geoff (WA)	1985–86
	Rod (WA)	1970–71
Massie	Hugh (NSW)	1881–82
	Bob (WA)	1972
Matthews	Chris (WA & Tas)	1986–87
	Greg (NSW)	1983–84
	Jimmy (Vic)	1911–12
Mayne	Edgar (SA & Vic)	1912
	Laurie (WA)	1964–65
Morris	Arthur (NSW)	1946–47
	Sam (Vic)	1884–85
Phillips	Wayne (SA)	1983–84
	Wayne (Vic)	1991–92
Richardson	Arthur (SA & WA)	1924–25
	Vic (SA)	1924–25
Robinson	Ray (NSW & SA)	1936–37
	Richie (Vic)	1977
Slater	Keith (WA)	1958–59
	Michael (NSW)	1993
Smith	Harry (Vic)	1912
	Steve (NSW)	1983–84
Taylor	John (NSW)	1920–21
	Mark (NSW)	1988–89
	Peter (NSW & Qld)	1986–87
Thomson	'Froggy' (Vic)	1970–71
	Jeff (Qld)	1972–73
	Nat (NSW)	1876–77
Turner	Alan (NSW)	1975
	Charlie (NSW)	1886–87
Walters	Frank (Vic & NSW)	1885–86
	Doug (NSW)	1965–66
Watson	Graeme (Vic, WA & NSW)	1966–67
	William (NSW)	1954–55

*Joe Darling is the great-uncle of Rick Darling

THE ANIMAL KINGDOM

Henry *Badger* (Yorkshire), Michael *Bear* (Essex), 'Dickie' *Bird* (Yorkshire & Leicestershire), Fred *Bull* (Essex & Scotland), Anthony *Catt* (Kent & Western Province), Martin and Jeff *Crowe* (New Zealand), Arthur *Dolphin* (England), Alonzo *Drake* (Yorkshire), Peter *Eele* (Somerset), Henry *Finch* (MCC), William *Fox* (Worcestershire), Aftab *Gul* (Pakistan), William *Hare* (Nottinghamshire), Ted *Herring* (Oxford University), Rodney *Hogg* (Australia), Allan *Lamb* (England), Beverley *Lyon* (Gloucestershire), James *Nightingale* (Surrey), John *Parratt* (Yorkshire), Joe *Partridge* (South Africa), Horace *Peacock* (MCC), Charles and Herbert *Pigg* (Cambridge University), Arthur *Pike* (Nottinghamshire), Reg *Raven* (Northamptonshire), Walter *Robins* (England), Gordon *Salmon* (Leicestershire), Alfred *Seal* (Sussex), Guy *Sparrow* (Derbyshire), Ray *Swallow* (Derbyshire), John *Swan* (Surrey), George *Whale* (Surrey), Louis *Woolf* (Victoria), Tim *Wren* (Kent)

AROUND THE HOME

Jack *Bannister* (Warwickshire), John *Binns* (Yorkshire), Joseph *Dawes* (Yorkshire), Edward *Fawcett* (Cambridge University & Sussex), Alf *Hall* (South Africa), John *Kettle* (New South Wales), Kingsmill *Key* (Surrey), Merv *Kitchen* (Somerset), Bill *Lampe* (New South Wales), Elisha *Light* (Hampshire), Tony *Lock* (England), Charles *Pool* (Northamptonshire), Robert *Porch* (Somerset), John *Shutter* (England), Theodore *Tapp* (London County), 'Tim' *Wall* (Australia), Anthony *Windows* (Gloucestershire & Cambridge University)

AROUND THE WORLD

Granger *Boston* (Cambridge University), Lance *Cairns* (New Zealand), Richard *England* (Oxford University), Bruce *French* (England), Harry *German* (Leicestershire), John *Hampshire* (England), Bob *Holland* (Australia), John *Ireland* (Cambridge University), John *Jordan* (Lancashire), Martin *Kent* (Australia), William *Kingston* (Northamptonshire), Oswawld *Lancashire* (Lancashire), William *Lithgow* (Oxford University), Cecil *Paris* (Hampshire), Fred *Poland* (Cambridge University), Tom *Richmond* (England), Ken *Scotland* (Scotland), Arthur *Somerset* (Sussex & MCC), Peter *Wales* (Sussex), Livern *Wellington* (Jamaica)

THE BODY

William *Back* (Western Australia), Graeme *Beard* (Australia), Daniel *Bottom* (Derbyshire & Nottinghamshire), Brian *Brain* (Worcestershire & Gloucestershire), Henry *Foot* (Victoria), Walter *Hand* (New South Wales), Harold *Hart* (Victoria), Tim *Head* (Sussex), Michael *Heal* (Oxford University), Geoff *Legge* (England), Allen *Limb* (Tasmania), J.G. *Navle* (India), Frank *Rist* (Essex)

•

A SELECTION OF FIRST-CLASS CRICKET'S UNUSUALLY-NAMED PLAYERS

	Teams	Career dates
Archibald Brabazon-Sparrow Acheson	MCC	1864
Threlfall Werge Talbot Baines	Cambridge University, Eastern Province and Transvaal	1930 to 1936–37
Edward William Bastard	Oxford University and Somerset	1882 to 1885
Rab Brougham Bruce-Lockhart	Cambridge University	1937 to 1938
Julius Caesar	Surrey and Lancashire	1849 to 1867
Leonidas De Toledo Marcondes De Montezuma	Sussex and London County	1898 to 1904
Nelson Zwingluis Graves	Philadelphia	1898 to 1908
Theophilus Greatorex	Middlesex and Cambridge University	1883 to 1892
Hophnie Hobah Hines Johnson	Jamaica and West Indies	1934–35 to 1950–51
John Devereaux Dubricious Pember	Leicestershire	1968 to 1971
George Arthur Adam Septimus Carter Trenchard Sale Pennington	Northamptonshire	1927
Albert Ennion Groucott ('Dusty') Rhodes	Derbyshire	1937 to 1954
Chevalier Epifanio Rodriguez	MCC	1900

BON APPETIT

John *Bacon* (Leicestershire), George *Bean* (Nottinghamshire & Sussex), Bob *Berry* (England), 'Harry' *Boyle* (Australia), George *Brann* (Sussex), Chris *Burger* (South Africa), Jimmy *Cook* (South Africa), Cecil *Currie* (Hampshire), William *Dines* (Essex), George *Figg* (Middlesex & Sussex), C.B. *Fry* (England), Richard *Garlick* (Lancashire & Northamptonshire), Stell *Haggas* (Yorkshire & Lancashire), J.P.S. *Jellie* (Gloucestershire), H.J.C. *Mutton* (South Australia), Richard *Nutt* (New South Wales), Tom *Oates* (Nottinghamshire), Martin *Olive* (Somerset), Ron *Oxenham* (Australia), Herbert *Peach* (Surrey), Cec *Pepper* (New South Wales), Lewis *Pickles* (Somerset), Thomas *Plumb* (North & South), Max *Raison* (Essex), George *Raw* (Cambridge University), Clive *Rice* (South Africa), Charles *Veal* (MCC)

CHARACTER TRAITS

Colin *Bland* (South Africa), Roger *Blunt* (New Zealand), Jack *Board* (England), Ray *Bright* (Australia), Graham *Cross* (Leicestershire), Henry *Faithfull* (New South Wales), Leslie *Gay* (England), Bartholomew *Good* (Nottinghamshire), William *Humble* (Derbyshire), Norman *Jolly* (Worcestershire), Fred *Keen* (Argentina), Cyril *Merry* (West Indies), Tom *Moody* (Australia), Ernest *Nice* (Surrey), Monty *Noble* (Australia), Roland *Proud* (Hampshire & Oxford University), John *Savage* (Leicestershire & Lancashire), Wilf *Slack* (England), Gerald *Sly* (Sussex), Chris *Smart* (Queensland), Warwick *Tidy* (Warwickshire), Bill *Whitty* (Australia), John *Wild* (Cambridge University)

CLOTHING

Jesse *Boot* (Derbyshire), Fred *Buckle* (Surrey), Peter *Capes* (Western Australia), *Cardigan* Connor (Hampshire), Jim *Coats* (Queensland), Leonard *Cuff* (Tasmania), Reg *Hankey* (Oxford University & Surrey), John *Hood* (Cambridge University), John *Mitten* (Leicestershire), Dennis *Silk* (Cambridge University & Somerset), Thomas *Tweed* (Cambridge University), John *Tye* (Derbyshire & Nottinghamshire), Shane *Warne* (Australia), Robert *Wiggs* (Cambridge University)

COLOURS

George *Black* (London County & New South Wales), Freddie *Brown* (England), Cecil *Gold* (Middlesex), Evan *Gray* (New Zealand), David *Green* (Lancashire & Gloucestershire), Horace *Hazell* (Somerset), Hubert *Pink* (Derbyshire), John *Reddish* (Nottinghamshire), D.L.S. de *Silva* (Sri Lanka), Jack *White* (England)

CRICKET

Ken *Ball* (Northamptonshire), William and Robert *Bayles* (Tasmania), A.R. *Bhat* (India), Peter *Bowler* (Leicestershire, Derbyshire & Tasmania), John *Bowles* (Gloucestershire & Worcestershire), Bill *Creese* (Hampshire), Cyril *Edge* (Lancashire), Arthur *Fielder* (England), Bill *Game* (Surrey & Oxford University), David *Hookes* (Australia), Bryan *Lobb* (Somerset), William *Over* (Victoria), Bradley *Player* (Orange Free State), Ian *Quick* (Victoria), Reg *Scorer* (Warwickshire), John *Seamer* (Somerset)

DEPARTMENT STORES

Percival *Coles* (Oxford University), *David Jones* (Nottinghamshire), *Grace Brothers*—E.M., G.F. and W.G. (England), Hubert *Myers* (Yorkshire & Tasmania)

LEGAL MATTERS

Richard *Court* (Hampshire), Fred *Crooke* (Lancashire & Gloucestershire), John *Deed* (Kent), Peter *Judge* (Middlesex, Glamorgan & Bengal), Stuart *Law* (Queensland), Joseph *Leese* (Lancashire), Tom *Wills* (Kent & Victoria)

LITERATURE

E.T. *Austen* (Victoria), William *Burns* (Worcestershire), Fred *Dickens* (Warwickshire), William *Hemingway* (Gloucestershire), Geoff *Lawson* (Australia), George *Macauley* (England), Francis *Marlow* (Sussex), Robert *Milne* (Lancashire), Arthur *Milton* (England), *William Shakespeare* (Worcestershire), *George Bernard Shaw* (Glamorgan), Peter *Thackeray* (Oxford University), Steve and Mark *Waugh* (Australia)

THE MILITARY

William *Cannon* (Victoria), George, John and William *Gunn* (England), Paul *Reiffel* (Australia), Craig *Serjeant* (Australia), Thomas *Shooter* (Nottinghamshire), John *Warr* (England)

MONEY MATTERS

Albert *Banks* (Western Australia), Kildare *Borrowes* (Middlesex), Miran *Bux* (Pakistan), Izak *Buys* (South Africa), Thomas *Coyne* (Western Australia), Herbert *Gamble* (Victoria & Queensland), 'Jackie' *Grant* (West Indies), Walter *Money* (Cambridge University), Tom *Penny* (Oxford University), John *Price* (England), Stanley *Proffitt* (Essex), Richard *Purchase* (Hampshire), Norman *Riches* (Glamorgan & Wales), Richard *Sale* (Warwickshire & Derbyshire), Hugh *Sells* (RAF), Arthur *Tanner* (Middlesex)

MOTOR VEHICLES

R.M. *Bentley* (Natal), Michael and Tony *Buss* (Sussex), Arthur *Carr* (England), Michael *Falcon* (Cambridge University), Percy *Fender* (England), Francis *Ford* (England), Cecil *Holden* (Lancashire), Phil *Horne* (New Zealand), Maurice *Leyland* (England), Ross *Morgan* (New Zealand), Arthur *Morris* (Australia), Jim *Valiant* (Essex), Denis *Vann* (Northamptonshire)

OCCUPATIONS

Glen *Baker* (Queensland), Bob *Barber* (England), Tom *Brewer* (London County), Basil *Butcher* (West Indies), Harold *Butler* (England), David *Carpenter* (Gloucestershire), Tom *Caterer* (South Australia), Bernard *Constable* (Surrey), Nari *Contractor* (India), Arthur *Dorman* (Cambridge University), Bill *Draper* (Kent), Jeremiah *Driver* (Yorkshire), Farokh *Engineer* (India), John *Farmer* (Oxford University), Jack *Gardiner* (Tasmania), Ghulam *Guard* (India), Frank *Hawker* (Essex), Malcolm *Marshall* (West Indies), Vijay *Merchant* (India), Keith *Miller* (Australia), Seymour *Nurse* (West Indies), John *Painter* (Gloucestershire), Peter *Plummer* (Nottinghamshire), Graeme *Porter* (Western Australia), Jack *Potter* (Victoria), George *Shoesmith* (Sussex), Michael *Slater* (Australia), Mark *Taylor* (Australia), Jehangir *Warden* (Parsis), Fred *Weaver* (Gloucestershire)

PLANT LIFE

Edward *Ash* (Cambridge University), Albert *Birch* (Kent), John *Cotton* (Nottinghamshire & Leicestershire), Richard *Elms* (Kent & Hampshire), Andy and Grant *Flower* (Zimbabwe), Arthur *Grass* (South Americans), Bernard *Hedges* (Glamorgan), Alfred *Ivey* (Oxford University), Mark *Lavender* (Western Australia), Jim *Leaf* (Army), Dennis *Lillee* (Australia), Jeff *Moss* (Australia), Archibald *Palm* (South Africa), Brian *Rose* (England), Frank *Thorn* (Victoria), Joseph *Vine* (England), Arthur *Wheat* (Nottinghamshire)

PRIME MINISTERS AND PRESIDENTS

Victor *Barton* (England), P.J. *Botha* (Border), James *Bush* (Gloucestershire), Dave *Callaghan* (Eastern Province), William *Churchill* (MCC), Grahame *Clinton* (Kent & Surrey), Pearce *Curtin* (Western Australia), Horace *Fisher* (Yorkshire), Angus *Fraser* (England), Francis *Gough* (Queensland), Neil *Hawke* (Australia), George *Edward Heath* (Hampshire), John *Holt* (West Indies), Kim

Hughes (Australia), Ian *Johnson* (Australia), James *Keating* (Victoria), *John Kennedy* (Warwickshire), 'J.J.' *Lyons* (Australia), *John McEwan* (Middlesex), *William McMahon* (Dublin University), *John Major* (Sussex), *Robert Menzies* (Canterbury & Wellington), Aziz *Mubarak* (Cambridge University), George *Nixon* (Middlesex & Cambridge University), Bruce *Reid* (Australia), Jonty *Rhodes* (South Africa), Allen *Thatcher* (New South Wales), L.P. *Vorster* (Transvaal B), John *Watson* (Somerset)

THE PUB

Douglas *Barr* (Scotland), Hector *Beers* (Northamptonshire), Frank *Belcher* (Gloucestershire), Dominic *Cork* (Derbyshire), John *Inns* (Essex), Alexander *Penfold* (Madras & Surrey), Ken *Sellar* (Sussex), Garry *Sobers* (West Indies), Peter *Toohey* (Australia)

RELIGION

Alan *Abbott* (Leicestershire), Ian *Bishop* (West Indies), Herbert *Chaplin* (Sussex), Greg, Ian and Trevor *Chappell* (Australia), Charles *Christ* (Queensland), Arthur *Christian* (Victoria & Western Australia), L. *Church* (D.R. Jardine's XI), Gordon *Lord* (Warwickshire & Worcestershire), Clifford *Monks* (Gloucestershire), John *Nunn* (Oxford University & Middlesex), Ray *Heaven* (Essex), John *Pentecost* (Kent), Roland *Pope* (Australia), Mark *Priest* (New Zealand), Wayne *Prior* (South Australia), Norman *Saint* (Essex)

SEX

William *Batchelor* (Cambridgeshire), Michael *Bissex* (Gloucestershire), David *Cock* (Essex), Gosnel *Cupid* (Windward Islands), 'Art' *Dick* (New Zealand), Des *Hoare* (Australia), 'Hal' *Hooker* (New South Wales), Ken *Fiddling* (Yorkshire & Northamptonshire), 'Hammy' *Love* (Australia), Raymond *Moan* (Ireland), Fred *Root* (England), Charles and George *Studd* (England), Roy *Virgin* (Northamptonshire, Somerset & Western Province), Peter *Willey* (England)

SHAPES AND SIZES

George *Bigg* (Lancashire), Chris *Broad* (England), Charles *Little* (Kent & Oxford University), Arnold *Long* (Surrey & Sussex), John *Lowe* (Oxford University & Warwickshire), James *Round* (Oxford University), Arthur *Short* (Eastern Province & Natal), Gladstone *Small* (England), John *Trim* (West Indies)

SHOWBIZ

Thomas *Bowie* (Scotland), *Michael Crawford* (Yorkshire), Richard *Elviss* (Oxford University), Edward *Gunston* (Victoria), *George Harrison* (Yorkshire), Tom *Hepburn* (Victoria), Samuel *Jagger* (Worcestershire, Sussex & Wales), *Paul Newman* (Derbyshire), *Eric Sykes* (Derbyshire), Walter *Vizard* (Gloucestershire)

THE WEATHER

Phil *Blizzard* (New South Wales & Tasmania), John *Dew* (Sussex), Jim *Fairweather* (Kent), Albert *Frost* (Tasmania), Robert *Gale* (Middlesex), Harold *Hale* (Gloucestershire & Tasmania), Colin Mc*Cool* (Australia), Billy *Midwinter* (Australia & England), Charles *Showers* (MCC), John *Snow* (England), William *Spring* (Surrey), Francis *Summers* (Worcestershire), Arthur *Winter* (Middlesex)

20 Bowling to Forget

In the second unofficial Test match at Cape Town in 1986–87, Australia used only four bowlers in the South Africans' first innings total of 493, and they each conceded over 100 runs—Rod McCurdy 3–133, Trevor Hohns 2–116, John Maguire 4–116 and Carl Rackemann 0–133. When South Africa made 533 in the fourth match at Port Elizabeth, again only four bowlers were employed, three of them conceding a century of runs with the other not far behind—Rod McCurdy 2–159, Terry Alderman 1–142, Trevor Hohns 2–109 and Rodney Hogg 5–97. The two South African totals are amongst the highest in all first-class cricket in which so few bowlers were used.

•

Malcolm Nash, a left-arm medium pacer, made the record books in 1968 when Garry Sobers belted him for 36 runs off a six-ball over at Swansea; the first time this had happened in first-class cricket. Nine seasons later it was almost a case of déjà vu when the Lancashire batsman Frank Hayes threatened to emulate Sobers' feat, hitting Nash for 34 runs (6,4,6,6,6,6) in a County Championship match, also at Swansea, in 1977.

•

During a Shell Trophy match at Christchurch in 1989–90, Wellington's Robert Vance was hit for the greatest number of runs off a single over in first-class cricket. Acting on the instructions of his captain Erwin McSweeney, Vance dished up a succession of full tosses to the Canterbury batsmen in the hope of narrowing the run gap and getting the last couple of wickets cheaply to win the match. The penultimate over was 22 deliveries long, included 17 no-balls, and conceded 77 runs (1,4,4,4,6,6,4,6,1,4,1,1,6,6,6,6, 6,0,0,4,0,1). Lee Germon, on his way to 160 not out, helped himself to 69 of the runs, while Roger Ford at the other end got just six. At the end of the match, with the scores level, it transpired that the over in question contained only five legitimate deliveries. Had the other ball been bowled Canterbury could well have taken the match.

•

Of the three Australian bowlers who made their Test debuts during the 1972–73 series against Pakistan, two of them failed to take a single wicket. Jeff Thomson received the call-up for the second Test at Melbourne and returned figures of 0 for 100 and 0 for 10, although it was later revealed he'd bowled with a broken foot bone. The next Test at Sydney, for which Thomson was not

considered, saw the debut of John Watkins, a right-arm leg-break bowler who sent down six extremely wayward and wicketless overs for 21 in his only appearance in top cricket.

•

A Victorian bowler by the name of Franklyn Pitcher had one of the worst starts to a cricketing career, being no-balled for throwing his first three balls in first-class cricket. Pitcher, in his only first-class match, against South Africa at Melbourne in 1910–11, was no-balled for throwing a total of five times.

•

Jack Marsh, the quick but questionable Aboriginal fast bowler from New South Wales, was no-balled 19 times for throwing by the same umpire during the course of two consecutive first-class matches against Victoria in 1900–01. In the first encounter at Melbourne, Bob Crockett no-balled Marsh twice in the second innings and a record 17 times in the return match a month later at Sydney. Crockett was the only umpire to call Marsh for throwing in his six-match first-class career. Another Aboriginal fast bowler consistently no-balled in a first-class match was Queensland's Eddie Gilbert. He was called 13 times in his three overs in the match against Victoria at the MCG in 1931–32. Marsh and Gilbert are amongst just three bowlers in Australian first-class cricket known to have been no-balled more than 10 times in a single first-class match.

•

Although John Warr took close to 1,000 wickets in first-class cricket, the Middlesex fast bowler was a big flop at Test level. On his Test debut at Sydney in 1950–51 he took 0 for 142, and 0 for 63 & 1 for 76 at Adelaide. And he was extremely lucky to gain his one and only Test scalp when Ian Johnson, given not out by the umpire, walked, knowing he'd snicked the ball through to the wicket-keeper Godfrey Evans.

Warr finished his two-match Test career with the unflattering average of 281.00. Others with an average of over 200 include Sri Lanka's Roger Wijesuriya (294.00), Mike Atherton (282.00), Sunil Gavaskar (206.00) and Nirode Chowdhury (205.00).

•

When Australia tallied a record 6 declared for 607 against New Zealand at Brisbane in 1993–94, five of the Kiwis' frontline bowlers conceded over 100 runs for only the second time in Test history. The first occasion was also against Australia, when five West Indians went for a century of runs in a total of 8 declared for 758 in the fifth Test at Kingston in 1954–55. The record-makers at Brisbane were Danny Morrison with 0 for 104, Chris Cairns 1 for 128, Simon Doull 2 for 105, Richard De Groen 1 for 120 and Dipak Patel 1 for 125. In the previous Test innings at Hobart, three of the New Zealand bowlers also conceded 100 runs with another missing out by the narrowest of margins—Morrison 1 for 125, Murphy Su'a 1 for 102, De Groen 2 for 113, with Doull taking 1 for 99. During the three-match series the Kiwis accounted for just 22 wickets and none of their bowlers came away with an average under 50. Morrison, who had next to no luck at all with several dropped catches, took three wickets in the three Tests at 140.67.

Two months later the hapless New Zealanders again had their bowling plundered, with Pakistan scoring 5 declared for 548 in the second Test at Wellington. Three of the four bowlers conceded more than 100 runs in the innings, the same who made the record books in Brisbane—Morrison 2–139, De Groen 0–104 and Doull 0–112.

21 At the Helm

When Wasim Akram was named as captain and senior batsman Javed Miandad was dropped for the Pakistan tour of New Zealand in 1993-94, 10 players refused to go unless both decisions were reversed. The uprising was led by vice-captain Waqar Younis who claimed Wasim lacked the ability to effectively lead the side, saying the team was 'feeling uneasy under his captaincy'. In a bid to defuse the crisis, Wasim was dumped as captain with Salim Malik taking over, although the original decision to drop Javed and two other players—Ramiz Raja and Aaqib Javed—remained.

Ironically, Javed Miandad faced a similar revolt himself in 1982, when all of the Pakistan Test side refused to serve under his leadership and demanded a new captain be appointed for the forthcoming tour of England. Although two withdrew their opposition, the others made themselves unavailable for the first two Tests of the series against Sri Lanka.

•

Queensland had the services of different official captains in five successive seasons between 1988 and 1993—Allan Border 1988-89, Greg Ritchie 1989-90, Trevor Hohns 1990-91, Carl Rackemann 1991-92 and Ian Healy 1992-93. Dirk Wellham found himself recalled for the Maroons in 1992-93 as stand-in captain while Healy was away on Test duty, while Stuart Law was chosen as Healy's temporary replacement the following season.

•

C. Aubrey Smith, who later found fame in Hollywood, uniquely captained England in his only Test match. It coincided with South Africa's introduction to the big league at Port Elizabeth in 1888-89; they were defeated by eight wickets, Smith taking 5 for 19 and 2 for 42.

•

During the West Indies-England Test match at Kingston in 1934-35, both captains were forced to retire through injury. England's Bob Wyatt's jaw was fractured by a short-pitched ball from 'Manny' Martindale, while 'Jackie' Grant suffered an ankle injury.

•

The opposing captains in the Australia-South Africa Test at Sydney in 1993-94 came out second best, with both undergoing hospital treatment on the second day of the match—Allan Border needed four stitches to an eye after

being struck by a ball while batting; Kepler Wessels broke a finger fielding in the slips. It was an injury that, coupled with a damaged knee, forced Wessels to return home. Earlier in the summer the other international captain touring Australia, New Zealand's Martin Crowe, also returned home for surgery on a troublesome knee and, like Wessels, missed the rest of the Australian season.

Hansie Cronje, who took over from Wessels as captain, was only 24 years of age and the youngest member of the side. His elevation to the position made him South Africa's youngest Test captain since the 22-year-old Murray Bissett in 1898-99.

Hansie Cronje captained Orange Free State at 21 and South Africa at 24

•

During a run of three consecutive matches in 1980, Worcestershire had three different captains in three days in three competitions. On 27 June Worcestershire, playing Essex in a Benson & Hedges Cup match, was captained by Norman Gifford. The following day they were up against Northamptonshire in a County Championship match, led this time by Glenn Turner. After one day's play of that game, Worcestershire then took on Northants in the John Player League with Ted Hemsley as skipper. They lost all three matches.

•

Waqar Younis, who took 13 wickets in his first Test as Pakistan captain

When Pakistan and Zimbabwe confronted each other for the first time at Test level both captains—Waqar Younis and Andy Flower—were leading their country for the first time. The scene was Karachi in 1993-94, and for Pakistan the 'Burewala Bombshell' bowled his side to victory capturing a record 13 wickets, the best bowling performance by a captain in Test history. Taking over from his injured partner Wasim Akram, Waqar took 7 for 91 and 6 for 44, all but one of his wickets bowled or lbw.

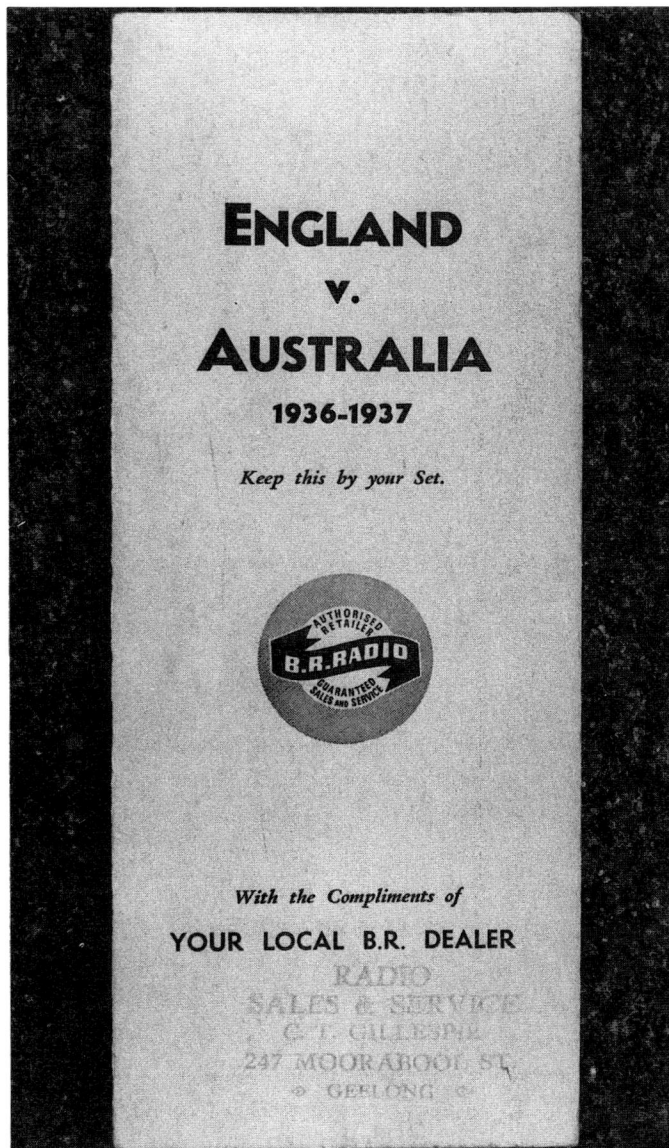

ENGLAND
v.
AUSTRALIA
1936-1937

Keep this by your Set.

With the Compliments of
YOUR LOCAL B.R. DEALER

In his first series as Australia's captain, against England in 1936-37, Don Bradman made history by becoming the only skipper to win a rubber after being two Tests down

•

MOST WICKETS BY A CAPTAIN IN A TEST MATCH

Captain	Wickets	Match
Waqar Younis	13–135 (7–91 & 6–44)	Pakistan v Zimbabwe at Karachi in 1993–94
Fazal Mahmood	12–100 (6–34 & 6–66)	Pakistan v West Indies at Dacca in 1958–59
Imran Khan	11–79 (3–19 & 8–60)	Pakistan v India at Karachi in 1982–83
Arthur Gilligan	11–90 (6–7 & 5–83)	England v South Africa at Birmingham in 1924
Allan Border	11–96 (7–46 & 4–50)	Australia v West Indies at Sydney in 1988–89
Imran Khan	11–121 (7–80 & 4–41)	Pakistan v West Indies at Georgetown in 1987–88
Intikhab Alam	11–130 (7–52 & 4–78)	Pakistan v New Zealand at Dunedin in 1972–73
'Buster' Nupen	11–150 (5–63 & 6–87)	South Africa v England at Johannesburg in 1930–31
Imran Khan*	11–180 (6–98 & 5–82)	Pakistan v India at Faisalabad in 1982–83
Imran Khan	10–77 (3–37 & 7–40)	Pakistan v England at Leeds in 1987
'Gubby' Allen	10–78 (5–35 & 5–43)	England v India at Lord's in 1936
Kapil Dev	10–135 (1–52 & 9–83)	India v West Indies at Ahmedabad in 1983–84
Intikhab Alam	10–182 (5–91 & 5–91)	Pakistan v New Zealand at Dacca in 1969–70
Bishen Bedi	10–194 (5–89 & 5–105)	India v Australia at Perth in 1977–78

*Imran Khan also scored a century (117), a unique all-round performance by a captain in a Test match

Although Don Bradman lost his first two Tests as captain, against England in 1936–37, he made history by bouncing back to win the series 3–2. Australia's captain on 24 occasions, Bradman was unbeaten in 21 of his last 22 Tests. He is also one of the few players who improved his batting record with the added responsibility of captaincy, and the only captain to finish his career with a batting average in excess of 100.

DON BRADMAN'S BATTING RECORD AS CAPTAIN/PLAYER							
	T	*I*	*NO*	*Runs*	*100s*	*HS*	*Avge*
Tests as captain	24	38	7	3147	14	270	101.51
Tests as player only	28	42	3	3849	15	334	98.69
Total	52	80	10	6996	29	334	99.94

•

Australia's Warwick Armstrong is the only player to win 10 or more Test caps as captain and never lose a match. In 10 Tests as captain, Armstrong won eight and secured two draws. All were against England in 1920–21 and 1921.

•

In consecutive Test matches in 1993, England was led by one of its oldest captains and then by one of its youngest. On the last day of the fourth Test against Australia at Leeds, England's captain Graham Gooch was 40 years and 3 days old. After stepping down, Gooch was replaced by Mike Atherton, at 25 years and 135 days, England's seventh-youngest captain and the youngest to lead an Ashes Test at home.

•

During the second round of the 1993 NatWest Bank Trophy in England, all eight captains chose to bat after winning the toss and in each match the side batting second won.

Brian Close, who skippered Yorkshire and Somerset, is one of the most successful captains in Test history, winning six matches out of seven. After he replaced Colin Cowdrey in 1966, England defeated the West Indies by an innings in his first Test at captain, and then secured five wins and a draw in the six Tests against India and Pakistan the following summer. For Close it was an awe-inspiring year, but one that eventually ended in huge disappointment. In a County Championship match against Warwickshire, prior to the last Test, it was alleged he indulged in deliberate time-wasting to deny his opposition the chance of victory—only two overs were bowled in the last 15 minutes. His strategy incurred the wrath of the selectors who were meeting to choose the captain for the forthcoming tour of the West Indies. Close, despite his huge win ratio, was replaced by Cowdrey. The final Test of the 1967 summer was his last until he was recalled 154 Tests later in 1976.

•

When Test cricket's longest-serving captain Allan Border scored 105 against New Zealand in 1993–94, it was his 15th century when in charge of Australia. With Don Bradman and Clive Lloyd both scoring 14 hundreds when captain, Border established a new Test record.

•

Herbert Wade appeared in 10 Test matches for South Africa, all as captain. Although he claimed victory only once, it was a memorable occasion, with the South Africans triumphing at Lord's in 1935, the first time they'd won in England.

•

When Somerset's captain Brian Rose was recalled to play against the West Indies in 1980 he had to serve under the leadership of his county vice-captain Ian Botham.

22 R.I.P.

Although Karachi won the 1958–59 Qaid-e-Azam Trophy, the victory was soured by the death of one of their players. Karachi's wicket-keeper Abdul Aziz collapsed while batting, after being hit in the chest by a delivery from Combined Services bowler Dildwar Awan. Abdul died before he reached hospital.

1958–59 Qaid-e-Azam Final—Karachi v Services

| First innings— | Abdul Aziz | retired hurt | 0 |
| Second innings— | Abdul Aziz | did not bat—dead | 0 |

●

Simon Kerr, a Rhodesian batsman who hit five unbeaten centuries in six innings for St Georges College in Salisbury in 1972, was stabbed to death in a thrill-killing at a party in Bristol two years later. Kerr had been recommended to the Gloucestershire County Cricket Club by Mike Procter, and was a member of the second XI squad at the time of his death.

●

One of the oddest obituaries to appear in *Wisden* can be found in the 1965 edition—an entry in memory of one of the best-known spectators at Lord's. Peter, a cat, lived at the ground for 12 years and was often seen on the ground during matches. On the passing of Peter, a senior MCC official said 'he was a cat of great character and loved publicity'. The Oval, too, had a famous feline and although Lucy, a resident at the ground for 15 years, did not make *Wisden*, her obituary did appear in a 1992 edition of the *Wisden Cricket Monthly* magazine.

●

Ian Folley, who was close to England Test selection in the late 1980s, lost his life in 1993 after being hit in the eye while batting in a Lancashire League match. The 30-year-old former County bowler, representing Whitehaven against Workington, missed an attempted hook, was hospitalised for treatment, but later died under anaesthetic.

●

One of New Zealand's most gruesome multiple murders involved a former first-class cricketer in 1965. Bill Frame, who had represented Otago in the late 1950s, murdered his girlfriend and both her parents in their home, and then turned the gun on himself. He was 32.

●

Don Bradman—erroneously reported dead by a Queensland newspaper in 1931

'DON BRADMAN DEAD'

Australia today mourns the loss of the greatest batsman the world has ever seen. During the progress of the Test match in Brisbane (Australia v South Africa) Don Bradman was attacked with dysentery, to which he succumbed on Saturday.

—Cooktown Independent

New South Wales batsman Claude Tozer was murdered in 1920 by his girlfriend after telling her that he wanted to end their affair. In a jealous rage she shot him in the head and chest and then turned the gun on herself. In his last first-class match, Tozer scored 51 and 53 for an Australian XI against the MCC at Brisbane, and just before his death had been nominated for the New South Wales captaincy.

•

TEST CRICKETERS KNOWN TO HAVE COMMITTED SUICIDE

Player	How died	Age	Date of death
William Scotton (E)	Cut his throat	37	9.7.1893
Arthur Shrewsbury (E)	Shot himself	46	19.5.1903
Vincent Tancred (SA)	Shot himself	29	3.6.1904
Albert Trott (A & E)	Shot himself	41	30.7.1914
Andrew Stoddart (E)	Shot himself	52	4.4.1915
'Billy' Zulch (SA)	Cut his throat	38	19.5.1924
William Bruce (A)	Drowned himself	61	3.8.1925
Aubrey Faulkner (SA)	Gassed himself	49	10.9.1930
Noel Harford (NZ)	Carbon monoxide poisoning	50	30.5.1936
Albert Relf (E)	Shot himself	62	26.3.1937
Norman Reid (SA)	Shot himself	56	10.6.1947
'Fen' Creswell (NZ)	Shot himself	50	10.6.1966
Jack Iverson (A)	Shot himself	58	24.10.1973
Sid Barnes (A)	Drug overdose	57	16.12.1973
Harold Gimblett (E)	Drug overdose	63	30.3.1978
Jim Burke (A)	Shot himself	47	2.2.1979
Glen Hall (SA)	Shot himself	49	26.6.1987
Joe Partridge (SA)	Shot himself	55	7.6.1988

Herbert Jenner-Fust, who played in a single first-class match for Gloucestershire in 1875, lived to the age of 99. His father, of the same name, played for Cambridge and Kent and lived to 98.

CRICKET'S FIRST-CLASS CENTURIONS

Player	Age and year of death	Team and career dates
Rupert de Smidt	102y & 252d—1986	Western Province—1912-13
Ted English	102y & 250d—1966	Hampshire—1898 to 1901
John Wheatley	102y & 102d—1962	Canterbury—1882-83 to 1903-04
Dinkar Deodhar	101y & 223d—1993	Maharashtra—1911-12 to 1947-48
George Harman	101y & 191d—1975	Dublin University—1895

•

Tom Burge, who managed the first Australian team to tour the West Indies in 1954–55, died two years later of a heart attack, while listening to the radio commentary of a cricket match in which his son Peter was batting. Appearing for R.N. Harvey's XI in a match against R.R. Lindwall's XI in Sydney, Burge immediately retired with his score on 43 on hearing the news of his father's death.

•

A.T. Paunce, who worked as a police magistrate in the New South Wales city of Queanbeyan, was the first player to die while playing in a cricket match in Australia. He collapsed and died fielding in a match for Married against Single in Sydney in 1837.

23 With Bat and Ball

Bill Roller, who represented Surrey, is the only player in first-class cricket to have scored a double-century and taken a hat-trick in the same match. His once-in-a-lifetime double came in 1885 in the match against Sussex at The Oval when he made 204 with the bat and took 4 for 28, including the hat-trick, and 2 for 21.

The feat of a hundred and a hat-trick has been achieved 10 times in first-class cricket, the last two occasions by the former South African all-rounder Mike Procter. He first did it in 1972 for Gloucestershire against Essex at Westcliff-on-Sea (102 & 5–30) and repeated the feat in 1979 against Leicestershire at Bristol (122 & 7–26). His acquisition of the double twice is unique in first-class cricket.

•

Ray Bright, Mike Whitney and Murray Bennett are among the few Australian Test cricketers to bowl left-arm and bat right-handed. Included in the short list of those who are left-hand batsmen and right-arm bowlers are Greg Matthews, Trevor Hohns and Peter Taylor.

•

During an Australian tour of New Zealand in 1949–50, Alan Davidson, who later became the first player to score a hundred runs and take 10 wickets in a Test match, served notice of what was to come in a match against Wairarapa. With the bat, Davidson hit an unbeaten 157 and with the ball took 10 for 29 in an innings. Only two players—V.E. Walker and W.G. Grace—have performed this extraordinary feat in first-class cricket.

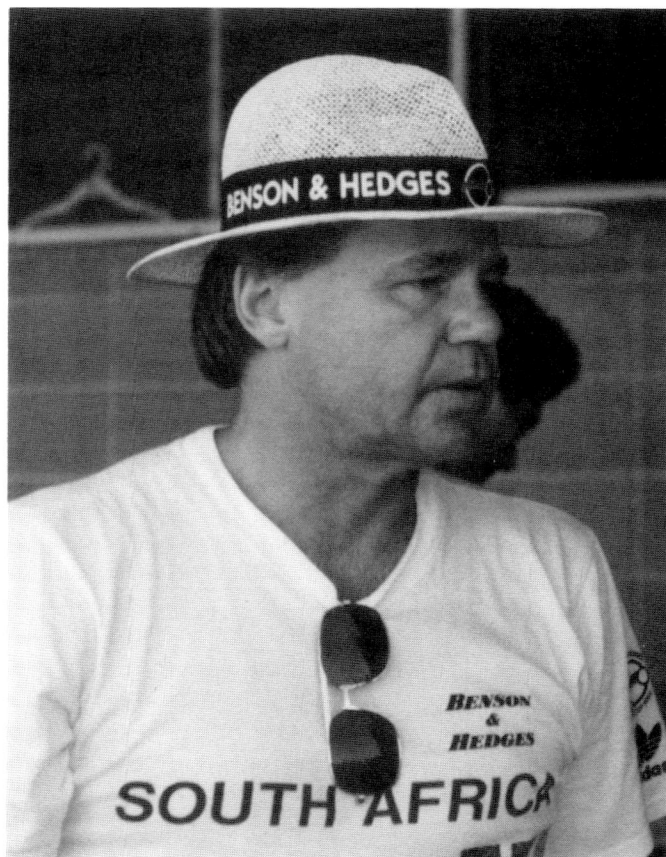

The South African all-rounder Mike Procter who scored a hundred and took a hat-trick in the same first-class match twice in his career

•

A CENTURY AND 10 WICKETS IN AN INNINGS IN A FIRST-CLASS MATCH		
Player	*Match details*	*Match*
V.E. Walker	108 & 10–74	England v Surrey at The Oval in 1859
W.G. Grace	104 & 10–49	MCC v Oxford University at Oxford in 1886

RECORDED INSTANCES OF TEST PLAYERS SCORING A CENTURY AND TAKING 10 WICKETS IN AN INNINGS IN ANY MATCH		
E.M. Grace (E)	119* & 10–?	Lansdown v Clifton at Bristol in 1861
	192* & 10–69	MCC v Gentlemen of Kent at Canterbury in 1862 (12-a-side match)
	131 & 10–?	Thornbury v Clifton at Alveston in 1881
W.G. Grace (E)	104 & 10–49	MCC v Oxford University at Oxford in 1886
George Giffen (A)	172* & 10–149	Norwood v Adelaide at Adelaide in 1892–93
Gilbert Jessop (A)	184* & 10–14	Beccles College v Norfolk Asylum at Thorpe in 1895
Jimmy Sinclair (SA)	157* & 10–103	Johannesburg v Stray Klips at Johannesburg in 1895–96
Bert Vogler (SA)	100 & 10–41	Woodbrook Club v Galway at Bray in 1909
Aubrey Faulkner (SA)	100* & 10–?	Hythe v Small Arms School at Hythe in 1921
'Gubby' Allen (E)	101 & 10–25	Cambridge Quidnuncs v Royal Artillery at Woolwich in 1925
Alan Davidson (A)	157* & 10–29	Australians v Wairarapa at Masterton in 1949–50
Graeme Pollock (SA)	117* & 10–25	Grey High School v Union High School at Graaf-Reinet in 1952–53

WITH BAT AND BALL

Steve Waugh set a unique record in 1993–94 when in consecutive Test series against the same opposition he topped both the batting and bowling averages. Against South Africa at home he scored 165 runs at 82.50 and took four wickets at 7.50. In the return series away he made 195 runs at 65.00 and claimed 10 wickets at 13.00. Before him, only Pakistan's Mushtaq Mohammad had performed a similar feat, topping both the batting and bowling averages against New Zealand and then England in 1972–73.

•

Steve Waugh only managed two wickets in the six-match Test series against England in 1993—openers Graham Gooch and Mike Atherton in the first innings of the last Test at The Oval. The first of those wickets gained him admission to a select group of Australian all-rounders who've scored 2,000 runs and taken 50 wickets in Test matches. With over 3,000 runs to his name, Waugh is only the fifth Australian, after Warwick Armstrong, Keith Miller, Richie Benaud and Bob Simpson, to have achieved the Test double.

•

On four occasions during his career, England's greatest modern all-rounder Ian Botham finished a Test series as the highest run-scorer and wicket-taker. He first performed the feat against New Zealand in 1977–78 and did it twice in consecutive Test series against Australia in the early eighties.

Series	T	R	HS	Avge	W	BB	Avge
New Zealand 1977–78	3	212	103	53.00	17	5–73	18.29
Pakistan 1978	3	212	108	70.66	13	8–34	16.07
Australia 1979–80	3	187	119*	37.40	19	6–78	19.52
Australia 1981	6	399	149*	36.27	34	6–95	20.58

•

In consecutive matches against Victoria, South Australian captain George Giffen twice recorded the exceptional feat of a double-century and 10 wickets. At Melbourne in 1890–91 he scored more runs and took more wickets than all of his team-mates put together, with 237 and 12 for 192. In their return match the following season at Adelaide he put in an even stronger performance, the greatest of all time in first-class cricket. With the bat he scored a career-best 271 and then took 16 wickets—9 for 69 in the first innings, 7 for 70 in the second.

Giffen scored a hundred runs and claimed 10 wickets in a match on seven other occasions in a career that boasted more than 10,000 runs and 1,000 wickets—a unique record in Australian first-class cricket.

'Hal' Hooker had a history-making time with both bat and ball in the course of successive first-class matches for New South Wales in 1928–29. Batting at No. 11 on Christmas Day in a Sheffield Shield match at the MCG he scored 62 in a world-record last-wicket stand of 307 with Alan Kippax (260*). In his next match, also against Victoria, he then produced some magic with the ball, taking four wickets with consecutive deliveries, the first time such a feat had been achieved in the Sheffield Shield.

•

Kim Hughes

On his first-class debut for Nottinghamshire in 1946, Fred Stocks hit 114 against Kent at Trent Bridge. In a match later that year, against Lancashire at Manchester, he took a wicket with his first ball in first-class cricket, at the time a unique double. Kim Hughes, in 1977–78, matched his feat when he too took a wicket with his first ball, against Guyana at Georgetown, having scored a hundred on his first-class debut for Western Australia in 1975–76.

•

AUSTRALIANS WITH 5,000 RUNS AND 500 WICKETS IN FIRST-CLASS CRICKET							
Player	Career dates	Runs	HS	Avge	Wkts	BB	Avge
Warwick Armstrong	1898–99/1921–22	16,158	303*	46.83	832	8–47	19.72
Richie Benaud	1948–49/1963–64	10,668	187	35.68	891	7–18	24.57
Alan Davidson	1949–50/1962–63	6,804	129	32.87	672	7–31	20.90
George Giffen	1877–78/1903–04	11,757	271	29.61	1,022	10–66	21.31
Jack Gregory	1918–19/1928–29	5,661	152	36.52	504	9–32	20.99
Monty Noble	1893–94/1919–20	13,975	284	40.74	625	8–48	23.11
Hugh Trumble	1887–88/1903–04	5,395	107	19.48	929	9–39	18.44

Eric Barbour, who played for New South Wales, was one of the most outstanding schoolboy cricketers of his time, recording the double in four consecutive seasons for Sydney Grammar. In 1906–07, at the age of 15, he scored 1,726 runs at 53.94 and took 142 wickets at 12.00. Barbour set a school batting record two seasons later, accumulating 2,146 runs, coupled with another haul of 142 wickets. In 1923–24 he set another record, in the Newcastle first-grade competition, scoring 1,154 runs, average 88.20 and taking 111 wickets at 9.90, the first such recorded double at this level.

•

Australia's Jack Gregory began his Test career in exemplary fashion in 1920–21, becoming the only player to score 400 runs and take 20 wickets and 15 catches in his first Test series. In five matches against England he aggregated 442 runs at 73.66, with a highest knock of 100 in the second Test at Melbourne, and put together scores of 78 not out, 77, 76 not out and 93 in his last four innings. In the same match that he scored his century, he also took 7 for 69 in England's first innings, the best return by a fast bowler in the series.

400 RUNS AND 20 WICKETS IN A TEST SERIES

Player	T	R	W	Series
George Giffen	5	475	34	Australia v England 1894–95
Aubrey Faulkner	5	545	29	South Africa v England 1909–10
Jack Gregory	5	442	23	Australia v England 1920–21
Keith Miller	5	439	20	Australia v West Indies 1954–55
Garry Sobers	5	424	23	West Indies v India 1961–62
	5	722	20	West Indies v England 1966
Tony Greig	5	430	24	England v West Indies 1973–74

Mike Whitney

During the 1992–93 season, New South Wales bowler Mike Whitney passed two diverse cricketing milestones—400 first-class wickets *and* 400 first-class runs.

24 Extra Extras

In a McDonald's Cup match in 1987–88, South Australia faced a cold reception from the Tasmanian bowling pair of Phil Blizzard and Allister de Winter. The two were the only successful Tasmanian bowlers in the match, with Glenn Bishop caught by Blizzard off de Winter.

•

In 1992 Richard Hadlee had, of all things, a pea named after him. The Hadlee Pea is a variety of the Blue Prussian Pea. Other Test cricketers to be so unusually honoured include Garry Sobers who had a variety of the heliconia plant named after him, Don Bradman, a dahlia, Greg Chappell, a rose and Don Tallon, a strain of barley.

•

South Australia's total of 554 at the Gabba in 1991–92 included a whopping 78 extras. Although there were 'only' 22 no-balls bowled by Queensland, eight were scored off, and under Australian Cricket Board rules, were added to the no-balls total and then doubled to make 60. Under regular playing conditions the number of extras would have been 40. Warwickshire's record total of 4 declared for 810 against Durham at Edgbaston in 1994 also included 78 extras.

•

The Maldives, an island group in the Indian Ocean, and a region not noted for its cricket, issued a cricket stamp in 1990 that featured, of all things, the Walt Disney character Mickey Mouse wielding a bat.

Cricketer Montague Druitt, who supposedly committed suicide by drowning in 1888, was considered by some, including the police, to be Jack the Ripper. When news of his death came to light, the police hunt for the murderer in London's East End was scaled down.

•

David Boon is so famous in his home-state of Tasmania that a specially commissioned car numberplate was produced in 1993 to coincide with the Hobart Test match against New Zealand in which he scored a century. The numberplate included his name, his picture and the number 100.

•

During the 1970s there were 82 official one-day internationals. In the 1980s there were 516. After the inaugural one-dayer, at Melbourne in 1970–71, 10 years went by before the 100th was played, but it took only three more years for the 200th.

•

Australian Test player Arthur Coningham represented both New South Wales and Queensland in first-class matches in 1893–94. Two years later, Coningham returned to the New South Wales colours, again representing both states in the same season. More recently, two South Australian players—Joe Scuderi and Paul Nobes—played for two states in the same summer. Scuderi appeared in two limited-overs matches for Queensland and nine first-class matches for South Australia in 1988–89, while Nobes played in two one-day matches for the Croweaters and seven first-class fixtures for Victoria in 1991–92.

•

Joe Scuderi (above) and Paul Nobes (below)

South African fast bowler Fanie de Villiers came up with an ingenious way of providing his team-mates with liquid refreshments during the World Series Cup in 1993–94. At a drinks break in the match against New Zealand at Perth he sent out the drinks on a motorised toy truck controlled remotely from the fence. The truck made it all the way to the middle with the drinks intact, did a few laps of Channel 9's 'Stumpcam', knocking off the bails and then menaced a few players by ramming their heels. De Villiers was able to put his $200 toy to good use in South Africa's next game—the Bushfire Relief Match against a NSW Invitational XI in Sydney. He collected more than $3,000 in its tray by guiding it around the entire SCG boundary.

•

Measuring 545 mm by 390 mm and weighing 12 kilograms, the leather-bound edition of *Men in White*, a history of New Zealand cricket, is the largest cricket book in the world. Published in 1985, the book, limited to 1,200 copies, contains over 500,000 words and 1,300 pictures. It was priced at approximately $1,200 and was sold out before publication.

•

SCOREBOARD

S. Africa v Australia
Third Test
In Durban
Australia 1st Innings 269
South Africa 1st Innings 422
Australia 2nd Innings

M TAYLOR lbw De Villiers	12
M SLATER lbw Donald	95
D BOON c P Kirsten b Donald	12
S WARNE c McMillan b Donald	12
M WAUGH not out	914
A BORDER not out	396
Sundries (3lb 3nb)	6
Total: (for four wkts)	**271**

Fall: 55 (Taylor), 81 (Boon), 109 (Warne), 157 (Slater). Bowling: A Donald 20-6-46-3 (1nb), F De Villiers 19-5-50-1 (2nb), B McMillan 13-4-30-0, C Matthews 13-5-26-0, H Cronje 10-3-22-0.

Batting time: 313 mins. Overs: 75.
Score at lunch on final day.

Geoffrey Greenidge was the last white player to appear in a Test match for the West Indies. He played five Tests, his last against Australia at Georgetown in 1972–73.

•

Allan Border retired from Test match cricket in a blaze of glory—with a triple-century in two hours—that is, according to the *Canberra Times*. Reporting on his last day in Test cricket, against South Africa at Durban in 1993–94, the newspaper stated that Border had 'stubbornly' ensured a draw by scoring an unbeaten 396 before lunch. At the other end, his batting partner Mark Waugh thumped 914 not out—not bad for a morning's work. For the record, Border scored 42 not out, Waugh 113 not out.

Another celebrated misprint occurred back in 1938 when the Reuters newsagency reported that England's Paul Gibb had scored 559 not out and Eddie Paynter 1,009 not out in the first Test against South Africa at Johannesburg.

•

England wicket-keeper Jack Russell found fame not only for his artistry behind the stumps, but also for his work with a paintbrush. Russell's artworks are recognised worldwide and his paintings have been displayed in London's Imperial War Museum, the Tower of London, the Lord's cricket ground and the Bradman Museum in Bowral. A self-taught artist, Russell's chosen subjects range from military history to cricket and landscapes.

Jack Russell, the artist

A cricket match halted by showers is a familiar occurrence at any time of the year in any part of the world. However, in 1981 one cricket game affected by rain in England was totally unexpected. It was an *indoor* cricket match in South Hampshire that had to be abandoned due to rain when the sports hall roof sprang a leak, flooding the playing area.

•

Whereas Mark Waugh needed 7,000 first-class runs to prove himself worthy of Test selection, Ian Davis—also from New South Wales—made his Australian debut with fewer than 700 runs under his belt. Davis had scored just 648 runs in eight matches before making his Test debut in 1973–74 against New Zealand, the season of his first-class debut. With a top score of just 86, Davis became one of the few specialist batsmen to get a Test cap without a first-class century to his name. Other batsmen to play in their first Test within 10 matches of their first-class debuts include Alan Fairfax (6), Graeme Wood (8) and Don Bradman (9).

•

Frank Gillingham, who appeared in over 200 first-class matches for Essex (1903–28), was born in Tokyo. The Japanese-born batsman died in Monaco in 1953.

The Victorian Trades Hall Council once called for a boycott of an Ashes Test match over the alleged anti-union actions of one of Australia's cricketers. In 1911–12 the union body claimed John McLaren had acted as a special constable during a bitter industrial dispute on the Brisbane wharves earlier in the year, an allegation rejected by the fast bowler. In any event, the proposed boycott of the fourth Test match in Melbourne did not eventuate as McLaren was omitted from the starting eleven and made 12th man.

•

In 1993 India's two star batsmen of the day—Vinod Kambli and Sachin Tendulkar—were honoured by the Tihar prison in Delhi. The facility named two of its cell-blocks Kambli and Sachin, in the hope of inspiring its young inmates.

•

Charles Studd, who made five Test appearances for England in the 1880s, later devoted his life to missionary work, spending much time in Africa, China, India and the United States. It was a cause his Test-playing brother George also pursued; he too worked in China and India, and from 1891 helped the destitute in the poorer parts of Los Angeles.

Frank Gillingham

Former England Test batsman Charles Studd, the founder of the World-Wide Evangelisation Crusade. Up until his death in 1931, he worked as a missionary in the Congo, where he helped construct a church—its aisle measured 22 yards.

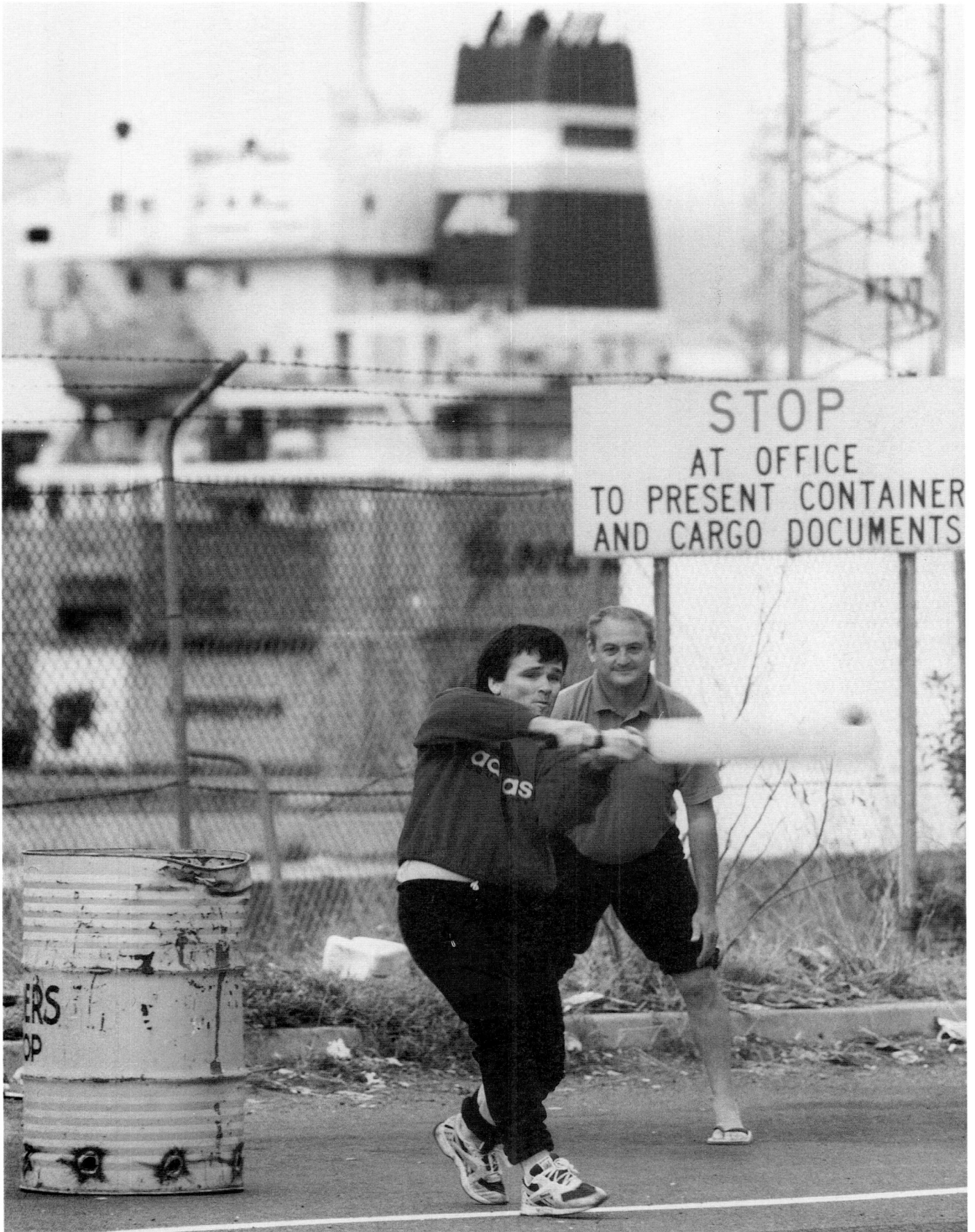

Waterside workers playing a game of cricket on a sticky picket at Port Melbourne during the national wharfies' strike in 1994

Cricket and advertising seem to go hand in hand, and have done so for well over a century. One of the earliest companies to take advantage of cricket was Colman's Mustard, which used W.G. Grace to promote its product in the 1890s. 'Colman's Mustard—like Grace Heads the Field'. Denis Compton became internationally known as the 'Brylcreem Boy'. Other cricketers associated with advertising include Tony Lock (Lucozade) and Ray Lindwall (Remington shavers). Tony Greig gained a certain amount of notoriety when he did an ad for cricket gear dressed only in a box and pads. In more recent years Ian Botham has been one of the most marketable players—promoting everything from dog food to Telecom. Greg Matthews found fame endorsing a hair replacement procedure while Allan Border sold Buttercup bread.

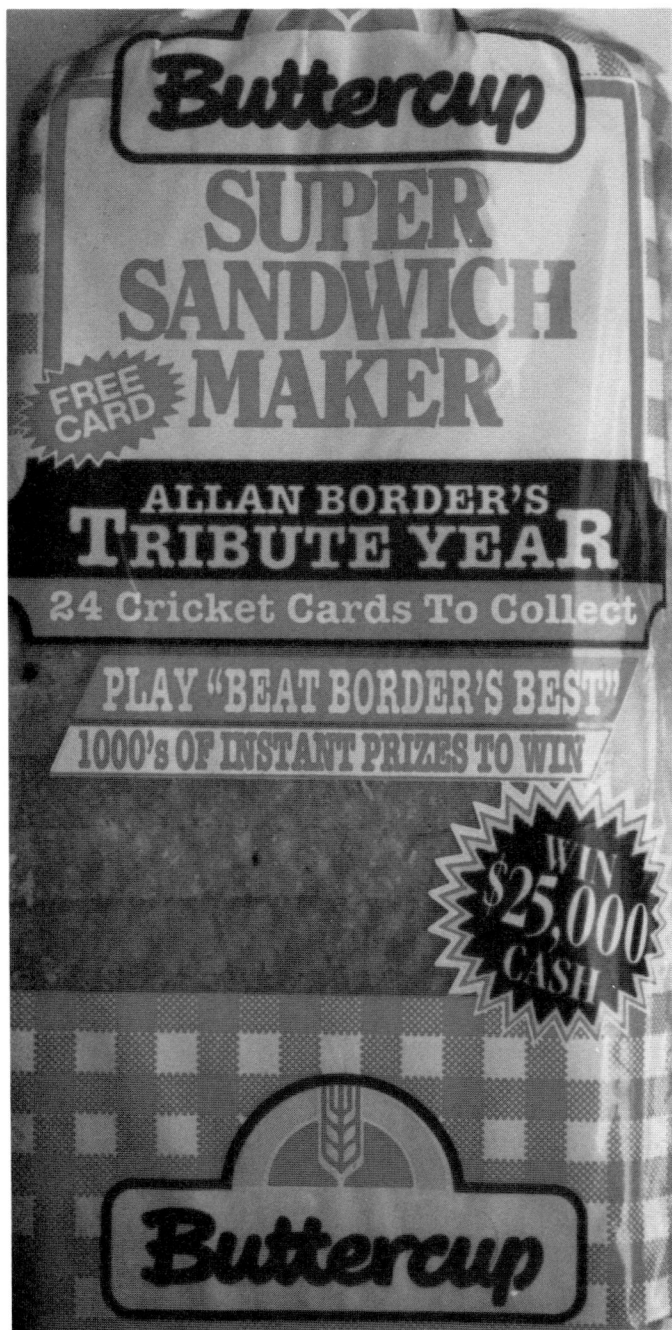

The Australian left-arm medium-pace bowler 'Dainty' Ironmonger was 45 when he made his Test debut in 1928–29. His first first-class match was for Victoria in 1909–10. The time span of 18 years and 299 days between first-class and Test debut is a record for an Australian player.

•

Two Australian Test cricketers played in their only Test match against the country of their birth. The first to do so was the Surrey-born Harry Musgrove who played against England at Melbourne in 1984–85; the other was Rex Sellers, born in Bulsar, who appeared in his sole Test against India at Calcutta in 1964–65.

AUSTRALIAN TEST CRICKETERS BORN OVERSEAS

	Birthplace	Test Debut
Charles Bannerman	England	1876–77
Bransby Cooper	India	1876–77
James Hodges	England	1876–77
Tom Kelly	Ireland	1876–77
Tom Kendall	England	1876–77
Billy Midwinter	England	1876–77
Tom Horan	Ireland	1878–79
Tom Groube	New Zealand	1880
Percy McDonnell	England	1880
Harry Musgrove	England	1884–85
'Sammy' Carter	England	1907–08
Clarrie Grimmett	New Zealand	1924–25
Archie Jackson	Scotland	1928–29
Rex Sellers	India	1964–65
Tony Dell	England	1970–71
Dav Whatmore	Sri Lanka	1978–79
Kepler Wessels	South Africa	1982–83
Brendon Julian	New Zealand	1993

•

In consecutive Sheffield Shield matches in the mid-1970s, wicket-keeper Dennis Yagmich twice achieved eight dismissals—for different states. In his only appearance for Western Australia in 1973–74 against Queensland in Perth, he took nine catches, but with Rod Marsh limiting his chances he moved to South Australia and made eight dismissals on his debut against Victoria.

•

A cricket match with a difference took place on 15 August 1877 when Gloucestershire, armed with broomsticks, took on Cheltenham with bats. Gloucestershire made 290 with their unorthodox implements—E.M. Grace hit 103, Billy Midwinter 58. In reply, Cheltenham reached 2 for 50 before time ran out.

•

In 1962 an annual cricket match in Hertfordshire organised by the BBC's Brian Johnston established some kind of bowling record when every member of his side took a wicket. It was a 12-a-side match involving Brian Johnston's XII and the Widford Cricket Club. The lucky eleven that contributed to what is perhaps a world record were Charles Gardner, Hugh Woodcock, John Warner, Robin Marlar, Trevor Howard, Major Rahman, Michael Melford, Russell Endean, Marshall Lee, J. Fellows-Smith and John Woodcock.

•

A century of cricket card collecting from the Wills cigarette cards of the 1890s (above) and 1920s (below) to the Futera cards of the 1990s (opposite)

One of the most popular and profitable pastimes associated with the game has been the collecting of cricket cards. The first ones, packaged in the United States, became available in Australia in the 1880s, while the first major set of cricket cards was issued by the Wills cigarette company in England in 1896. At a recent auction in England a set of 50 Wills cards from 1901 went for £460, while another lot comprising six cards fetched £110. A single 1902 Charlesworth & Austin card featuring W.G. Grace auctioned at Christie's went under the hammer for a staggering £220.

In 1993 a new series of cricket cards was produced in Australia, and within a few months they were changing hands at huge prices. A limited edition Don Bradman card sold for $210, while a New Zealand collector offered $750 for an autographed card depicting Allan Border.

•

One of Australia's leading women cricketers claimed she was sexually discriminated against when she was dropped from the 1993–94 tour of New Zealand. Denise Annetts, the holder of several batting records, said sexual preference had been a factor in her non-selection, claiming the only reason she was dropped was because she was heterosexual and married.

•

One of the highlights of the 1994 Sydney Gay and Lesbian Mardi Gras was the sight of about 30 female 'Merv Hughes' dressed in creams, bowling their way down Oxford Street—part of the record 11,000 participants and 137 floats in the event.

•

England's Wilfred Rhodes and India's Vinoo Mankad both batted at every position in the order, 1 to 11, during their Test careers.

•

Western Australia's Ken MacLeay, who appeared in 16 one-day internationals but never in a Test

Shaun Graf, an all-rounder who played for both Western Australia and Victoria, is one of the few Australians to have played in a one-day international but never in a Test. He appeared in a total of 11 one-dayers during the early 1980s, scoring 24 runs and taking eight wickets. The closest Graf came to playing Test cricket was in 1980–81, when he was twice 12th man for Australia.

AUSTRALIA'S 12TH MEN NEVER TO HAVE PLAYED IN A TEST

Player and state	Test in which 12th man
Les Poidevin (NSW)	First Test v England at Sydney in 1901–02
Les Hill (SA)	Third Test v England at Adelaide in 1907–08
Colin McKenzie (Vic)	Fourth Test v England at Melbourne in 1907–08
'Mick' Waddy (NSW)	Fifth Test v England at Sydney in 1907–08
Syd Hird (NSW)	First Test v England at Sydney in 1932–33
Bert Tobin (SA)	Fourth Test v England at Brisbane in 1932–33
Ian Quick (Vic)	Fourth Test v England at Manchester in 1961
Ian McLachlan (SA)	Fourth Test v England at Adelaide in 1962–63
Jack Potter (Vic)	Second Test v South Africa at Melbourne in 1963–64
	First Test v England at Nottingham in 1964
	Third Test v England at Leeds in 1964
Sam Trimble (Qld)	Fifth Test v West Indies at Port-of-Spain in 1964–65
Geoff Davies (NSW)	First Test v West Indies at Brisbane in 1968–69
Jock Irvine (WA)	Fifth Test v India at Madras in 1969–70
Shaun Graf (Vic)	Second Test v New Zealand in Perth in 1980–81
	First Test v India at Sydney in 1980–81
Darren Lehmann (SA)	Third Test v Pakistan at Sydney in 1989–90

Some of the Sheffield Shield players to appear in a one-day international for Australia but never a Test include Graeme Porter, Rod McCurdy, Glenn Trimble, Andrew Zesers, Jamie Siddons and Ken MacLeay.

•

Ian Healy, who worked in the garment industry before his Test-playing days, launched his own fashion label, Gloves Off, in 1994. The range of sports leisurewear items included shorts, T-shirts, track pants, polo shirts and caps.

•

A religious group in Pakistan once petitioned the President to have cricket matches banned from television, claiming attendances at mosques had diminished during the TV coverage of the 1982–83 Test series against India.

•

Queensland wicket-keeper Wade Seccombe was sidelined from the Mercantile Mutual Cup match against Western Australia in 1993–94 after injuring his wrist and failing a fitness test. His replacement? Gavin Fitness.

•

Brian Trubshaw, a former first-class cricketer, was awarded the CBE and OBE for his services to aviation. He became internationally known as the main test pilot for the Concorde.

•

Kepler Wessels has the unique distinction of having played for two countries in inaugural Test matches against Sri Lanka—for Australia at Kandy in 1982–83 and for South Africa at Colombo in 1993–94.

•

A match between Launceston and the Old Suttonians in Cornwall in 1984 was interrupted four times when camels, which had escaped from a nearby circus, invaded the playing field.

•

Allen Allen & Hemsley, Australia's oldest law firm, was founded in 1822 by the family of England Test captain 'Gubby' Allen. One of the firm's partners was Reginald Allen, an uncle of 'Gubby', who played in a Test match for Australia, against England in 1886–87.

•

Lord Tennyson, Australia's second Governor-General, 1902–04, was the father of Lionel Tennyson who captained England in three Tests in 1921.

•

During the 1993–94 season in South Africa, Lulama Mazikazana, a wicket-keeper, was forced to delay making his first-class debut for Eastern Province because he had to take part in the Xhosa tribe's circumcision ceremony.

Kepler Wessels

Members and staff of the Allen Allen & Hemsley cricket team at a match in the early 1920s. Reginald Allen, who played for Australia, is in the centre of the middle row.

How sweet it is. In the same week that Shane Warne was named the 1993–94 International Cricketer of the Year, he came out on top in another poll, one conducted by the Confectionery Manufacturers of Australasia. A nationwide survey of female teenagers revealed that most would like Warne to deliver them a box of chocolates on St Valentine's Day. Warne (119) beat Hollywood heart-throbs Keanu Reeves (101), Richard Gere (83), Christian Slater (78) and Mel Gibson (71).

Another illustration of his popularity with women came during the third World Series final at the SCG that summer when, fielding near Bay 19, he was confronted by a young autograph-hunter dressed in a very revealing, luminous orange tank-top. And in what may just be a world first, the Australian leg-spinner, egged on by the crowd, autographed not the usual scrap of paper or miniature cricket bat, but her chest!

•

On his first-class debut against South Australia at East Melbourne in 1880–81, Victoria's Robert Pateman only made four with the bat, but scored them in rather bizarre fashion. When team-mate Fred Baker was dismissed late on the first day Pateman came out and batted in his street clothes.

•

While sunglasses are now an accepted on-field player accessory, back in 1981–82 it was not the done thing to wear them. The touring Australians, who were upset at a delayed flight from Christchurch, took on Canterbury in a 45-overs match in a decidedly light-hearted fashion, much to the annoyance of the crowd. Jeff Thomson fielded in sunglasses, while Kim Hughes wore a tie.

It's believed that indoor cricket originated in Denmark during the late 1960s. An indoor tournament, arranged by the Husum Cricket Club, was played at a sports hall in South Slesvig in the winter of 1968–69, possibly the first organised indoor match in the world.

•

Les Favell had an unusual day's cricket on 5 January 1957, playing in *two* first-class matches in different cities—a unique occurrence. On the last day of the South Australia–Tasmania match being played in Hobart, Favell was summoned to appear in a testimonial match in Sydney when two players withdrew at the last minute.

•

Searching for an excuse to explain England's loss to Australia at Lord's in 1993, the then Chairman of Selectors, Ted Dexter, suggested that 'Venus may be in the wrong juxtaposition with something else'. His statement won the John Smith's No Nonsense Prize for the most baffling remark of 1993 at the annual Plain English Campaign Awards.

•

Jack Russell signed a novel sponsorship agreement with the Heinz food company for the 1990–91 Ashes series—a can of baked beans for every run scored and a case (24 cans) for each catch or stumping.

•

Refined gentleman wishes to meet widow with two tickets for the third Test, view to matrimony. Kindly send photo of tickets.
—advertisement, *World Sport*

Picture Credits

ACT Cricket Association, Craig Abraham, Advertiser Papers Ltd, David Rayvern Allen, Allen Allen & Hemsley, Australian Broadcasting Corporation, Australian Sports Cards Pty Ltd, Bank of England, Senator Michael Baume, Richie Benaud, Channel 9, Channel 10, Don Chipp, The Duke of Edinburgh, The Fingleton Family, Kate Fitzpatrick, George Patterson Pty Ltd, Government Photographic Service, Vic Grimmett, Sir Richard Hadlee, Hampshire County Cricket Club, Harper Collins Publishers, Andy Hooper, Lyndon Howe, Indian High Commission, Jack Russell Fine Art Publishing, Lancashire County Cricket Club, The Liberal Party, Lord Home of the Hirsel, Middlesex County Cricket Club, National Library of Australia, New South Wales Cricket Association, Nottinghamshire County Cricket Club, Office of the Hon R.J.L. Hawke, Pakistan Cricket Board, Bill Peach, Eric Piris, PolyGram Music Publishing, South Pacific Pictures Limited, Somerset County Cricket Club, South Australian Cricket Association, Sri Lankan Cricket Board, Surrey County Cricket Club, Tasmanian Cricket Association, Tobasgo Design Consultants, Victorian Cricket Association, West Australian Cricket Association, Jean Wong, Zimbabwe High Commission.

Every effort has been made to trace copyright owners, however if there have been any omissions apologies are extended, and acknowledgments will be made in any subsequent editions.

Bibliography

Books

Philip Bailey, Philip Thorn and Peter Wynne-Thomas, *Who's Who of Cricketers*, Guild Publishing, London 1984

Rowland Bowen, *Cricket: A History of its Growth and Development Throughout the World*, Eyre & Spottiswoode, London 1970

Robert Brooke and Peter Matthews, *Guiness Cricket Firsts*, Guiness Publishing Ltd, Enfield 1988

Graham Dawson and Charlie Watt, *Test Cricket Lists*, Five Mile Press, Balwyn 1992

Ross Dundas and Jack Pollard, *Highest, Most and Best: Australian Cricket Statistics 1850–1990*, Augus & Robertson, Sydney 1990

Leslie Frewin, *The Boundary Book: Second Innings*, Pelham Books, London 1986

Leslie Frewin, *The NatWest Boundary Book*, Macmillan, South Melbourne 1988

Bill Frindall, *The Wisden Book of Cricket Records*, Headline Book Publishing, London 1993

Bill Frindall, *The Wisden Book of Test Cricket*, Macdonald & Co Ltd, London 1985

Benny Green, *The Illustrated Wisden Anthology: 1864–1989*, Angus & Robertson, London 1988

Benny Green, *The Wisden Book of Cricketers' Lives*, Macdonald & Co Ltd, London 1986

Peter Haining, *LBW: Laughter Before Wicket*, Allen & Unwin, London 1986

Allan Miller, *Allan's Australian Cricket Annual*, Allan Miller, Busselton, various years

Mudar Patherya and Barry O'Brien, *The Penguin Book of Cricket Lists*, Penguin, New Delhi 1988

Derek Salberg, *Much Ado About Cricket*, K.A.F. Brewin Books, Studley 1987

Don Selth, *The Prime Minister's XI*, Don Selth, Canberra 1990

Charlie Watt, *Australian First-Class Cricket*, Five Mile Press, Knoxfield 1993

Ray Webster and Allan Miller, *First-Class Cricket in Australia: 1850–51 to 1941–42*, Ray Webster, Glen Waverley 1991

Marcus Williams, *Double Century: 200 Years of Cricket in The Times*, Collins, London 1985

Wisden Cricketers' Almanack, John Wisden & Co. Ltd, Guildford, various years

Magazines

ABC Cricket Book
Australian Cricket
Cricketer
The Cricketer International
The Cricketer Quarterly
Inside Edge
Wisden Cricket Monthly

Newspapers

The Australian
The Canberra Times
The Daily Telegraph Mirror
The Sun-Herald
The Sunday Telegraph
The Sydney Morning Herald

Index

Smith, Chris, 102
Smith, Harry, 120
Smith, Ian, 25
Smith, Peter, 35
Smith, Robin, 18, 37, 42, 90, 102
Smith, Steve, 104, 120
Smith, Wilbur, 18
Smithers, Sir W., 52
Smithies, Karen, 51
Snagge, John, 90
Snow, John, 73
Sobers, Garry, 14, 16–7, 22, 24–6, 29, 39, 46, 48, 59, 73, 77–8, 82–3, 86, 111, 123, 132–3
Sohail Fazal, 92
Solway, Peter, 41
Sparling, John, 64
Spencer, Fifth Earl, 118
Spofforth, Fred, 66, 68, 71, 97
Squire, J.C., 13
Sridhar, M.V., 96
Srikkanth, Kris, 31
Stackpole, Keith, 91, 111, 115
Staples, Sir Robert Ponsonby, 85
Stephenson, Heathfield, 13
Sterling, Peter, 38
Stevens, 'Lumpy', 10
Stevens, Jon, 63
Stevenson, Graham, 35
Stewart, Alec, 18, 42, 90
Stillman, Les, 39
Stimpson, Peter, 30
Stocks, Fred, 131
Stockton, Edwin, 56
Stoddart, Andrew, 38, 129
Stollmeyer, Jeffrey, 31
Stoppard, Tom, 88
Street, Tony, 53
Stuart, Ricky, 40–1
Studd, Charles, 136
Studd, George, 136
Su'a, Murphy, 124
Such, Peter, 18, 68
Surti, Rusi, 19
Sutcliffe, Herbert, 20, 24, 31–2, 105, 111, 119
Swan, Colin, 99
Swan, Ken, 99
Sweet, Gary, 77

Tallon, Don, 16, 46, 59, 133
Tamsett, F., 10
Tancred, Vincent, 129
Tarrant, Frank, 60
Tavaré, Chris, 23, 31
Taylor, Bruce, 19
Taylor, Elizabeth, 82
Taylor, John, 120
Taylor, Johnny, 96

Taylor, Mark, 24, 26, 31, 34–5, 70, 98, 106, 115, 119–20,
Taylor, Peter, 119–20, 130
Tendulkar, Sachin, 12, 108, 136
Tennyson, Lionel, 13, 142
Tennyson, Lord, 13, 142
Terry, Paul, 119
Thatcher, Margaret, 48, 52
Theroux, Paul, 18
Thomas, David, 113
Thomas, Jimmy, 47
Thomson, 'Froggy', 66, 120
Thomson, Jeff, 38–9, 69, 90, 111, 120, 123, 144
Thomson, Nat, 120
Thorpe, Graham, 36
Timms, Michelle, 42
Tobin, Bert, 142
Tolkein, J.R., 18
Toshack, Ernie, 70
Townley, Athol, 48
Townsend, Charlie, 107
Tozer, Claude, 129
Travers, Ben, 80–1
Treloar, Arthur, 88
Trent, Bruce, 81
Trim, John, 45
Trimble, Glenn, 142
Trimble, Sam, 142
Trott, 'Harry', 37, 96, 110
Trott, Albert, 66, 72, 129
Trott, Stuart, 37
Trubshaw, Brian, 142
Trueman, Fred, 87
Trumble, Hugh, 70–1, 96–7, 131
Trumper, Victor, 28, 96, 101, 115
Tuckett, Len, 29
Tuckwell, Bert, 114
Tufnell, Phil, 90
Turner, Alan, 66, 120
Turner, Charlie, 66, 69, 97, 108, 120
Turner, Glenn, 31, 126
Twopenny, 9
Tyson, Frank, 53

Udal, John, 44
Underwood, Derek, 69, 82, 110
van Ryneveld, Clive, 56
Vance, Robert, 123
Vautin, Paul, 38
Veletta, Mike, 45, 97
Vengsarkar, Dilip, 42, 106
Verity, Hedley, 59, 68, 102
Visser, Peter, 112
Viswanath, Gundappa, 24, 32, 119
Vogler, Bert, 130

Waddy, 'Mick', 142
Wade, Herbert, 127
Waite, Mervyn, 93
Wales, Prince of, 116
Walford, Mike, 37
Walker, Max, 74, 90
Walker, Peter, 62
Walker, V.E., 130
Wallach, Eli, 78
Walsh, Courtney, 90
Walsh, F., 71
Walters, Doug, 25, 120
Walters, Frank, 120
Walters, Steve, 41
Waqar Younis, 69, 114, 125–6
Ward, William, 55
Warne, Shane, 9, 37, 41, 56, 69, 70, 77, 80, 90, 98, 114–15, 144
Warner, 'Plum', 52, 80, 98
Warner, Aucher, 52
Warner, H.B., 73
Warner, John, 80, 139
Warr, John, 123
Washbrook, Cyril, 31, 74, 77
Wasim Akram, 46, 125
Wasim Bari, 106, 110
Waters, John, 78
Watkin, Steve, 55
Watkins, John, 123
Watson, Graeme, 120
Watson, Sir Brooke, 50
Watson, William, 120
Watts, Charlie, 85
Watts, Pat, 104
Watts, Peter, 104
Waugh, Alec, 13, 17
Waugh, Danny, 102
Waugh, Dean, 66, 102
Waugh, Mark, 23, 35, 42, 66, 80, 90, 98, 119, 135–6
Waugh, Steve, 32, 34, 66, 80, 98, 108, 114, 119, 131
Wayne, Naunton, 77–8
Wazir Mohammad, 104
Webber, Andrew Lloyd, 75
Webber, Darren, 41
Webster, Rudi, 66
Weekes, Everton, 24–5, 119
Wellham, Charlie, 99
Wellham, Dale, 99
Wellham, Dirk, 24, 44, 99, 125
Wellham, Greg, 99
Wellham, Wally, 99
Wenham, E.G., 23
Wessels, Kepler, 9, 125, 139, 142–3
Westbrook, Keith, 101
Westbrook, Norman, 101
Westbrook, Roy, 101
Westbrook, Tom, 101
Westbrook, Walter, 101

Wettimuny, Sidath, 111
Wharton, Alan, 23
Whatmore, Dav, 139
Wheatley, John, 129
Whitaker, Mark, 112
White, 'Butch', 68
White, Jack, 68
White, the Hon. Luke, 117
Whitney, Mike, 74, 86, 89, 130, 132
Whittacker, Forrest, 78
Whitty, Dame May, 78
Wijesuriya, Roger, 123
Wiley, John, 47
Williams, Basil, 111
Williams, Eric, 51, 55
Williams, Kenneth, 78
Willis, Bob, 88, 106
Willis, Evan, 43
Willis, Ralph, 44
Wilson, Betty, 9–10
Wilson, G.T.O., 112
Wilson, George, 71
Wilson, Jeff, 36
Windsor, Duke of, 117
Wishart, Warren, 102
Wodehouse, P.G., 16–17
Wogan, Terry, 86
Wood, Graeme, 31, 90, 136
Woodcock, Hugh, 139
Woodcock, John, 139
Woodfull, Bill, 97, 112
Woods, Donald, 17
Woods, Sammy, 28
Woolley, Frank, 24, 85
Woolmer, Bob, 71
Woosnam, Ian, 42
Wordsworth, Charles, 17
Wordsworth, William, 17
Worontschak, Yuri, 86
Worrall, Jack, 96
Worrell, Frank, 25, 54–5, 85
Worsley, Sir William, 118
Worthington, Tom, 102
Wright, Alby, 110
Wright, Doug, 66
Wright, John, 111
Wyatt, Bob, 125
Wynyard, W.T., 9

Yagmich, Dennis, 139
Yallop, Graham, 29, 32, 86, 90
Yardley, Bill, 85
York, Michael, 78
York, Susannah, 78

Zaheer Abbas, 12, 27
Zesers, Andrew, 107, 142
Zoehrer, Tim, 90, 97
Zulch, 'Billy', 129